Abraham Lincoln's
Most Famous Case

Abraham Lincoln's Most Famous Case

THE ALMANAC TRIAL

George R. Dekle, Sr.

PRAEGER

AN IMPRINT OF ABC-CLIO, LLC
Santa Barbara, California • Denver, Colorado • Oxford, England

Library of Congress Cataloging-in-Publication Data

Dekle, George R., 1948- author.
  Abraham Lincoln's most famous case : the Almanac Trial / George R. Dekle, Sr.
    pages cm
  Includes bibliographical references and index.
    ISBN 978–1–4408–3049–5 (hardback) — ISBN 978–1–4408–3050–1 (ebook)
1. Armstrong, Duff, 1833–1899—Trials, litigation, etc. 2. Lincoln, Abraham, 1809–1865—Career in law. 3. Trials (Murder)—Illinois—Beardstown. I. Title.
KF223.A47D45   2014
345.773'0252309773553—dc23   2013044678

ISBN: 978–1–4408–3049–5
EISBN: 978–1–4408–3050–1

18 17 16 15 14   1 2 3 4 5

This book is also available on the World Wide Web as an eBook.
Visit www.abc-clio.com for details.

Praeger
An Imprint of ABC-CLIO, LLC

ABC-CLIO, LLC
130 Cremona Drive, P.O. Box 1911
Santa Barbara, California 93116-1911

This book is printed on acid-free paper ∞

Manufactured in the United States of America

To my wife, Lane, without whose help and support
this book would not have been possible.

Contents

Preface

Ecclesiastes 12:12 says that "of the making of many books there is no end," and those words seem to describe the situation with the literature on our sixteenth president. The flow of books about Abraham Lincoln began almost immediately upon the heels of his death, and it continues unabated to this day. Every aspect of his life and thought has seen treatment in print, from his health to his religious beliefs to his practice of law. Why, then, another book on Lincoln? Will Rogers once said that we know a lot of things that just aren't so, and that is certainly the case with Lincoln's famous defense in the Almanac Trial. The history of the trial has acquired so many accretions over the years that it is hard to tell where the legend ends and the truth begins. If this book can dispel the confusion about the trial and extract the fact from the fiction, then its modest contribution to the history of our greatest president might make it worthy of a place in the literature on Lincoln.

Any practicing lawyer who has ever attended a continuing legal education class on trial advocacy knows some version of the story of Lincoln's performance in the trial. Whenever the topic turns to cross-examination, the speaker will likely describe how Lincoln saved an innocent man from the gallows by using an almanac to expose the perjury of a villainous witness. The speaker will sometimes even quote portions of the cross-examination to demonstrate exactly how Lincoln accomplished his spectacular feat. Shortly after I retired from the active practice of law, I sat in such a class listening to the speaker expound on Lincoln's cross. As the speaker dissected the examination question by question, it occurred to me that his transcript did not agree with another transcript of the cross I had recently seen. I resolved to do a little research and see if I could reconcile the discrepancies between the two transcripts. The more deeply I looked into the matter, the more confused the issue became. I uncovered what I felt to be good evidence that Lincoln not only did not cross-examine the witness, he did not cross-examine anyone. Many sources claimed that a lawyer named William Walker conducted the cross-examination while Lincoln sat silently at counsel table. I also found a strong undercurrent of suspicion that Lincoln achieved the acquittal of his client with a forged almanac.

The literature on the trial presented a nice murder mystery. Did Lincoln use chicanery to unjustly free a murderer, or did he use his considerable skill as a trial lawyer to engineer the brilliant defense of an innocent man? Although I am neither a historian nor a Lincoln scholar, I felt equal to the task of unraveling the Almanac Trial because if I learned anything during my three decades as a criminal trial lawyer, I learned how to investigate, prosecute, and defend murder cases. In the spirit of those scholars who quest for the historical Jesus, I began a quest for the historical Almanac Trial. My quest did not reveal a cardboard saint with superhuman legal skills, but a human being who possessed good trial skills and impeccable ethics. Many nonlawyers and even some lawyers have questioned the propriety of several things that Lincoln did during the trial, but I hope to show that none of his actions warrant reproach. Did Lincoln save an innocent man, or did he knowingly free a killer? You must decide that for yourself. I will, however, attempt to demonstrate that the guilt or innocence of his client is irrelevant to the question of whether Lincoln behaved ethically.

Two other aspects of the book should be mentioned. During the nineteenth century even the well educated used nonstandard spelling and punctuation. In quoting letters and court documents from that era, I have standardized their spelling and punctuation. There were many interesting aspects of the case that could not be fitted into the word limit. I have set up a blog, almanac-trial.blogspot.com, that the curious reader can visit to learn more about these things.

Such an undertaking as this cannot be the product of one writer's unassisted effort. I owe a debt of gratitude to many people who have helped me in my quest to learn the facts of the Almanac Trial. Professor Ron J. Keller, the director of the Lincoln Heritage Museum at Lincoln College rendered invaluable assistance in providing me with back issues of the *Lincoln Newsletter*. Michael Burlingame, the Chancellor Naomi B. Lynn Distinguished Chair in Lincoln Studies at the University of Illinois, graciously shared some of his personal research with me. Professor Brian Dirck of Anderson University answered my questions and helped me through some problems with my research. David Joens, the director of the Illinois State Archives, helped me locate the pardon papers for James H. Norris, the co-defendant who went to prison for the murder. Christine Colburn, Rena Schergen, and Thomas Whittaker of the Special Collections Research Center of the University of Chicago Library assisted me with tracking down William E. Barton's papers on his research of the trial. Kathryn Harris of the Abraham Lincoln Presidential Library helped to locate references on the trial. Joshua Caster at the University of Nebraska assisted me in obtaining a copy of the photograph taken of Lincoln on the afternoon of the trial. Camille Apodaca, from the Permission and Licensing Department of PARS International Corporation; Dennis Anderson of the *Peoria Journal Star*; and Carolyn Conklin of the Peoria Public Library all helped me track down reprints of archival news articles. Jane Westenfeld, of the Pelletier Library at Allegheny College, helped me find my way through Ida Tarbell's papers on the trial, and Brent Abercrombie, the Manuscript Librarian at Indiana State Library, rendered the same sort of help with Albert Beveridge's papers. Doug Hansen and Ardis Nelson of Hansen Wheel and Wagon Shop in Letcher, South Dakota, gave me an education on wagon hammers and neck yokes, two items that figured prominently in the story of the murder. When I could not find an authentic old-fashioned wagon hammer, Terry Moore of Texas Wagon Works in Gonzalez, Texas, used his blacksmithing skills to make one for me. Katherine Duncan, a barrister in Bell Yard Chambers, London, explained the nuances of cross-examination in England. Sarah A. Kiley of the C. A. Pound Human Identification Laboratory at the University of Florida consulted on issues relating to blunt force trauma to the head. Dr. Sharon Packer, assistant clinical professor of Psychiatry and Behavioral Sciences at Albert Einstein College of Medicine, consulted with me on issues relating to memory. Amy Mills, of Amy Mills Portrait Designs in Lake City, Florida, took the photographs of the slungshot for me. Duffy Soto of Hunter Graphics in Lake City, Florida, helped in the preparation of the other illustrations for the book. Rachel Williams of Easton, Illinois, helped me to find the defendant's grave in the Walnut Grove Cemetery. Corky Kinstle gave me a tour of the old Beardstown courthouse where the trial was held and showed me the jail where the defendant awaited trial. I was saved from numerous errors by those who graciously gave of their time to read and critique the manuscript: I have already mentioned Professor Brian Dirck, Professor Michael Burlingame, Professor Ron J. Keller, and Dr. Sharon Packer.

Others who read and critiqued the manuscript were Ron Clark, distinguished practitioner in residence at Seattle University Law; Professor Daniel Stowell, director and editor of *The Papers of Abraham Lincoln*; and my wife, Lane Dekle, who not only read and critiqued the manuscript, but also gave me moral support through the entire process of bringing this book to publication. This is a better book for the contributions of all these people.

Chapter 1

Murder at a Whiskey Camp

It is a summer night in antebellum Mason County, Illinois. It is unseasonably cool, with a temperature of 56 degrees. A soft wind blows from the northwest, and stars twinkling in a cloudless sky[1] form a jeweled canopy over the stand of trees known to history as Walker's Grove,[2] Walnut Grove,[3] or sometimes Virgin's Grove.[4] Two encampments disturb the usual tranquility of this unpopulated area. At one encampment worshippers have gathered to hear evangelical sermons, sing hymns of praise, and refresh their souls. At the other encampment men have gathered to drink, gamble, and race horses. Some of them even intend to harass the camp of worship, which lies a mile distant from the camp of whiskey. A big man strides through the whiskey camp like an angry bear. He is tall, broad, and strong, and he is confident of his ability to handle himself. Sure that he cannot be defeated, he is looking for a fight. And just in case he chooses an adversary who proves too much of a challenge, he carries a loaded whip[5]—a whip with the lash braided around pellets of buckshot.[6] It is a formidable weapon, with the lash retaining its flexibility but packing a heavier wallop.

A small man has come to the camp to drink whiskey and race horses. Tonight the small man concentrates on the whiskey. Having drunk his fill, he looks for a place to sleep off the effects of the alcohol. Finding a place that seems suitable, he lies down and soon falls asleep. He does not sleep long. The big man wakes him up and curses him. The small man tries to ignore the big man's bullying, but finally he has enough. He hits the big man in the face. The big man closes with the smaller and

A camp meeting. (From *Camp Meeting Manual: A Practical Book for the Camp Ground* by B. W. Gorham, 1854)

begins to grapple with him, trying to take him to the ground.[7] Although overmatched in size and strength, the small man is no weakling, and he knows how to fight. Like his father before him, the small man is an accomplished wrestler. Using his own considerable strength and his superior knowledge of grappling, the small man throws the big man. The victory is short lived. The big man arises, grabs the small man, and throws him to the ground. Mounting the prostrate body of his foe as one would mount a horse, he begins to pummel the small man. He does not need the whip and does not use it. Bystanders intervene and pull the big man off his victim.[8]

The big man is not finished. He tries to restart the fight, but others intervene again, and he goes off, perhaps to sleep, perhaps to bully others. He fights at least one other man on this evening, and possibly more. Testosterone and alcohol form a lethal combination, and the loser of such a fight often will not let things stand. Retribution must be exacted, and that retribution sometimes gets meted out when the loser arms himself and strikes unexpectedly. It is a common pattern of behavior re-enacted countless times.[9] Later that night someone takes vengeance on the big man.[10] Using a deadly weapon, the attacker strikes. Although he does not intend to kill, he has dealt the big man a mortal injury. The big man now demonstrates just how strong he is. Suffering from fatal wounds, he mounts his horse and rides for home. The wounds so debilitate the big man that he has trouble staying in the saddle. He falls off his horse once, maybe twice, but each time he remounts and continues his journey. When he arrives at his home, he takes to his bed. He languishes for three days, and then he dies.

The big man's relatives complain to the local constabulary, the investigation begins. One of the revelers at the whiskey camp comes forward and says he saw the fatal assault. He not only saw the assault, he retrieved the abandoned murder weapon.[11] The witness turns the weapon over to the authorities and names the assailant. It was the small man who threw the deceased and was repaid with a savage beating. The officers of the law question the small man. He admits fighting the deceased and admits striking a mighty blow but says he used nothing more lethal than his bare fist. The officers arrest the young man and take him to jail. The charge is murder, a capital offense.

The small man's father, though once a strong man, is now used up by a life of poverty and hard work. He lies sick and near death, and the news of his son's arrest is too much for him to take.[12] Although he has little to show for his lifetime of toil, his last words to his wife are to sell everything they have, hire a lawyer, and save their son's life.[13] Their son will not go without a lawyer even if she cannot hire one. Illinois law does not allow one charged with a capital crime to face trial without a lawyer. The court appoints a lawyer to represent indigents charged with capital murder, but the lawyer must perform the defense without compensation.[14] With the privilege of practicing law as a member of the Illinois bar comes the duty to defend the penniless who are accused of capital crimes. It is an unfortunate fact of life, however, that underpaid lawyers often do not defend their clients with the zeal displayed by well-paid lawyers. To give her son his best opportunity to escape the gallows, the newly widowed mother must hire a lawyer. She buries her husband, takes stock of her meager assets, and raises as much money as she can to pay her son's legal fees. It is a pitiful sum, no more than a widow's mite, but with it she seeks a lawyer.

This chain of events, which begins with a rather nondescript murder at a whiskey camp and leads to a penurious widow selling all she has to save her son, culminates in one of the most celebrated jury trials in the history of American jurisprudence—Abraham Lincoln's Almanac Trial. Lincoln takes the case and wins an acquittal; and scores of Lincoln biographers have told the dramatic story of how Lincoln achieved this great victory. Unfortunately, they cannot agree about how Lincoln won the case. Just as there are three names for the grove in which the killing occurred, there are three versions of what happened in the trial. It seems there are at least three versions of every event in Lincoln's life.

What really happened at the trial? What really happened that night in Walker's Grove? The scenario set forth earlier in this chapter recites the facts in the light most favorable to the prosecution. It may not set them forth with complete accuracy, and you would be accurate to say that they are not complete. Its lack of completeness results from two factors. First, I have withheld certain details, such as the names of the parties, for reasons that will become clear in the next two chapters. Second, certain important details are unknown and unknowable, and we can fill in those gaps only by inference from the evidence. These gaps in knowledge plague both the killing and the resulting trial, and reasonable analysts can draw diametrically opposed inferences from the evidence. Before we can fill the gaps in our knowledge by drawing inferences from the available evidence, we must make some judgments about which evidence to use as the foundation for our inferences. For these reasons, when we examine the evidence about the killing and the resulting trial, we will not determine what really happened. Although myriads of books on the market promise to tell "what really happened" in this or that historic event, in point of fact they cannot deliver on such promises—they can only tell us what their authors believe to have happened. When we talk about an event that occurred over 100 years ago, we can never know what really happened. It is often hard enough to determine what really happened last week. Anyone who has ever watched a National Football League (NFL) game knows that it is sometimes impossible to determine what really happened even when you have a video review of the event. In our study of the Almanac Trial, we will therefore set a more realistic goal—to determine what probably happened. But "probably happened" can mean 50.001 percent or 99.999 percent. How high a degree of probability should we require? To answer this question, we turn to jurisprudence, which does not measure degrees of probability with percentage points.

Different types of legal proceedings require different degrees of probability—called burdens of proof—depending on the objective of the proceeding. An application for an arrest warrant requires a comparatively low burden of proof—probable cause, which is "a reasonable ground of suspicion, supported by circumstances sufficiently strong in themselves to warrant a cautious person in the belief that a particular person is guilty of a particular crime."[15] Civil cases require proof by either "a preponderance of evidence" or "the greater weight of the evidence"—sometimes popularly described as a probability of 51 percent. Even capital murder cases do not require absolute certainty, just proof beyond a reasonable doubt. We will not attempt to define "reasonable doubt" because the precise meaning of the term is elusive. Indeed, many worthy jurists have declared it impossible to define.[16] The Florida Supreme Court finds the task of defining reasonable doubt so difficult that it "defines" the term by saying what a reasonable doubt is not rather than by describing what it is.[17] Other types of proceedings (sexually violent predator commitments, for example) require proof by clear and convincing evidence—a standard somewhere between the greater weight of the evidence and proof beyond a reasonable doubt. Clear and convincing evidence is somewhat easier to define—it is "evidence that is precise, explicit, lacking in confusion, and of such weight that it produces a firm belief or conviction, without hesitation, about the matter in issue."[18] In our investigation we will strive to establish the facts of the killing and the trial to meet the standard of clear and convincing evidence. Having described the problem and set our standard of proof, we are almost ready to begin the task of unraveling the evidence and determining the probable course of the Almanac Trial.

What is our evidence? Scores, if not hundreds, of books and articles describe the events we are investigating. We will look at as many as we can, separating the wheat from the chaff and using only the wheat. Those works that give evidence of careful research command greater weight than those that do not. As much as possible, we will go behind those works to the sources they relied upon. Because we have access to the source materials used by many of the better authors, we can learn what the witnesses to the killing and the trial have to say by reading their actual letters, statements, and interviews.[19] We must be careful as we work with these sources, keeping ever mindful of the limitations of human memory. Daniel W. Stowell succinctly stated the problems we will confront when he wrote:

Reminiscences by participants in or observers of specific historical events are among these complicated source materials. Often recorded years or decades after the events they describe, these reminiscences can be colored by nostalgia, influenced by other people's accounts of the same event, and refracted through their later attitudes toward the participants. Reminiscences are frequently distorted by the sheer passage of time, clouded by poor memories, and imperfectly recorded by interviewers.[20]

As we evaluate our sources, we will use common law rules of evidence, but we will have no exclusionary rules.[21] Exclusionary rules often mechanically reject perfectly reliable evidence. Exclusionary rules have no place in historical investigation, and we do not *a priori* reject any relevant evidence. We may reject it if we weigh it and find it wanting, but first we must weigh it. The fact that a piece of information violates an evidentiary rule of exclusion will cause us to give it less weight, but if it has sufficient indicia of reliability, we will take it into account. We must investigate the court records, such as they are, and see what we can learn from them. We will look at collateral evidence that can give us a context for evaluating the more direct evidence. We will do our best to get to the bottom of things and determine what probably happened. Let us now begin our quest. We will start by looking at three very different stories that have been told about the trial. By the end of the book, we should be able to tell which, if any, of those stories is probably true.

Chapter 2

Lincoln the Cross-Examiner

Francis Wellman, a New York lawyer and former prosecutor, popularized our first version of the story of the Almanac Trial. In 1901 he wrote *The Art of Cross-Examination*, a book that became one of the most famous trial advocacy manuals ever published. The fourth edition is still in print,[1] and many modern lawyers swear by it as the fount of knowledge for learning how to cross-examine. I discovered the book while in law school and re-read it from cover to cover several times. Wellman wrote in an easy, informal style, illustrating his points with incidents from famous and not-so-famous trials.

In his chapter titled "Cross-Examining the Perjured Witness," Wellman told of a legendary cross-examination conducted by a young, unproven lawyer named Abraham Lincoln. This cross-examination has entered the pantheon of great moments in the history of American trial advocacy. It rivals the cross-examination of Oscar Wilde by the barrister Edward Carson,[2] and the story has been told and retold over the years in biographies of Lincoln and in books on law, legal ethics, and trial advocacy. It has even been the centerpiece of several works of fiction, the most well known being the 1939 John Ford epic *Young Mr. Lincoln*. Modern trial advocacy books still make reference to this famous cross, which was the climactic event in the Almanac Trial.[3] One recent handbook on cross-examination devotes no fewer than three pages to analyzing Lincoln's handling of the cross.[4] The story has had such staying power because it is not only an exciting tale, it serves as a striking example of a frequently employed cross-examination technique sometimes called commit and contradict.

Perhaps the best-known recent example of this technique comes from O. J. Simpson's trial for the murders of Nicole Simpson and Ron Goldman. In that case, Detective Mark Fuhrman discovered a piece of evidence containing DNA that matched Simpson's DNA profile. To combat this damning evidence, the defense needed to discredit Fuhrman to make the jury more receptive to the argument that Fuhrman had planted the evidence. F. Lee Bailey cross-examined Fuhrman, attacking almost every assertion Fuhrman made, but the most telling blow against Fuhrman's credibility came long after he had left the witness stand. Bailey repeatedly questioned Fuhrman about whether he had ever uttered a particularly offensive racial slur. Fuhrman steadfastly denied doing so, and the papers at the time said Fuhrman had held up well under Bailey's all-out attack. Bailey had, however, planted the seeds of Fuhrman's destruction, and they bore fruit when the defense later introduced irrefutable evidence of Fuhrman's repeated use of that particular racial epithet.[5]

The point Bailey scored against Fuhrman dealt with a side issue, and his actual cross-examination of Fuhrman produced little drama. Carson's cross of Oscar Wilde gives a somewhat more dramatic example of the technique because Carson did not wait until Wilde had left the witness stand to contradict him. During his direct examination Wilde committed himself to the fact Carson sought to impeach. Carson began his examination by repeating the commitment and then immediately confronting Wilde with documentary contradiction:

Q: You stated your age was thirty-nine? I think you are over forty. [Carson displays a birth certificate to the witness.] You were born on 16 October 1854?

A: I had no wish to pose as being young. I am thirty-nine or forty. You have my birth certificate and that settles the matter.

Q: But being born in 1854 makes you more than forty? [Forty-one, to be precise.]

A: Ah, very well.[6]

Carson achieved a somewhat more dramatic effect than Bailey did because he could immediately confront Wilde, but still the impeachment of the witness came on a matter peripheral to the main issue of the case. Wellman's account portrays Lincoln's contradiction as going to the heart of the prosecution's case and destroying the witness while he was still on the stand.

Although Wellman made the cross-examination famous, he took it verbatim from an earlier book written by Judge J. W. Donovan. Because the story originates with Donovan, we repeat his account of the Almanac Trial:

In the July *Century* [magazine] appears the end of a story of a long case, and includes what is vaguely known as Lincoln's first defense in a murder trial. The details need not be repeated. The pith of the story is instructive to lawyers.

Grayson was charged with shooting Lockwood at a camp meeting, on the evening of August 9, 18—, and with running away from the scene of the killing, which was witnessed by Sovine. The proof was so strong that even with an excellent previous character, Grayson came very near being lynched on two occasions soon after his indictment for murder.

The mother of the accused, after failing to secure older counsel, finally engaged young Abraham Lincoln, as he was then called, and the trial came on to an early hearing. No objection was made to the jury, and no cross-examination of witnesses, save the last and only important one, who swore that he knew the parties, saw the shot fired by Grayson, saw him run away, and picked up the deceased, who died instantly.

The evidence of guilt and identity was morally certain. The attendance was large, the interest intense. Grayson's mother began to wonder why Abraham remained silent so long and why he didn't do something!

The people finally rested. The tall lawyer (Lincoln) stood up and eyed the strong witness in silence, without books or notes, and slowly began his defense by these questions:

[Q:] And you were with Lockwood just before and saw the shooting?

[A:] Yes.

[Q:] And you stood very near to them?

[A:] No, about twenty feet away.

[Q:] May it not have been ten feet?

[A:] No, it was twenty feet or more.

[Q:] In the open field?

[A:] No, in the timber.

[Q:] What kind of timber?

[A:] Beech timber.

[Q:] Leaves on it are rather thick in August?

[A:] Rather.

[Q:] And you think this pistol was the one used?

[A:] It looks like it.

[Q:] You could see defendant shoot—see how the barrel hung, and all about it?

[A:] Yes.

[Q:] How near was this to the meeting place?

Lincoln cross-examines Allen. (From *Anecdotal Lincoln: Speeches, Stories, and Yarns from the "Immortal Abe,"* by Paul Selby, 1900)

[A:] Three-quarters of a mile away.

[Q:] Where were the lights?

[A:] Up by the minister's stand.

[Q:] Three-quarters of a mile away?

[A:] Yes,—I answered ye twiste.

[Q:] Did you not see a candle there, with Lockwood or Grayson?

[A:] No. What would we want a candle for?

[Q:] How, then, did you see the shooting?

[A:] By moonlight!

[Q:] You saw this shooting at ten at night—in beech timber, three-quarters of a mile from the lights—saw the pistol barrel—saw the man fire—saw it twenty feet away—saw it all by moonlight? Saw it nearly a mile from the camp lights?

[A:] Yes, I told you so before.

The interest was now so intense that men leaned forward to catch the smallest syllable. Then the lawyer drew out a blue-covered almanac from his side coat pocket—opened it slowly—offered it in evidence—showed it to the jury and the court—read from a page with careful deliberation that the moon on that night was unseen and only arose at one the next morning![7]

Donovan concludes his story by saying Lincoln moved for the arrest of the perjured witness. According to Lincoln, "Nothing but a motive to clear himself could have induced him to swear away so falsely the life of one who never did him harm." When the judge ordered Sovine's immediate arrest, the witness broke down and confessed to firing the fatal shot.[8]

Norman Rockwell immortalized that historic moment in a dramatic portrait. The portrait shows the lawyers had doffed their coats in the hot courtroom, and Lincoln's suspenders were plainly visible, with one of them fallen from his shoulder. Lincoln stands tall and erect in his white suit, his right hand clenched in a fist and resting on a law book on counsel table, his left holding both the opened almanac and his glasses. Behind him sits the forlorn Grayson, his manacled hands clasped in prayer and his face downcast in despair. Lincoln looks intently at the witness as he prepares to use the almanac to devastating effect.

Donovan goes on to heap hyperbolic praise on Lincoln's high ethical standards and skill as a cross-examiner. He says:

This lesson to lawyers, who may not read the whole story, is a good law lecture. It may be added that Lincoln first determined his client was not guilty, and having settled that point he knew the story was one made up for a purpose, and that purpose he was bound to discover, and did discover in his own original manner.

As a reader of trials for years, this one presents as keen interest and displays as much sagacity of counsel as any I have found—even Choate or Webster could have done no better—many other trials are more elaborate in detail, many contain passages of wit and arguments of rare eloquence—they are lessons from life and full of wisdom—some of masterful logic, yet none are so great or were so ably conducted as to overshadow this simple victory by a young country lawyer, who lived to be the leader of a nation and filled with honor the highest station in the world.[9]

Version one of the Almanac Trial tells a remarkable story of courtroom heroics that should ensure Lincoln's fame as a consummate cross-examiner. But is it true? As Lincoln himself is supposed to have said, "History is not history unless it is true."[10] How heavily should we rely on Donovan's testimony? Donovan was a trial lawyer, not a historian, and he wrote at the dawn of the twentieth century about a trial that occurred at the middle of the nineteenth. Although sometimes we must satisfy ourselves with the testimony of a single witness, in this case we can easily check Donovan's facts against versions two and three of the Almanac Trial, both of which predate Lincoln's election to the presidency. Version two comes from David W. Bartlett's pretentiously titled work *The Life and Public Services of Hon. Abraham Lincoln: To Which Is Added a Biographical Sketch of Hon. Hannibal Hamlin,*[11] a shameless piece of campaign propaganda masquerading as a biography. It includes an eyewitness account of the trial by an anonymous "Western Republican."[12] Bartlett's account, like Donovan's, heaped lavish praise upon Lincoln's performance, but they agree on little else. Version three portrays Lincoln's performance in the Almanac Trial as decidedly less than heroic.[13]

Chapter 3

Lincoln the Orator

Version two of the Almanac Trial first saw widespread publication fresh on the heels of one of the most momentous events of the nineteenth century. On May 18, 1860, the Republican National Convention in Chicago nominated Abraham Lincoln as its candidate for president on the third ballot.[1] The very next day the *Cleveland Leader* published version two of Lincoln's defense in the Almanac Trial.[2] Shortly after that, on May 25, 1860, the *Janesville Daily Gazette* reprinted the anonymous article from the *Cleveland Leader* under the title "Thrilling Episode from the Life of Abe Lincoln,"[3] and papers all over the Northeast and Midwest followed suit.[4] The source of the story claimed to be an eyewitness to the trial,[5] and two of Lincoln's official campaign biographies included almost verbatim copies of the eyewitness's account.[6] The biography by David W. Bartlett identified the source as a "Western Republican,"[7] and that is how we will refer to him as we discuss his testimony. The Western Republican said:

Mr. Lincoln, or "Old Abe," as his friends familiarly call him, is a self made man. A Kentuckian by birth, he emigrated to Illinois in his boyhood, where he earned his living at the anvil, devoting his leisure hours to study. Having chosen the law as his future calling, he devoted himself assiduously to its mastery, contending at every step with adverse fortune. During this period of study, he for some time found a home under the hospitable roof of one Armstrong, a farmer, who lived in a log-house some eight miles from the village of Petersburg, Menard County. Here, clad in homespun, with elbows out, and knees covered with patches, young Lincoln would master his lessons by the firelight of the cabin, and then walk to town for the purpose of recitation. This man Armstrong was himself poor, but he saw the genius struggling in the young student, and opened to him his rude home, and bid him welcome to his coarse fare.

How Lincoln graduated with promise, how he has more than fulfilled that promise, how honorably he acquitted himself alike on the battle-field, in defending our border settlements against the ravages of the savage foes, and in the halls of our national legislature, are matters of history, and need no repetition here. But one little incident of a more private nature, standing as it does as a sort of sequel to some things already alluded to, I deem worthy of record. Some few years since, the oldest son of Mr. Lincoln's old friend Armstrong, the chief support of his widowed mother—the good old man having some time previously passed from earth—was arrested on the charge of murder. A young man had been killed during a riotous melee, in the night-time, at a camp-meeting, and one of his associates stated that the death-wound was inflicted by young Armstrong. A preliminary examination was gone into, at which the accuser testified so positively that there seemed no doubt of the guilt of the prisoner, and, therefore, he was held for trial. As is too often the case, the bloody act caused an undue degree of excitement in the public mind. Every improper incident in the life of the prisoner—each act which bore the least semblance to rowdyism—each school-boy quarrel—was suddenly remembered and magnified, until they pictured him as a fiend of the most horrid hue. As these rumors spread abroad, they were received as gospel truth, and a feverish desire for vengeance seized upon the infatuated populace, while only prison-bars prevented a horrible death at the hands of a mob. The events were heralded in the county papers, painted in the highest colors, accompanied by rejoicings over the certainty of punishment being meted out to the guilty party. The prisoner, overwhelmed by the circumstances under which he found himself placed, fell into a melancholy condition, bordering upon despair; and the widowed mother, looking through her tears, saw no cause for hope from earthly aid.

At this juncture, the widow received a letter from Mr. Lincoln, volunteering his services in an effort to save the youth from the impending stroke. Gladly was his aid accepted, although it seemed impossible for even his sagacity to prevail in such a desperate case; but the heart of the attorney was in his work, and he set about it with a will that knew no such word as fail. Feeling that the poisoned condition of the public mind was such as to preclude the possibility of impaneling an impartial jury in the court having jurisdiction, he procured a change of venue, and a postponement of the trial. He then went studiously to work unraveling the history of the case, and satisfied himself that his client was the victim of malice, and that the statement of the accuser was a tissue of falsehoods.

When the trial was called on, the prisoner, pale and emaciated, with hopelessness written on every feature, and accompanied by his half-hoping, half-despairing mother—whose only hope was a mother's belief of her son's innocence, in the justice of the God she worshipped, and in the noble counsel, who, without hope of fee or reward upon earth, had undertaken the cause—took his seat in the prisoner's box, and with a "stony firmness" listened to the reading of the indictment. Lincoln sat quietly by, while the large auditory looked on him as though wondering what he could say in defense of one whose guilt they regarded as certain. The examination of witnesses for the State was begun, and a well-arranged mass of evidence, incidental and positive, was introduced, which seemed to impale the prisoner beyond the possibility of extrication. The counsel for the defense propounded but few questions, and those of a character which excited no uneasiness on the part of the prosecutor—merely, in most cases, requiring the main witness to be definite as to time and place.

When the evidence of the prosecution was ended, Lincoln introduced a few witnesses to remove some erroneous impressions in regard to the previous character of his client, who, though somewhat rowdyish, had never been known to commit a vicious act; and to show that a greater degree of ill-feeling existed between the accuser and accused than the accused and the deceased. The prosecutor felt that the case was a clear one, and his opening speech was brief and formal. Lincoln arose, while a deathly silence pervaded the vast audience, and in a clear but moderate tone began his argument. Slowly and carefully he reviewed the testimony, pointing out the hitherto unobserved discrepancies in the statements of the principal witness. That which had seemed plain and plausible, he made to appear crooked as a serpent's path. The witness had stated that the affair took place at a certain hour in the evening, and that, by the aid of the brightly shining moon, he saw the prisoner inflict the death blow with a slungshot.[8] Mr. Lincoln showed that at the hour referred to, the moon had not yet appeared above the horizon, and consequently the whole tale was a fabrication.

An almost instantaneous change seemed to have been wrought in the mind of his auditors, and the verdict of "not guilty" was at the end of every tongue. But the advocate was not content with this intellectual achievement. His whole being had for months been bound up in this work of gratitude and mercy, and, as the lava of the overcharged crater bursts from its imprisonment, so great thoughts and burning words leaped forth from the soul of the eloquent Lincoln. He drew a picture of the perjurer so horrid and ghastly that the accuser could sit under it no longer, but reeled and staggered from the court-room, while the audience fancied they could see the brand upon his brow. Then in words of thrilling pathos, Lincoln appealed to the jurors as fathers of sons who might become fatherless, and as husbands of wives who might be widowed, to yield to no previous impressions, no ill-founded prejudice, but to do his client justice; and as he alluded to the debt of gratitude which he owed to the boy's sire, tears were seen to fall from many eyes unused to weep. It was near night when he concluded by saying that, if justice were done—as he believed it would be—before the sun should set, it would shine upon his client a free man.

The jury retired, and the court adjourned for the day. Half an hour had not elapsed, when, as the officers of the court and the volunteer attorney sat at the tea-table of their hotel, a messenger announced that the jury had returned to their seats. All repaired immediately to the court-house, and while the prisoner was being brought from the jail, the court-room was filled to overflowing with

Almanac Trial courtroom today. (Photograph by George R. Dekle, Sr.)

citizens of the town. When the prisoner and his mother entered, silence reigned as completely as though the house was empty. The foreman of the jury, in answer to the usual inquiry of the court, delivered the verdict of "Not Guilty!" The widow dropped into the arms of her son, who lifted her up, and told her to look upon him as before—free and innocent. Then, with the words, "Where is Mr. Lincoln?" he rushed across the room and grasped the hand of his deliverer, while his heart was too full for utterance. Lincoln turned his eyes toward the West, where the sun still lingered in view, and then, turning to the youth, said, "It is not yet sundown, and you are free." I confess that my cheeks were not wholly unwet by tears, and I turned from the affecting scene. As I cast a glance behind, I saw Abraham Lincoln obeying the divine injunction by comforting the widowed and the fatherless.[9]

The Western Republican tells a stirring tale, but it bears little resemblance to Donovan's. A cursory examination of the two stories reveals many obvious discrepancies, including disagreement about the identities of the parties involved, but the most interesting discrepancies come from things the Western Republican doesn't say. He says nothing about the two things for which the trial is best remembered—the cross-examination of the defendant's accuser and Lincoln's use of the almanac to impeach him. The Western Republican simply says that Lincoln showed the accuser to be incorrect about the position of the moon, but because he does not describe how Lincoln impeached the accuser, the reader must infer that Lincoln used an almanac.

If these were our only two accounts of the trial, the glaring discrepancies could cause the skeptical reader to doubt whether the Almanac Trial ever occurred, but the actual records of the case have been scanned and placed online, and they may be examined at a website entitled *The Law Practice of Abraham Lincoln*.[10] The killing occurred just outside a camp meeting held in rural Mason County, Illinois. The trial judge ordered a change of venue to Cass County, and the case was tried at the courthouse in Beardstown, Illinois. The trial itself made such an impression on the citizens of Cass County that the Beardstown Woman's Club placed a plaque commemorating the trial on the wall of the courthouse.[11] It reads: "The Beardstown Woman's Club erected this Tablet February 12, 1909, In Memory of ABRAHAM LINCOLN Who for the sake of a mother in distress, cleared her son, Duff Armstrong, of the charge of murder, in this Hall of Justice, May 7, 1858."[12] At the unveiling of the plaque, the president of the woman's club gave a speech describing the events of the Almanac Trial, and her description tallies quite well with the account of the Western Republican.[13] Her description carries weight because she knew people who witnessed the trial, and as late as 1920 she was able to escort William E. Barton, a Lincoln biographer, around Beardstown introducing him to people with personal recollections of the trial.[14] The old courthouse has been turned into a museum and the courtroom restored to look as it might have looked when Lincoln made his famous defense.[15] On the wall to one side of the judge's bench hangs a photograph of Lincoln taken on the afternoon of the trial, and on the wall to the other side hangs a painting depicting Lincoln as he shows the almanac to the jury.[16]

We can be sure that the trial occurred and that Lincoln was involved in it, but the two sources we have examined so far give very different accounts of the trial. They even disagree about how Lincoln won his famous victory. Donovan paints Lincoln as the consummate cross-examiner and sagacious trial advocate. The Western Republican describes him as an eloquent orator whose impassioned appeal could move the most cold-hearted juror. In the next chapter we will look at version three of the Almanac Trial, which casts Lincoln in an entirely different light.

Chapter 4

Lincoln the Trickster

"Thrilling Episode from the Life of Abe Lincoln" got an almost immediate answer. On June 26, 1860, the *Chicago Times* published a vitriolic letter maintaining that the Western Republican had told a "pack of lies, in which there is scarcely a shadow of truth."[1] The writer, who identified himself as an apolitical observer from Menard County, Illinois, took issue with almost everything the Western Republican had said. He alleged: Lincoln did not write Mrs. Armstrong offering his services, but just happened to be in town when the trial began. Lincoln did not obtain a change of venue; the court had changed venue before Lincoln came into the case. Armstrong was not pale and emaciated at the trial; he was "robust and healthy and looked as though he didn't care a 'fig' how the trial went." Lincoln played no major part in the trial; a local attorney served as lead counsel at the trial. In his argument to the jury Lincoln did not draw "a picture of the perjurer so ghastly and horrid, that [the perjurer] actually reeled from the courtroom." Lincoln was not in the courtroom when the jury returned its verdict; he was in a saloon drinking beer.[2] Finally, the "Apolitical Observer" thought it "decidedly rich" to say Mrs. Armstrong's "only hope was in the God she worshipped"; he did, however, admit "[t]he old lady *probably* knows that there is a God, and that's about it" [emphasis in original].

Even more serious allegations against Lincoln arose during his run for the presidency. A Democratic newspaper in Oregon printed an article calling Lincoln a third-rate lawyer who used trickery to win his cases. The article bolstered its claim with a vague affidavit purporting to be from one of the jurors on the case. The affidavit claimed that Lincoln had made fraudulent use of the almanac he presented at the trial.[3] Some of the locals had always suspected something was not quite right about the almanac Lincoln used. They remembered that on the night of the crime, the moon was high overhead and shining brightly at the time of the killing.[4] Inability to reconcile the conflict between Lincoln's almanac and the popular memory led to a widespread belief that Lincoln faked the almanac.[5] Some of the spectators at the trial remembered two almanacs were produced in court, and this led to the belief that Lincoln engaged in some sort of sleight of hand. He must have shown the correct almanac to the court but slipped an almanac for another year to the jury.[6] Many defenders of Lincoln did not deny that the jury saw the wrong almanac but instead contended that Lincoln mistakenly handed them the wrong almanac.[7] Lincoln's detractors countered by saying Lincoln could have made no mistake because he actually forged the almanac handed to the jury. When court recessed on the evening before the trial closed, Lincoln took an almanac for another year and changed the date on the cover to the year of the crime.[8] One of the spectators at the trial, an attorney named Carter, said he examined the almanac after the trial and determined it was for the wrong year.[9] The sheriff, James Dick, said Lincoln had handed him the almanac during a recess and asked Dick to hold it until it was called for. Lincoln's detractors sought to add weight to the bogus almanac claim by using Dick's testimony to suggest chicanery. Why had Lincoln handed the almanac to Dick if not to deflect suspicion from himself if the forgery were discovered? Dick's inability to remember whether the almanac was for 1857 or some other year compounded the suspicion. Somehow Lincoln's enemies transformed Dick's inability to remember the date into proof positive that the date was not 1857.[10] When Lincoln produced the almanac, the prosecutors sent for another to compare with it, and none could be found in the courthouse. Why couldn't they find another almanac in the courthouse? Because Lincoln had gone around and stolen all the almanacs in the courthouse to prevent comparison.[11]

There are two stories about what happened to Lincoln's almanac. In one story, the almanac simply disappeared. After the trial, skeptics looked up the night of the crime in several old almanacs and they all agreed—the moon shone brightly on the night of the killing. When they went to the court records to consult the almanac Lincoln had used, they discovered it had vanished.[12] The second version has the almanac winding up in the hands of J. Henry Shaw, one of the prosecutors in the case. When Shaw died, the almanac came into the possession of John Husted, who was a deputy sheriff at the time of the trial.[13] Husted sold the almanac

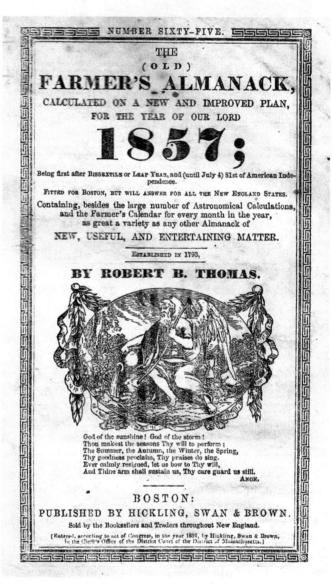

1857 Almanac cover. (George R. Dekle, Sr.'s personal library)

to J. P. Hodge for $5. The year of the almanac had been changed from 1853 to 1857, and Husted assured Hodge he knew for a fact that Lincoln did the changing.[14] The almanac floated around Illinois for two decades being sold and resold for higher and higher prices.[15] The last purchaser donated it to the Chicago Historical Society, where it remained until it disappeared sometime in the early 1920s.[16]

Ward H. Lamon, one of Lincoln's early biographers (who had practiced with Lincoln for a time),[17] added weight to the accusation by citing the testimony of two seemingly unimpeachable sources— Shaw, whom we have already met as one of Armstrong's prosecutors, and E. J. Loomis, the assistant in charge of the Nautical Almanac Office in Washington, DC.[18] According to Lamon, Shaw had this to say about the incident:

Mr. Lincoln, previous to the trial, handed an almanac of the year previous to the murder to an officer of the court, stating that he might call for one during the trial, and, if he did, to send him that one. An important witness for the People had fixed the time of the murder to be in the night, near a camp-meeting; that the moon was about in the same place that the sun would be at ten o'clock in the morning, and was nearly full, therefore he could see plainly, &c. At the proper time, Mr. Lincoln called to the officer for an almanac; and the one prepared for the occasion was shown by Mr. Lincoln, he reading from it, at the time referred to by the witness *The moon had already set;* that in the roar of laughter the jury and opposing counsel forgot to look at the date. ... My own opinion is that when an almanac was called for by Mr. Lincoln, *two* were brought, one of the year of the murder, and one of the year previous; that Mr. Lincoln was entirely innocent of any deception in the matter [emphasis in original].[19]

Loomis informed Lamon that at the time of the killing, "The moon was within one hour of setting."[20] If, as Shaw recalled, Lincoln's almanac showed the moon had already set, then we are confronted with apparently unimpeachable evidence Lincoln produced a bogus almanac. Shaw's excuse that Lincoln mistakenly showed the wrong almanac to the jury seems rather lame, as does his assertion that the judge and prosecutors were so incompetent they neglected to inspect the almanac to determine its authenticity. The 1870 edition of *Ram on Facts* tells a similar story about an English barrister who obtained an acquittal by using a counterfeit almanac. The victim testified positively that he saw the defendant's face clearly by the light of the moon, but on cross-examination the barrister produced an almanac showing the night to be moonless. According to the story, the barrister had a fake almanac printed for use in impeaching the victim. Ram denounced the story as "a pure fiction, 'a thing devised by the enemy,' an enemy to the good fame of the bar." Ram gave two excellent reasons for dismissing the story as fiction:

[F]irst, that the witness having once sworn positively to the moonlight, it is improbable counsel would by a second question hazard a less positive and favorable answer, reducing, perhaps, the moonlight to starlight, to light enough still to see and identify the prisoner by; and, secondly, it is not to be supposed that for a "fellow," a highway robber, any one would venture to practice, and brave the punishment of, such an extreme contempt of court and profanation of justice.[21]

Although Ram's objections to the story of the barrister's counterfeit almanac weight just as heavily against the story of Lincoln's faked almanac, the editors of the fourth American edition of his work credited the story of Lincoln's perfidy. They described the incident in a footnote and indexed it as "LINCOLN, *President Abraham*, how he procured an acquittal by fraud."[22] Perhaps they did so because they believed the testimony of Loomis and Shaw sufficient to defeat Ram's objections.

We thus have three competing versions of Lincoln's performance in the Almanac Trial. In the first version he wins the case with a brilliant cross-examination of the state's star witness. In the second he wins by using his skill as an orator to deliver an impassioned final argument that moves the courtroom to tears. In the third he subverts justice by counterfeiting an almanac and then carousing in a saloon while the jury deliberates the fate of his client. These three pictures of Lincoln do not necessarily conflict and may all be true, but the various stories give widely divergent details of the trial. They do, however, seem to be in agreement on the broad outline of the Almanac Trial: A murder occurs outside a camp meeting. An eyewitness identifies Lincoln's client as the killer. The eyewitness claims to have seen the accused strike the fatal blow by the light of the moon high overhead. Lincoln wins an acquittal by using an almanac to discredit the testimony of the accuser.

Over the next two chapters we will trace the transformation of our three pictures of Lincoln as the story of the trial was told and retold over the decades. We will begin with a study of the earliest nineteenth-century sources, almost none of which qualify as serious scholarship. From there we will move to the more sober appraisals that began appearing in the late nineteenth and early twentieth centuries. We will look at how the three strains of tradition made their way through the later years of the twentieth century, and we will study how the three strains continue through to the twenty-first century. Then we will sift the evidence to determine the course of the trial.

Chapter 5

The Hagiography of the Trial

As we have already seen, Donovan and the Western Republican could not agree as to the names of the parties, the weapon used, or the position of the moon, and the Apolitical Observer showed more interest in hurling insults than enlightening his audience. We should be cautious in accepting the Apolitical Observer's story for two reasons: he tells us next to nothing about the facts of the case, and he displays such bias toward Lincoln that we should reject what he says unless it is corroborated by more impartial witnesses. Standing alone, the Western Republican's story also merits suspicion. His bombastic style and the lavish praise he heaps upon Lincoln betray his story for what it really is—not sober history but campaign histrionics. Donovan wrote near the end of the nineteenth century, fully 40 years after the trial, plenty of time for the facts of twice told tales to become twisted, and biographers were not idle between 1861 and 1898. The last four decades of the nineteenth century saw the publication of at least 18 accounts of the trial, the earliest one coming in 1866. Where the Western Republican and the Apolitical Observer engaged in campaign rhetoric and Donovan wrote a trial advocacy manual, the writers between Lincoln's death and the end of the nineteenth century produced another type of literature altogether—hagiography, a distinct form of literature first used in the early Christian church. *Foxe's Book of Martyrs* stands as the best-recognized work in this form of literature, but many similar works preceded it. Hagiography almost invariably recounted the noble acts of saintly men and women, extolling their virtues and ascribing preternatural abilities to them, and no hagiography would be complete

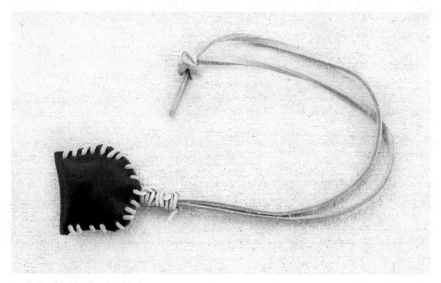

A slungshot. (Made by George R. Dekle, Sr. from descriptions of J. Henry Shaw and Nelson Watkins)

without a detailed account of the saint's tragic death at the hands of ruthless villains.

Lincoln had led the country through its most difficult period and had died a martyr's death at the time of his greatest triumph. There were a few dissenting voices, but most nineteenth-century writers were careful to polish Lincoln's image, some to the point of making him a cardboard character displaying impossibly high morals, ethics, and abilities. Those who dared to swim against the tide of praise were, for the most part, careful to mute their criticism. Whatever their perspective, though, they give us scant reason to credit Donovan's account.

Some versions fail to name any of the principals in the murder;[1] others name only the defendant;[2] fewer name the victim; and only one names the eyewitness.[3] We can, however, sort out the names easily. Court records name the parties as James Preston Metzker, the victim; William Duff Armstrong, the defendant; and Charles Allen, the accuser. We can also rest assured that the weapon was not a firearm. Most sources report that Armstrong used either a slingshot[4] or a slungshot.[5] This discrepancy in nomenclature presents a problem only if we apply the modern definition to the term "slingshot." Originally "slingshot" and "slungshot" meant the same thing—a deadly weapon consisting of a heavy weight fixed on the end of a cord or flexible handle.[6] Probably the most famous variety of slungshot is the medieval "morning star," a spiked ball on the end of a chain attached to a handle.[7] In more modern times prison inmates will sometimes improvise slungshots by putting a bar of soap in a sock[8] or affixing a combination lock from a footlocker onto the buckle of a belt.[9] When we read "slingshot" in the older sources we should remember that they refer to the deadly weapon, not the modern toy.

Let us now look at the sources chronologically to determine how the story morphed in the retelling. Not counting the campaign biographies, we have three accounts from the 1860s—those of J. G. Holland (1866), Isaac N. Arnold (1866), and Harriet Beecher Stowe (1868). Bartlett the campaign biographer had described how Lincoln felt obligated to undertake the defense of Armstrong because of a debt of gratitude he felt toward Armstrong's parents.[10] Holland elaborates on this explanation by giving the history of Lincoln's meeting with Armstrong's father. It seems that Lincoln and the elder Armstrong engaged in a wrestling match as young men, and their competition had given them such regard for each other that they became lifelong friends.[11] Holland tells how Lincoln learned of the arrest of Armstrong and undertook the defense because of his debt of gratitude to Armstrong's widowed mother. Holland says nothing about the conduct of the trial itself, describing only Lincoln's argument to the jury. To refute the eyewitness's testimony that he saw the murder by the light of the moon, Lincoln produced an almanac showing that there was no moon at all when the crime occurred. The jury deliberated a mere half hour before it returned a not guilty verdict.[12] Isaac N. Arnold, a Republican congressman from Illinois and a friend of Lincoln, describes the trial in a few sentences, giving three brief facts—that the chief witness for the state said he saw the death-blow struck by the light of the moon, that Lincoln showed he was wrong by references to an almanac, and that Lincoln made a powerful speech to the jury.[13] Harriet Beecher Stowe's account follows Bartlett's closely but omits much of the bombast. Stowe tells of the conclusive evidence of guilt adduced by the prosecution and describes how Lincoln met that evidence by "cross-examin[ing] very lightly." Stowe then describes Lincoln's argument to the jury, dividing it into four parts. In the first part Lincoln examined the testimony of the state's chief witness, pointing out "first one discrepancy, and then another, and then another." In the second part of his speech Lincoln turned to the key portion of the witness's testimony. Lincoln reminded the jury how the witness had sworn he saw the incident by the light of the moon and then produced an almanac showing that at the time of the killing the moon had not yet risen. In the third part of his speech, having demolished the witness's testimony, Lincoln demolished his character. Stowe tells how Lincoln, his wrath "fully kindled," described the witness "in such a horrid picture of guilt and shame that the miserable fellow, stunned and confounded, actually fled from the face of the incensed lawyer out of the court room." Lincoln ended his speech with an impassioned plea, telling the jury of his deep gratitude to Armstrong's father and asking them to "lay aside any temporary prejudices, and to do simple justice." His speech moved his audience to tears, and the jury quickly acquitted.[14]

Our next informant, Ward H. Lamon (1872), working with a ghost writer by the name of Chauncey Black, based his account on the testimony of people who attended the trial. Lamon tells how Duff Armstrong and James H. Norris were indicted for the murder of a gentleman named "Metzgar" at a camp meeting in Mason County, Illinois. Norris stood trial for the murder in Mason County and was duly convicted of manslaughter. Armstrong's lawyers, feeling that the sentiment in Mason County was too much against their client, took a change of venue to Cass County. Lincoln, because of his high regard for Armstrong's parents, associated himself with the defense team. At the trial Lincoln served in an auxiliary capacity. An attorney named Walker cross-examined the witnesses for the state, with Lincoln taking notes and suggesting questions. Lincoln took no active part before the jury until both sides had rested; then he delivered the final argument and used the almanac to devastating effect.[15] Lamon quotes J. Henry Shaw, one of the prosecutors, as saying, "Armstrong was not cleared by any want of testimony against him, but by the irresistible appeal of Mr. Lincoln in his favor."[16] As we saw in the preceding chapter, Lamon also swam against the tide of adulation by asserting that Lincoln used a bogus almanac to destroy the witness's credibility.

The 1880s saw the publication of no fewer than 10 accounts of the trial. J. B. McClure (1880) briefly describes how Lincoln discredited the state's chief witness by using an almanac to show that there was no moon at the time of the killing. McClure tells how, as the sun sank in the West and the jury retired to consider its verdict, Lincoln remarked that if justice was done "before the sun set it would shine on his client a free man." When the jury returned its verdict of not guilty, the defendant first fell weeping into his mother's arms and then turned to thank Lincoln, who said, "It is not yet sundown and you are a free man."[17] Charles Godfrey Leland (1881) devotes a mere nine lines to describing the Almanac Trial and adds nothing to our stock of information.[18] Goldwyn Smith (1881), although he accuses Lincoln of using a fraudulent almanac, gives us very little information about the conduct of the trial other than to say, "The witness whose testimony bore hardest on the prisoner swore that he saw the murder committed by the light of the moon. Lincoln put in an almanac, which, on reference being made to it showed that at the time stated by the witness there was no moon. This broke down the witness and the prisoner was acquitted."[19]

W. M. Thayer (1882) gives us our most circumstantial account of the trial yet, telling us of Lincoln's great love and respect for "Aunt Hannah," Armstrong's mother, and of how Lincoln rocked young Armstrong to sleep when he was a baby. Aunt Hannah, despairing for her wrongly accused son, wrote Lincoln a plaintive letter asking for his help. Lincoln immediately answered, accepting the case. He then moved for a continuance and a change of venue. When Aunt Hannah objected to lengthening her son's stay in jail, Lincoln told her, "I need more time to unravel the affair. I want to produce evidence that shall vindicate William to the satisfaction of every reasonable man." Thayer then tells how the prosecution called witness after witness to testify to Armstrong's "previous vicious character" and to describe the events of the fatal night. He gives us a transcript of Lincoln's cross-examination of the key witness, and it bears little resemblance to the one quoted by Donovan.[20] Thayer then recounts Lincoln's final argument, following Harriet Beecher Stowe's outline but giving more dramatic detail. After picking the witness's testimony to pieces, Lincoln produced the almanac with the following words: "And he testifies that the moon was shining brightly when the deed was perpetrated, between the hours of ten and eleven o'clock, when the moon did not appear on that night, as your Honour's almanac will show, until an hour or more later, and consequently the whole story is a fabrication." Lincoln concluded his argument with a stirring appeal to the jury's sympathy and ended his plea by telling them, "If justice is done, as I believe it will be, before the sun sets, it will shine upon my client a free man." And it did.[21]

Isaac N. Arnold (1885), who gave his first sketchy account of the Almanac Trial in 1866, returned to the story almost two decades later, giving much more detail. Arnold relates that according to Armstrong's accuser a nearly full moon shone brightly from about the position the sun would be at 10:00 in the morning.[22] Arnold then describes the final argument by quoting Lincoln's co-counsel, William Walker:

At first he spoke slowly and carefully, reviewed the testimony, and pointed out its contradictions, discrepancies, and impossibilities. When he had thus prepared the way, he called for the almanac, and showed that, at the hour at which the principal witness swore he had seen, by the light of the full moon, the mortal blow given, there was no moon at all. ... The last fifteen minutes of his speech was as eloquent as I ever heard. ... The jury sat as if entranced, and when he was through, found relief in a gush of tears.[23]

Arnold records no accusation of perjury against Armstrong's accuser but details the emotional appeal Lincoln made to the sympathies of the jury. He thus follows Harriet Beecher Stowe's outline of the speech but omits the diatribe against the eyewitness.

William O. Stoddard (1885), who served as a personal aide to President Lincoln during the Civil War,[24] tells us that Lincoln took no active part in the defense of Armstrong. Walker served as lead counsel, with Lincoln doing little more than suggesting questions for cross-examination. Lincoln came into his own, however, when he summed up for the defense. His keen analysis of the evidence, which shredded the state's case, culminated in the production of an almanac to show that "instead of the splendor of moonlight sworn to by the prosecuting witnesses, there was no moon at all and darkness reigned." At this revelation, "Court, jury, [and] lawyers burst into a roar of astonished laughter." Having achieved the desired effect, Lincoln then turned to a melodramatic description of the kindnesses done to him by Hannah Armstrong. Stoddard concludes that Lincoln's emotional appeal "without reference to the testimony so skillfully pulled to pieces" saved Armstrong from the gallows.[25]

The next two chroniclers of the Almanac Trial, Noah Brooks (1888) and John Robert Irelan (1888) add nothing, except that Brooks contends Lincoln believed Armstrong to be innocent[26] while Irelan says Lincoln "perhaps" thought Armstrong guilty.[27]

William H. Herndon (1889), who used Jesse Weik to ghost write his biography, should be our most reliable informant yet. Although he was Lincoln's law partner at the time of the trial,[28] he disappoints us by devoting a single paragraph to the event. His sole addition to our store of information is the fact that when Hannah Armstrong asked how much she owed him, Lincoln replied, "Why, Hannah, I shan't charge you a cent, and anything else I can do for you, will do it willingly and without charge." What is probably most interesting about Herndon's account is what he doesn't tell us. Although he was in the best position of all our informants to have gotten the story of the trial from Lincoln's own lips, he quotes J. Henry Shaw (one of the prosecutors) and Hannah Armstrong as sources for his description of the trial.[29] Trial lawyers love to regale each other with tales of their courtroom heroics. If Lincoln played such a pivotal role in the trial, it is passing strange that he never uttered a word to Herndon about it. Others among our informants had the opportunity to get the story from the ultimate source, but none quote a single word from Lincoln about the trial. Many of the early biographers were close associates of Lincoln during his presidency. Because the Almanac Trial became a bone of contention during the election campaign, it seems only natural that they would have gotten Lincoln's version of the event.

We close out the century with the accounts of Charles Wallace French (1891), Charles Carleton Coffin (1892), and Ernest Foster (1893). Foster says Metzker died from a stab wound to the heart and that Lincoln discovered through thorough investigation that Armstrong was the victim of a vicious conspiracy. Lincoln won the case during final argument by displaying the almanac to show that the moon had not yet risen at the time of the stabbing.[30] French says that Lincoln "asked but few questions and produced no witnesses, except one or two to prove the previous good character of the young man" and won the case in final argument by displaying the almanac.[31] Coffin, on the other hand, gives us a transcript of the cross-examination that culminates when Lincoln confronts the witness with the almanac:

Q: You say that you saw him strike the fatal blow?

A: Yes.

Q: What time was it?

A: About eleven o'clock in the evening.

Q: Was it a bright night?

A: Yes, the moon was nearly full.

Q: What was its position in the sky?

A: It was just about the position of the sun at ten o'clock in the forenoon.

Q: You say that the moon was nearly full, and shining so bright that you could see Bill strike the blow?

A: Yes.
   [Lincoln produces an almanac from his pocket and shows it to the jury].

By Mr. Lincoln: Gentlemen, either this witness is wrong or this almanac is wrong, for it says there was no moon that night. Which will you believe?[32]

Except for Coffin and Donovan, the early sources seem to unanimously agree that Lincoln first produced the almanac during final argument. If Lincoln cross-examined at all, he cross-examined only "lightly," with no forensic fireworks. It looks as though Donovan's tale of a tour-de-force cross-examination has no basis in fact. Although the early sources thoroughly undermine the story of Lincoln's cross-examination, many twentieth- and twenty-first-century sources perpetuate it. Albert Woldman (1936),[33] Reinhard H. Luthin (1960),[34] Stephen B. Oates (1977),[35] David Herbert Donald (1995),[36] John Evangelist Walsh (2000),[37] Allen D. Spiegel (2002),[38] Christopher G. Ritter (2004),[39]

Michael Burlingame (2008),[40] Brian Dirck (2009),[41] Ronald C. White (2009),[42] and Arthur L. Rizer (2010)[43] all give us vivid descriptions of Lincoln's cross, and all have Lincoln confronting Allen with the almanac at the climax of the examination. Walsh, Spiegel, Ritter, Burlingame, and Rizer all give us transcripts of the cross-examination. The transcripts have this in common: They disagree with Donovan and Coffin. We will revisit these transcripts in detail in Chapter 11 when we try to reconstruct whether Lincoln actually cross-examined Allen at all and what questions, if any, he asked.

Writers of fiction have preferred the version of the story that has Lincoln using the almanac during cross-examination. Edward Eggleston (1887), who appears to be the first novelist to fictionalize the Almanac Trial, portrays Lincoln as a fledgling attorney defending his first murder case. Lincoln obtains an acquittal of the falsely accused youth by means of a brilliant cross-examination in which he confronts the accuser with an almanac. Eggleston's description of the cross-examination should sound familiar:

"How far away were you from Lockwood when the murder took place"

"Twenty feet."

"You said 'or more' awhile ago."

"Well, 't wusn't no less, p'r'aps," said Dave, showing signs of worry. "You don't think I measured it, do yeh?"

"There were no lights nearer than three-quarters of a mile?"

"No," said the witness, the cold perspiration beading on his face as he saw Lincoln's trap opening to receive him.

"You don't mean to say that the platform torches up by the preacher's tent gave any light three-quarters of a mile away and in the woods?"

"No, of course not."

"How could you see Tom and know that it was he that fired, when the only light was nearly a mile away, and inside a circle of tents?"

"Saw by moonlight," said Sovine, snappishly, disposed to dash at any gap that offered a possible way of escape.

"What sort of trees were there on the ground?"

"Beech."

"Beech-leaves are pretty thick in August?" asked Lincoln.

"Ye-es, rather," gasped the witness, seeing a new pitfall yawning just ahead of him.

"And yet light enough from the moon came through these thick beech-trees to let you know Tom Grayson?"

"Yes."

"And you could see him shoot?"

"Yes."

"And you full twenty feet away?"

"Well, about that; nearly twenty, anyhow." Dave shifted his weight to his right foot.

"And you pretend to say to this court that by the moonlight that you got through the beech-trees in August you could even see that it was a pistol that Tom had?"

"Ye-es." Dave now stood on his left foot.

"And you could see what kind of a pistol it was?" This was said with a little laugh very exasperating to the witness.

"Yes, I could," answered Dave, with dogged resolution not to be faced down.

"And just how the barrel was hung to the stock?" There was a positive sneer in Lincoln's voice now.

"Yes." This was spoken feebly.

"And you twenty feet or more away?"

"I've got awful good eyes, an' I know what I see," whined the witness, apologetically.

At this point in the cross-examination, Lincoln produces an almanac and says "But may it please the court, before proceeding with the witness I would like to have the jury look at the almanac which I hold in my hand. They will here see that on the night of [the crime] the moon did not rise until half-past one in the morning." Lincoln then tells Sovine, "You may have a chance to explain when the jury get done looking at the almanac. For the present you'd better keep silent." Lincoln concludes by asking the judge to order the arrest of the accuser, and the accuser breaks down and confesses to the murder.[44]

Donovan's and Eggleston's accounts agree as to the names of the parties, the weapon used, and the eventual confession of the accuser. They also give remarkably similar descriptions of the questions and answers. Donovan referred to an article in *Century* magazine as his source for the transcript of Lincoln's cross-examination. Before Eggleston published his novel, he serialized it in *Century* magazine.[45] From these facts we infer that Donovan read Eggleston's installment on the trial in *Century* magazine and mistook it for history rather than fiction. We can understand Donovan's mistake when we consider the fact that in addition to being a novelist, Eggleston was a prolific author of works on American history.[46] Thus, one of the earliest historical references to Lincoln using an almanac during cross-examination comes from a work of fiction. This fact further undermines the proposition that Lincoln used the almanac during his cross-examination of Allen, but it does not render the proposition impossible.[47] Whether Lincoln actually cross-examined Allen, or whether he confronted Allen with the almanac, make little difference to his legacy as an honorable lawyer. If it didn't happen, then we simply have a myth about a great man that doesn't diminish his greatness. But if Lincoln used a bogus almanac, the nickname "Honest Abe" is more than harmless fiction, it is a lie. Thus far, our investigation casts serious doubt on Lincoln's honesty. The vast majority of our witnesses say that the almanac showed no moon at the time of the murder, while Lamon has given us strong evidence that the moon was one hour away from setting when the killing occurred. Perhaps the sources we will study in the next chapter can shed more light on these two problems.

Chapter 6

The Historiography of the Trial

As we saw in the preceding chapter, Lincoln's early biographers showed more interest in polishing the image of the martyred president than in relating a sober history of his career. They took the story of the Almanac Trial, which began its life as a piece of campaign rhetoric, and spun it into a dramatic tale of exemplary integrity, loyalty, and heroism. These early stories emphasized Lincoln's oratorical skill and almost uniformly ignored the cross-examination of Charles Allen, Armstrong's principal accuser. Then at the end of the nineteenth century the story of the dramatic cross-examination sprang fully formed from the pen of J. W. Donovan. Francis Wellman repeated it, and the story of the dramatic cross-examination largely supplanted the story of the dramatic final argument. Whichever version they told, though, the biographers painted Lincoln as a larger-than-life hero.

Two authors discussed in the preceding chapter, Ward H. Lamon and William H. Herndon, swam against the tide of hagiography. They both practiced law with Lincoln, and their biographies tend to validate the old Victorian proverb that no man is a hero to his valet. Herndon, who began collecting material for his biography almost immediately after the death of Lincoln, relied heavily on interviews and correspondence with people who knew him in life. Herndon's methods have come under fire from modern historiographers, but it cannot be denied that he tried his best to determine the facts and to write an accurate account.[1] Although Herndon held Lincoln in high regard, he did not believe Lincoln to be a saint or superman, and he tried to tell the story of a very human man who succeeded against great odds. He was deeply disappointed when his efforts met with censure from those who would turn Lincoln into a demigod. Lamon, who used Herndon's notes in writing his own biography, also portrayed Lincoln as a fallible human being and was roundly criticized for his iconoclasm.[2]

Although the stream of laudatory books continues unabated into the twenty-first century, as the nineteenth century drew to a close some writers began to look at Lincoln with a more discerning eye. One of the most discerning pairs of eyes had to be those belonging to Ida M. Tarbell (1898/1907), an investigative journalist who wrote for *McClure's* magazine. Although she did not approve of the characterization, she became known as one of the foremost of the "muckrakers," a group of Gilded Age journalists who specialized in exposing graft and corruption in government and big business. Her most influential work, *The History of the Standard Oil Company*, is credited with setting in motion the chain of events that culminated in the Supreme Court's 1911 decision to break up Standard Oil.[3] She unleashed her investigative talent upon Abraham Lincoln in a series of 20 articles for *McClure's*[4] and later collected the articles into a four-volume work.[5] Tarbell was objective enough to recognize and report both the good and the bad about her subjects. Her *History of Standard Oil* exposed many illegal practices by John D. Rockefeller, but she also praised him for his positive contributions to the oil industry.[6] Despite the criticism of Lincoln biographer Albert J. Beveridge that Tarbell's work was an attempt to "fumigate" Lincoln,[7] we can expect that she would be just as even-handed in her treatment of Lincoln.

Tarbell's account of the Almanac Trial, which is based on interviews with eyewitnesses to the trial, has the murder occurring between 10:00 p.m. and 11:00 p.m. and the moon setting before midnight. She rejects the story of the fake almanac by stating that reference to any authentic almanac from the time would show that the moon set precisely when Lincoln's almanac said it did. Although her language is somewhat ambiguous, she does not appear to claim that there was no moon at the time of the murder. Although she does say that the moon was "not in the heavens," she could have meant that the moon was on the horizon at the time of the killing and not high overhead and shining brightly as claimed by Allen.[8]

Tarbell's main witnesses to the events of the trial seem to be William A. Douglas, who testified for the prosecution, and Duff Armstrong himself. Douglas, one of the first witnesses to testify, was allowed to stay in the courtroom after testifying and apparently saw the entire trial. Although it is hard to tell for certain, it appears that Tarbell's description of

Lincoln's cross comes from Douglas. Douglas merely reports that Lincoln had Allen repeat several times that the moon was high in the sky and shining brightly. According to Tarbell, "Under Lincoln's questioning he repeated the statement until it was impossible that the jury should forget it." Viewed in isolation, the cross-examination appears quite amateurish. Lincoln drills the most damning part of Allen's testimony indelibly into the memories of the jurors. Prosecutors sometimes jokingly call this type of cross-questioning "supplemental direct examination." This is neither dramatic nor effective in isolation, but as F. Lee Bailey did with Mark Fuhrman, Lincoln was getting the commitment he would later contradict with the almanac. Tarbell goes on to describe Lincoln's stirring final argument and says it was during his final argument that he produced the almanac.[9] Thus it appears that examination by an expert investigative reporter supports the Western Republican's account against the other two versions. Tarbell may have been the first to engage in critical analysis of the trial, but she certainly wasn't the last.

James L. King (1898) took a close look at the Almanac Trial in an article written for the *North American Review*. The article, which sought to assess Lincoln's legal abilities, defended Lincoln against the allegations of fraud. King relied upon the testimony of an eyewitness to the trial, a judge by the name of Abram Bergen. Bergen had been a young lawyer at the time of the Almanac Trial and had attended the trial to learn as much as he could from watching Lincoln perform in court. As a wide-eyed rookie watching what was probably his first murder trial, Bergen should have been a keen observer and should have made an excellent witness to the events of the trial despite the passage of many decades. Bergen pronounced the story of the fake almanac to be "absolutely untrue." Bergen remembered that Lincoln first mentioned the almanac during the presentation of the defense evidence. He asked the judge to take judicial notice of the almanac and offered the almanac into evidence so that "there might be no question on that point." The judge accepted the almanac into evidence and held that either side might use it during final argument. Apparently the prosecution saw no danger in Lincoln's maneuver because they did not immediately inspect the almanac. Bergen's description suggests that Lincoln finessed the prosecution by nonchalantly offering the almanac as though it meant very little. The prosecutors apparently were taken in by the ploy and let the almanac go uninspected. Lincoln then gave the almanac to Sheriff Dick to hold until he called for it. When Lincoln dramatically produced the almanac and read from it during final argument, he threw the prosecution team into disarray. They objected to the authenticity of the almanac and obtained another almanac from the office of Probate Judge Arenz. The prosecutors, after carefully comparing their almanac to the one produced by Lincoln, had to admit that Lincoln's almanac was genuine. At first they thought they had found a discrepancy, but further investigation showed that they were mistaken. If Bergen's description is accurate, Lincoln outsmarted the prosecutors by saving the damning evidence of the almanac for final argument, but he did absolutely nothing wrong. It is not the duty of the lawyer for one side of a case to point out to the other side the significance of evidence that is readily available for inspection. Bergen went on to say that the story of the bogus almanac first surfaced during Lincoln's campaign for the presidency and that Lincoln's detractors tried to support their allegation of trickery with an affidavit by Sheriff John Dick that he, Dick, did not notice the date on the almanac.[10] King, who was the state librarian in Topeka, Kansas, gleaned his information from the text of a speech given by Judge Bergen to the Kansas State Bar Association in 1897. Judge Bergen's speech was reduced to writing and immediately published in the *American Lawyer*. A comparison of King's text with the published text of Bergen's speech shows that the wording of the two is almost identical.[11]

The next historian in chronological order is T. G. Onstot, an Illinois businessman who published an oral history of Menard and Mason Counties in 1900, which he compiled from a series of news articles he had written on local history.[12] Although not a Lincoln biographer, he did include reminiscences of Lincoln in his work. John G. Nicolay and John Hay describe Onstot's account of Lincoln as "deliciously artless and not very accurate, but worthy of a place in Lincoln collections."[13] His account of the Almanac Trial is noteworthy because he bases it upon correspondence he received from William Walker, who was intimately involved in the trials of both Armstrong and his co-defendant James H. Norris. According to Walker, Lincoln was very much in the background during the actual taking of testimony. Walker conducted the examinations of the witnesses, and Lincoln took notes. Walker recalls Lincoln insisting that all the witnesses be called upon to repeat that the murder occurred at 10:00 p.m. and that it was as light as day. Lincoln made the final argument for the defense. He supposedly told the jury, "These witnesses have all perjured themselves and I can prove it." He then brought out the almanac and showed that at 10:00 p.m. the moon had not yet risen. Onstot tells us that the fight occurred in a heavily wooded ravine, which would have kept the site in darkness unless the moon was high overhead.

Although J. T. Hobson (1909) can best be described as a Lincoln hagiographer, he is included in this chapter because of some excellent spadework he did in sorting out the facts of the Almanac Trial. Hobson was a minister of the Gospel, and his primary interest in Lincoln was driven by the desire to use Lincoln's life and works to inspire moral behavior. His first book on Lincoln bore the title *The Lincoln Year Book: Containing Immortal Words of Abraham Lincoln Spoken and Written on Various Occasions, Preceded by Appropriate Scripture Texts and Followed by Choice Poetic Selections for Each Day in the Year, with Special Reference to Anniversary Dates.*[14] His next book, *Footprints of Abraham Lincoln: Presenting Many Interesting Facts, Reminiscences and Illustrations Never Before Published,*[15] gives evidence of careful investigation. He reproduces in full a letter from Lyman Lacey, one of Duff Armstrong's lawyers. Lacey gives a complete account of the trial, but we must take his assertions with a grain of salt for two reasons. First, it was written in 1908, fully 50 years after the trial; and second, Lacey did not attend the trial. Lacey says nothing about a dramatic cross-examination but describes Lincoln as using the almanac in final argument. He goes on to say that his partner, William Walker, would certainly have told him if Lincoln had used a bogus almanac.

Hobson does his best work on the trial in tracing the history of the legend of Lincoln's cross-examination, making a highly significant finding that has gone virtually ignored. Hobson tells us how Edward Eggleston came to write his account of the cross-examination. Hobson learned from Eggleston's brother, George Carey Eggleston, that

the story arose from an incident connected with a trial in the early 'fifties at Vevay, Indiana, witnessed by himself and his brother Edward, the author of the "Hoosier Schoolmaster," and other popular novels. He says his brother, in writing the novel, entitled "The Graysons," exercised the novelist's privilege, and attributed this clever trick to Abraham Lincoln in the days of his obscurity.[16]

According to Edward Eggleston's brother, the dramatic confrontation with the witness was performed by another lawyer in another trial, transposed by Eggleston's imagination into Lincoln's Almanac Trial and not based on any information relating to the actual facts of the Almanac Trial itself. It may be that Hobson's contribution went largely unnoticed because *The Lincoln Year Book* ruined his reputation as a serious Lincoln scholar.

Not long after J. N. Gridley (1910) moved to Beardstown, Illinois, the scene of the Almanac Trial, he heard a local citizen tell the story of how Lincoln faked the almanac to show that there was no moon on the night of the killing. Gridley initially accepted the story at face value but eventually decided to investigate whether it was true. He first wrote Joel Stebbins, professor of astronomy at Illinois University, asking the position of the moon on the night of the murder. Stebbins replied that on August 29, 1857, the moon crossed the meridian at 7:44 p.m. and set within 15 minutes of midnight. Gridley concluded that if Lincoln showed an almanac saying there was no moon that night, he perpetrated a fraud on the court.[17] Gridley determined to dig deeper and sought out members of the jury. He learned that only one juror was still living, John T. Brady. He wrote Brady and learned that as Brady remembered, Lincoln produced an almanac that showed the moon to be setting on the horizon at the time of the killing. Brady distinctly recalled that the prosecutors examined the almanac and that one of the prosecutors said the almanac showed that the moon was just coming up as the killing occurred. Lincoln replied, "It serves my purpose just as well, just coming up, or just going down, as you admit it was not over head as Mr. Allen swore it was."[18] Brady's memory was somewhat jumbled as to whether Lincoln first produced the almanac during cross-examination or during final argument. He clearly remembered, though, that Lincoln had Allen repeat several times that the moon was overhead and that "Mr. Lincoln was very careful not to cross Mr. Allen in anything, and when Allen lacked words to express himself, Lincoln loaned them to him."[19] Brady's memory may have been faulty in at least one other material respect—Brady stated that Allen was the only witness called by the prosecution, but court records show that 15 other witnesses received subpoenas on behalf of the prosecution.[20] Perhaps it was not Brady's memory but his ability to express himself that was at fault. He may well have meant that of all the witnesses called by the prosecution, Allen was the only one who directly incriminated Armstrong.

William E. Barton (1925) began his career as a circuit-riding preacher in Tennessee. In 1902 he accepted an offer to become the pastor of the First Congregational Church of Oak Park, Illinois, where he served from 1902 until 1924. After his retirement, he served as a lecturer for Vanderbilt University. Barton wrote prodigiously during his entire career, authoring several books on Lincoln and amassing a huge volume of notes and papers concerning his research of Lincoln's life. Those notes and papers now reside in the Special Collections Research Center of the University of Chicago Library.[21] Barton interviewed several witnesses to the trial, reviewed James Norris's application for pardon for the killing of Metzker, and conducted a thorough investigation of the Chicago Historical Society's bogus almanac, going so far as to examine it with a microscope. He found that although someone had taken great pains to scratch out the numeral 3 everywhere 1853 appeared and replace it with a 7, the change was not done well enough to fool an alert observer. Barton determined from his investigation that the almanac played only a small part in the trial of Armstrong; that the key evidence exonerating Armstrong came in the form of testimony by other witnesses who swore that Allen was somewhere else in the whiskey camp when the fight occurred and could not have seen what he claimed; and that Lincoln's high ethical standards would have prevented him from using a bogus almanac at the trial.[22] The defense of alibi is well known to anyone familiar with criminal prosecutions—it simply means that the accused was somewhere else when the crime occurred and could not possibly have committed it. This form of reverse alibi, proving that the eyewitness was somewhere else and could not have seen the event, is far less common. The ancient Hebrews called it the defense of confutation, and Talmudic law provided that if any defendant was exonerated by confutation, the confuted witnesses could suffer the penalty prescribed for the crime.[23] It is hard to see how the confutation of Allen played a pivotal role in Armstrong's acquittal—the confuting witnesses testified on behalf of Norris to no avail. It is also hard to see how an examination of the Chicago Historical Society's almanac could prove that Lincoln did not use another bogus almanac. The almanac examined by Barton may simply have been a double fraud invented by someone who wanted ill-gotten profit.

Carl Sandburg (1926) is best remembered as a poet, but he also wrote a six-volume biography of Lincoln. Sandburg has been criticized for not being as good a researcher as some other Lincoln biographers,[24] but his account of the Almanac Trial is both thorough and consistent with other diligent researchers. Sandburg does not have Lincoln confronting Allen with the almanac but has him producing the almanac after calling at least one defense witness.[25] Sandburg disposed of the story of the fake almanac by rejecting the testimony of those witnesses who said the almanac showed no moon at all and accepting Brady's statement that the almanac had the moon on the horizon. Sandburg said with the moon setting just before midnight, it was hard to believe that Allen had enough light to see at 11:00 p.m.[26]

After Albert J. Beveridge (1928) won the 1920 Pulitzer Prize for his four-volume life of John Marshall, he turned his considerable talents to the task of writing a biography of Lincoln. Although he died before he could finish the project, he managed to publish two volumes dealing with Lincoln's career prior to becoming president. Beveridge prepared for his project by surveying the currently existing literature on Lincoln, and he did not like what he saw. Pronouncing these previous efforts to be "trash,"[27] he set out to write "the facts, the exact facts and all the facts" about the slain president.[28] Initially Beveridge believed that Lincoln likely used a "doctored almanac" to discredit Allen's testimony, but he planned not to say so in his book because he was not positive.[29] When it came time to write, however, he had satisfied himself that Lincoln used an almanac for the correct year.[30] Unlike previous Lincoln biographers,

Beveridge gives a catalog of the sources upon which he bases his description of the trial.[31] Given the sources he cites, it is hard to understand his description of the cross-examination. Beveridge says that Armstrong testified the moon was where the sun would be at 10:00 a.m. "Thereupon," he says, "Lincoln produced [the almanac]."[32] This gives the impression that Lincoln confronted Allen with the almanac while Allen testified on cross-examination. Beveridge may have gotten the impression that this was the case because his sources say the almanac "floored" the witness. They probably meant that Lincoln's use of the almanac during final argument floored Allen, who had stayed to watch the conclusion of the trial. Shaw, Walker, and Bergen, whose testimony Beveridge held in highest regard, all say Lincoln produced the almanac after the prosecution had rested its case. Beveridge was not impressed by Lincoln's use of the almanac, thinking that any competent trial attorney would have done the same. Nor did he think the almanac played an important role in the case. Beveridge cited a number of things the defense did to substantially weaken the prosecution's case, but he felt the most telling thing in Armstrong's favor was Lincoln's speech to the jury.

At the dawn of the twentieth century, careful investigation had raised serious questions about the tale of the dramatic cross-examination, and by the second quarter of the twentieth century, the stories of both the brilliant cross and the faked almanac were thoroughly undermined. We will recall that Francis Wellman included Donovan's account of the cross in *The Art of Cross Examination*, using it in his chapter on cross-examining the perjured witness.[33] Although Wellman kept Donovan's story in his book even after he learned of its falsity, he kept it as an example of the fallibility of testimony, saying that the tale of Lincoln's cross had been told and retold so many times that the oral tradition transformed the story into Donovan's version.[34] Wellman apparently knew nothing of the history of how Eggleston's fiction got repeated by Donovan as fact and thus drew the logical but erroneous inference that Donovan's version was the product of faulty transmission of twice told tales. Even European biographers had discounted the stories of Lincoln's dramatic cross. In England Lord Charnwood (1917) had Lincoln producing the almanac after the prosecution rested,[35] and in Germany Emil Ludwig (1930) wrote that Lincoln first used the almanac in final argument.[36] How, then, could the story of the dramatic cross-examination survive to be repeated in so many late twentieth- and early twenty-first-century accounts of the trial?

Let us answer that question by first stating the obvious— "undermined" is not a synonym of "untrue." Although we have thoroughly demolished Donovan as a basis for crediting the story of the dramatic cross, we may very well be able to find other sources that will support it. Even the story of the faked almanac is not completely refuted by our evidence. If, as many witnesses to the trial say, Lincoln produced an almanac showing that the night was moonless, then the fake almanac story still has support. One early source who lends credence to the story of the dramatic cross-examination is Frederick Trevor Hill (1905). Hill was one of the first Lincoln biographers to write a book solely about Lincoln's law practice.[37] In his book, Hill reports that Lincoln worked his cross-examination of Allen to the point that Lincoln:

demanded that he inform the jury how he had managed to see so clearly at that time of night. "By the moonlight," answered the witness, promptly. "Well, was there light enough to see everything that happened?" persisted the examiner. The witness responded "that the moon was about in the same place that the sun would be at ten o'clock in the morning and was almost full,["] and the moment the words were out of his mouth the cross-examiner confronted him with a calendar showing that the moon, which at its best was only slightly past its first quarter on August 29, had afforded practically no light at eleven o'clock and that it had absolutely set at seven minutes after midnight.

Hill cited no less a witness than J. Henry Shaw, one of the prosecutors, as the source of his information.[38] Hill set a precedent for books on Lincoln as a lawyer. Most of them seem to follow Hill's lead in having Lincoln confront Allen with the almanac. Albert A. Woldman's book *Lawyer Lincoln* (1930),[39] John J. Duff's *A. Lincoln: Prairie Lawyer* (1960),[40] and Brian Dirck's *Lincoln the Lawyer* (2009)[41] all have Lincoln craftily setting Allen up before dramatically confronting him with the almanac. Having traced the history of the telling and retelling of the tale of the Almanac Trial, we will turn to the task of attempting to discern the facts of the case, including the circumstances of the killing and the course of the actual trial itself.

Chapter 7

Lincoln and the Clary's Grove Boys

The chain of events that led Abraham Lincoln to represent Duff Armstrong on a charge of murder began when he came to New Salem in Sangamon County, Illinois in 1831. Up to this point in his young life, Lincoln had done little to indicate that he would achieve any more success than his father, an illiterate backwoodsman who could barely sign his name. Lincoln's father had handed him an axe when he was eight years old, and Lincoln would later write that "from that time until [my] twenty-third year [I] was almost constantly handling that most useful instrument. . . ."[1] Handling an axe from daylight until dark for a period of 12 years will produce tremendous strength, and we shall see that if Lincoln's contemporaries recognized him for anything during his youth, they recognized him for his strength. The residents of New Salem, upon first encountering Lincoln, would little suspect that this tall and rangy young man possessed such a quality. At 6 feet 4 inches tall and weighing 214 pounds,[2] and looking more like Ichabod Crane than Paul Bunyan, Lincoln first gained the admiration of New Salem with neither his looks nor his strength, but with another attribute.

Lincoln made his first appearance in New Salem as a boatman on the Sangamon River. Navigating the tributaries of the Mississippi was a tricky business. Boats constantly ran aground in the shallows of the rivers, and extricating them proved no small task. When Lincoln and his crewmates ran their flatboat onto a dam near New Salem in Sangamon County, it stuck fast and began taking on water at the stern. A number of Sangamon Countians gathered, not to help Lincoln, but to enjoy the spectacle of the young men trying to save a wrecked boat. Lincoln first tried manfully to lift the boat over the low dam. When his strength failed him, he impressed the crowd by drawing upon a hidden resource—his ingenuity. Offloading enough cargo to allow the boat to ride higher in the water, he bored a hole in the bottom of the boat with a borrowed auger. The crowd might have wondered how boring a hole in the bottom of the boat would improve its seaworthiness, but Lincoln knew what he was doing. The water that threatened to swamp the boat ran out through the hole, the boat lost enough weight to be lifted over the dam, Lincoln plugged the hole, and the boat continued on its way to New Orleans. At least that is the story told by John Hanks, one of the men who helped Lincoln sail the flatboat to New Orleans.[3]

Lincoln never forgot his experiences as a boatman. Although he became a respected lawyer and a successful politician, he continued to worry about the plight of boatmen on the Mississippi River system. He did more than wring his hands over the problem; he put them to solving it. Devising a mechanical method of lifting boats over shallows, he made a model of his invention and took it to Washington during his time as congressman. In Washington he applied for and received a patent. Although nobody ever built the mechanism or put it into operation, it gave Lincoln the distinction of being the only elected president ever to patent an invention. The model can be seen today at the Smithsonian Institution.[4]

Denton Offutt, the capitalist who bankrolled Lincoln's voyage to New Orleans, was so impressed with the young man's ingenuity that he hired Lincoln to work as a clerk in the store he planned to open in New Salem. This job opportunity may well have changed the course of Lincoln's life. It marked the beginning of his transition from blue-collar laborer to white-collar professional. When Lincoln returned to Sangamon County to take up his duties at Offutt's store, he almost immediately had another opportunity to display his intellectual prowess. He had not long been in New Salem before he had the chance to render service in a local election. They needed a clerk and were casting about looking for someone who could read and write well enough to do the job when someone suggested that they enlist the aid of the tall, thin newcomer. Upon being asked if he could read and write, Lincoln replied, "Yes, a little." They quickly put him to work, and he performed so well in this, his first public office, that he again won the admiration of the locals.[5]

It goes without saying that Lincoln possessed a keen mind, but what evidence do we have that he possessed near-Herculean strength? Our first indication comes from his weight. When he went to Washington as president-elect, he weighed in at around 180 pounds.[6] As men become older and less active, they tend to gain weight rather than lose it. What caused the sedentary, middle-aged Lincoln to weigh more than 30 pounds less than the young, physically active Lincoln? We can reasonably infer that his shrinkage indicated a loss of muscle mass. Lincoln had a classic ectomorphic body type. Ectomorphs normally have little muscle and less body fat. Almost any personal trainer in almost any gym will tell you that to gain weight the ectomorph must eat hearty, and if he wants that weight to be muscle, he must train hard. If he stops eating and training, he shrinks. Lincoln the lawyer didn't work as hard as Lincoln the log splitter, and unused muscle tends to atrophy. As he became less active, his muscle mass shrank, and because he was an ectomorph he did not put on fat.

Lincoln had not been in Sangamon County long before he began to give evidence of his physical prowess. Many stories are told about his feats of strength, but two of his exploits border on the unbelievable. William Greene, who worked in Offutt's store with Lincoln, loved to gamble but was not very good at it. Lincoln admonished him to quit, but he protested that he couldn't until he paid off a $0.90 gambling debt to a man named Estep. Upon Greene's promise to quit, Lincoln arranged for a bet with the creditor to cancel the debt. To win the bet, Lincoln would have to lift a 40-gallon barrel of whiskey and take a sip from the bung hole. A whiskey barrel weighs around 110 pounds empty,[7] and whiskey weighs approximately 8 pounds to the gallon,[8] meaning that Lincoln would be lifting and drinking from a tankard that could weigh no less than 110 pounds and no more than 430 pounds. Ward Lamon commented on this feat in the following words: "It was even said he could easily raise a barrel of whiskey to his mouth when standing upright, and take a drink out of the bung-hole; but of course one cannot believe it."[9] Lamon, who was a strong man in his own right, was correct to disbelieve the story as he heard it. Of course, Lincoln didn't lift and drink the whiskey as you would lift and drink from a pitcher. He laid the barrel on its side, squatted, grabbed the barrel by the chimes,[10] and hoisted it onto his knees, much as a World's Strongest Man competitor begins to lift an Atlas Stone. From that position, Lincoln was able to hoist and tilt the barrel so that whiskey could pour out of the bung hole in the side of the barrel and into his mouth. Upon accomplishing this feat, Lincoln spit the whiskey out and gave his friend a severe lecture on the evils of gambling. Greene took the temperance pledge.[11] Greene may have been sincere in his resolve to stop gambling, but he soon relapsed into his old habits. Later, when they were both serving in the Black Hawk War, Greene induced Lincoln to help him win a $10 bet by replicating his feat with another whiskey barrel. Lincoln repeated the barrel lift and afterward gave Greene another lecture on the evils of gambling.[12] Greene would later credit Lincoln's lecture for putting him on the straight and narrow path. Could it be that these two stories are actually doublets of a single incident? The chances are good that the two stories recount two different incidents because Lincoln did not mind flexing his muscles for his admirers. When William Herndon was researching his biography of Lincoln, he received the assurance of R. B. Rutledge, another Sangamon Countian, that "I have frequently seen [Lincoln] take a barrel of whiskey by the chimes and lift it up to his face as if to drink out of the bung-hole."[13]

Lincoln's second feat is just as impressive. A number of witnesses attested to the fact that he lifted a box of rocks weighing in at a little over 1,000 pounds.[14] At first blush, this seems impossible. After all, Zydrunas Savickas, who has won multiple World's Strongest Man titles, set the strongman competition world record for the dead lift at the 2012 Arnold Strongman Classic—1,117 pounds.[15] How could Lincoln, an untrained man, lift a weigh comparable to that of a world-class weightlifter? He didn't do a dead lift, he did a somewhat "easier" lift called a harness lift. In the dead lift, the lifter stands before a barbell loaded with weights, stoops to grab it, and stands erect, lifting the bar from the ground to above his knees, moving the weight a distance of two feet or more. In the harness lift, the lifter puts a harness on his shoulders, mounts a platform over the weight, bends his knees, attaches the harness to the weight, and stands up, merely clearing the ground with the weight. The weight need move no more than a centimeter in a harness lift. Lamon, who has no difficulty believing this tale of Lincoln's prowess, tells us that Lincoln regularly performed the lift, using between 1,000 and 1,200 pounds. He then tells us, "Frequent exhibitions of such strength doubtless had much to do with his unbounded influence over the rougher class of men."[16]

Newcomers to small towns can expect to be tested, and if the newcomer is a man, the test sometimes comes in hand-to-hand combat. Lincoln had to prove himself against Jack Armstrong, the leader of a gang of roughnecks known as the Clary's Grove Boys. Although Lincoln's early biographers tried to portray the Clary's Grove Boys as a group of mischievous, fun-loving young men,[17] their descriptions of the gang's exploits clearly depict them as bullies and petty criminals. One newcomer to Sangamon County shrugged off a warning about the Clary's Grove Boys. He was a rather large man by the name of Radford who planned to open a store. One of Radford's new friends advised him to be wary of the Clary's Grove Boys or they would "smash him up." Because he was a huge man, he confidently declared that he had no fear of them. His friend reiterated the warning "they don't come alone. If one can't whip you two or three can." Not long after that, a clerk in Radford's employ insulted the boys by refusing to sell them liquor. They took the liquor by force and smashed the contents of the store. When they satisfied themselves that they had demolished the store's contents, they mounted their horses and rode off whooping and yelling. Radford sold what remained of his store and moved on.[18]

Before Lincoln arrived, Jack Armstrong enjoyed a reputation as the strongest man in Sangamon County, a distinction that Lincoln certainly threatened. Lincoln threatened Armstrong in another area as well. He posed a threat to Armstrong's reputation as the best wrestler in Sangamon County. Lincoln enjoyed a reputation as a talented wrestler himself, largely due to his recent defeat of a famous wrestler by the name of Daniel Needham. This match had occurred during Lincoln's return from his flatboat trip to New Orleans,[19] and it is sure to have been trumpeted about Sangamon County by Lincoln's employer, Denton Offutt, who was something of a loudmouth. Offutt proclaimed that his young clerk could defeat any man in Sangamon County at running, jumping, or wrestling.[20] It was only a matter of time before Lincoln would be called upon to make good on Offutt's boast. Offutt was finally given an ultimatum to put up or shut up, and he wagered $10 that Lincoln could throw Jack Armstrong. Although Lincoln could certainly handle himself in a scuffle, he was reluctant to take on the leader of the Clary's Grove Boys, probably because "they don't come alone. If one can't whip you two or three can." Offutt insisted, however, and Lincoln reluctantly agreed to the match.

Modern Americans are most familiar with professional "rassling," but several styles of wrestling are contested in American schools and colleges—folkstyle, freestyle, and Greco-Roman. Lincoln and his rival engaged in none of these styles of wrestling. From the descriptions given of the Lincoln-Armstrong match, it appears that frontiersmen in Illinois contested a variant of the style of wrestling practiced in the British Isles. This style is best known as collar and elbow, but it went by other names as well. Because all these styles were contested in similar fashion, we will speak mainly of collar and elbow wrestling. The sport originated in Northern Ireland[21] and apparently came to the United States with Scots-Irish immigrants. Over the years, the style evolved from a strictly standup game to a ground fighting game, and the rules varied from place to place. To appreciate the story of Lincoln's bout with Armstrong, we need to have some understanding of the rules of the sport. Based upon the descriptions of Lincoln's wrestling matches as a young man[22] and upon the rules of the various forms of British wrestling from the available sources,[23] I present here a conjectural reconstruction of the rules observed in antebellum Illinois. The contestants confronted each other, with each

Lincoln wrestles Jack Armstrong. (From *Abraham Lincoln and the Downfall of American Slavery*, by Noah Brooks, 1894)

grasping his opponent in an agreed-upon manner. At a given signal, the combat would commence, with each man trying to throw the other to the ground. The first person to touch the ground with anything other than the soles of his feet lost the round. If both contestants hit the ground at the same time, it was called a dog fall, and the round was considered drawn. If a contestant intentionally broke his hold (let go of his opponent), he lost the round. A match consisted of the best two out of three falls. The contestants took turns prescribing the type of hold with which to contest the round. The popularity of the collar and elbow hold or square hold, which called for the contestants to grab their opponent by the collar with one hand and the elbow with the other, may be what caused the style to be known by that name. The side hold, which called for the contestants to grab each other at the waist, was Lincoln's favorite hold.[24] I do not believe that there was ground fighting in the antebellum Illinois form of the sport. If there were ground fighting, a throw would not end the fight. It would continue until one or the other contestant was pinned. When ground fighting was introduced into the sport, the opponents could lawfully break their hold and seek another hold to try to pin their adversary by putting him on his back with either both shoulders and one hip on the ground or both hips and one shoulder on the ground. All of our sources speak of Lincoln and Armstrong trying to throw each other, not pin each other.

Although undoubtedly a strong man, Armstrong could not match Lincoln physically. At 5 feet 6 inches and 160 pounds,[25] he ceded a 10-inch height advantage and a 54-pound weight advantage to Lincoln, and his arm span could not possibly have equaled Lincoln's enormous arm span, which has been estimated at 6 feet 10 inches.[26] In his youth Lincoln seldom lost a wrestling match, and even when president, he could still physically eject disagreeable petitioners from his office. On one occasion he took a belligerent ex-soldier by the collar and tossed him out of his office with the admonition, "Sir, I give you fair warning, never to show yourself in this office again."[27] Lincoln could anticipate no trouble in defeating Armstrong, but given the gang's tendency for group violence he had reason to fear the aftermath.

William Herndon,[28] Ida Tarbell,[29] and Noah Brooks[30] give us the "*textus receptus*" of the encounter, and it reads like the script of a modern professional wrestling match. When we combine the details of their accounts, the following story emerges.

The two men met on open ground near Offutt's store. All Clary's Grove and New Salem came to watch and bet on the contest, with the betting going decidedly in Armstrong's favor. The two men grasped each other in the prescribed manner and began the tussle. They wrestled long and hard, but they were so evenly matched that both kept their feet. When Armstrong began to realize that he could not defeat Lincoln by fair means, he resorted to foul. Enraged by Armstrong's cheating, Lincoln grabbed his antagonist by the throat with both hands, lifted him off the ground, and shook him like a rag doll. As Lincoln cast his vanquished foe to the ground, the remainder of the Clary's Grove Boys broke through the ring of spectators and advanced menacingly upon Lincoln. Facing such a large number of foes, Lincoln placed his back to the wall of the store and prepared for their attack. Before his crowd of assailants could come to grips with him, Armstrong had regained his feet. Armstrong stepped in front of the mob and declared, "Boys, Abe Lincoln is the best fellow that ever broke into this settlement! He shall be one of us!" As a child fan of professional wrestling, I saw hundreds of bouts that followed this script: (1) Hero and villain are evenly matched. (2) Villain cheats and gains an advantage over hero. (3) Hero becomes angry, defeats villain with ease. It defies logic that Lincoln could move so suddenly from evenly matched to overwhelmingly dominant.

If you remove the bombastic language, Ward Lamon's version of the bout agrees with the general course of the contest as recounted by the textus receptus, but he avers that the stalemate at the beginning of the bout did not result from the combatants being evenly matched. According to Lamon, Lincoln feared the reaction of the gang should their champion be defeated. To forestall a riot, Lincoln "pulled his punches" to make the match more even. After holding Armstrong at bay for a while, he suggested they agree to a draw. Rather than agreeing to a draw, Armstrong broke his hold and tried an illegal maneuver called legging. When Armstrong broke his hold, according to the rules of the game, Lincoln should have been declared the winner. Lincoln became so angry that his "prudence deserted him," and he thrashed Armstrong. The gang took this as a signal to move into action, and they filled the air with cries of "Fight!" Lincoln, still angry, offered to fight any one of the gang. At this juncture James Rutledge, one of New Salem's most respected men, rushed into the melee and restored peace. Who, then, won the fight? Some have Lincoln winning,[31] some have the men agreeing to a draw,[32] and some have Armstrong throwing Lincoln by cheating.[33] No witness reports that Armstrong defeated Lincoln by fair means. A majority report that Armstrong broke his hold and legged Lincoln, but they disagree as to what happened next. There is yet another version of the match, and it comes from Lincoln himself. When campaigning for president, Lincoln had occasion to reminisce about a wrestling match he contested against a man named Thompson during the Black Hawk War. Lincoln said that both he and his opponent were undefeated at the time they wrestled and that Thompson threw him twice. He ended the story by saying, "that man could throw a grizzly bear."[34] This roundabout assertion that Armstrong did not defeat him is not the only evidence we have from Lincoln. In 1860, at the request of Samuel Parks, Lincoln penciled corrections into one of his campaign biographies.[35] Although he made a number of changes to the biography, he left the account of his match with Armstrong unedited. In that account, Lincoln was on his way to victory when the Clary's Grove Boys intervened to save their leader. Lincoln became angry and offered to race or fight any one of them singly. The bout ended amicably when Armstrong agreed to call the match a draw.[36]

After weighing all the sources, it seems that the bout probably occurred in this fashion:[37] Denton Offutt and Bill Clary wagered a rather large sum on the outcome of the bout ($5 to $10); other spectators wagered lesser sums. The combatants initially disagreed on how to contest the bout, with Armstrong wanting an informal "scuffle" and Lincoln wanting the bout to be contested according to settled rules. Lincoln's view prevailed, and they fought according to the rules outlined earlier in this chapter. Lincoln was virtually assured of a win when he prevailed on the issue of how the match would be contested. In an informal scuffle the combatants were free to break their holds, and Armstrong's superior speed and agility might have given Lincoln trouble. In a collar and elbow match, Armstrong's speed and agility would count for little, and Lincoln's enormous strength would ensure a win. The two men took side holds, and the bout commenced. Lincoln won the first fall. Taking side holds again, they started the second round. Armstrong found himself faced with the dilemma Mike Tyson confronted in his second bout with Evander Holyfield—he could either lose gracefully or cheat. Tyson resolved his dilemma by clenching with Holyfield and biting off a portion of Holyfield's ear; Armstrong by breaking his hold and legging Lincoln, throwing him to the ground. The foul brought on a near-riot, but James Rutledge restored order through the force of his personality. Lincoln offered a draw, magnanimously overlooking the foul, and Armstrong accepted.[38]

However the bout went, it proved a watershed moment in young Lincoln's life. John T. Stuart, his first law partner, called it "the turning point."[39] W. D. Howells, one of Lincoln's three campaign biographers, wrote that it "seems to have been one of the most significant incidents of his early life."[40] It led directly to Lincoln's obtaining his first elective office. Not long after the wrestling match, Black Hawk, a war chief of the Sauk and Fox tribes, led a group of followers across the Mississippi River into Illinois. The governor called up the militia, and the Black Hawk War began. Lincoln joined a company of his friends and neighbors, a large number of whom were Clary's Grove Boys. During the organization of the company, the Clary's Grove Boys rallied behind Lincoln and elected him captain. The newly commissioned officer appointed his good friend Jack Armstrong to be company first sergeant.[41] Lincoln's closest encounter with combat during the Black Hawk War came when an elderly Indian wandered into the camp carrying a letter of safe conduct from General Cass. The men wanted to kill him, but Lincoln intervened. The men said they had enlisted to kill Indians, here was an Indian, and they were going to kill him. Lincoln's continued refusal to allow the murder raised the ire of his men, and one of them called him a coward. Lincoln thereupon let it be known that they would have to kill him before they could kill the prisoner.[42] Lincoln's view prevailed, and the old man's life was spared.

Lincoln expanded his circle of friends during the Black Hawk War, and he made one friendship that helped to direct his career path. He formed a fast friendship with John T. Stuart, the lawyer who reputedly steered Lincoln away from a career as a blacksmith[43] and into a career as a lawyer. Stuart has been credited with giving Lincoln his first law book, but other sources have Lincoln coming into possession of his first law book by other means.[44] No matter where Lincoln obtained his first law book, Stuart encouraged Lincoln's interest in the law and made him the loan of several law books to study. After his admission to the bar, Lincoln became a partner of Stuart for a time. Lincoln's legal career began in Stuart's shadow, but he so far outstripped his former mentor that Stuart once complained to a friend, "Carrie, I believe I am going to live to posterity only as the man who advised Mr. Lincoln to study law and lent him his law books."[45]

The story of how Lincoln learned the law and became a lawyer has been told elsewhere and is beyond the scope of this book, but there is one small aspect of his education that we should review before moving on with our investigation. The wrestling match with Jack Armstrong produced not only a fast friendship between the two men, it led to the development of a strong friendship between Lincoln and Armstrong's wife, Hannah. Lincoln frequently visited in the Armstrong home and often stayed overnight with them. While staying with the Armstrongs, Lincoln would play with the Armstrong children, and Hannah would perform domestic services for him. It is said that in addition to mending his clothes, Hannah encouraged Lincoln in his efforts at self-education, particularly his study of law.[46] Contrary to the claims of the Apolitical Observer, whose assessment of Hannah Armstrong we read in Chapter 4, among those who knew her, "[s]he was distinguished for her quaint sayings, her plain manner of speaking the truth, and her honesty and integrity. She had hosts of friends wherever she was known."[47] We must now turn to the end rather than the beginning of Lincoln's legal career. Lincoln had begun preparations for his historic Senate race against Stephen A. Douglas when he learned that this lady who had supported him in his youth and encouraged him in his education, now a widow, was in dire need.

Chapter 8

The Camp Meeting

By the end of the eighteenth century, Christianity in the United States had fallen upon hard times. The Great Awakening's tide of revival, which had peaked during the 1740s, had begun to ebb. Deism, transcendentalism, universalism, and downright apostasy had so eaten away at church membership that by 1795 one traveler through Kentucky complained that "the universalists, joining with the Deists, had given Christianity a deadly stab hereabouts." Indeed, during the six years leading up to 1800, the Methodist Church lost over 6,000 members nationwide.[1] Although the year 1800 may have marked the nadir of early American Christianity, the seeds of its renaissance had begun to sprout the year before. In 1799 John and William McGee set out from their home in western Tennessee and went through Kentucky as they traveled to Ohio. Both had taken the cloth as preachers, but John served as a Methodist minister, while his brother William entered the ministry as a Presbyterian. They stopped at a settlement on the Red River, where they found a Reverend McGready holding an open-air camp meeting. He invited them to preach at the meeting, and the brothers held forth so eloquently that they extended the meeting for several days. The locals, hearing that the Spirit was moving at the services, flocked to the scene in large numbers. Pleased by the enthusiastic response, they organized another camp meeting at a place called Muddy River. When that meeting met with the same resounding success as the first, they held another at the Ridge. At the Ridge some of the attendees cried for mercy, some shouted praises, and others retired to the woods to fall on their knees in prayer. It was an exhilarating experience where people followed the injunction of Ephesians 5:18 to "be not drunk with wine, wherein is excess; but be filled with the Spirit." No fewer than 100 worshipers made professions of faith.[2]

The McGee brothers held their next meeting on Desha's Creek, near the Cumberland River, and thousands came out to hear them. One participant reported that

the people fell under the power of the word "like corn before a storm of wind," and that many who were thus slain, "arose from the dust with divine glory beaming upon their countenances," and then praised God in such strains of heartfelt gratitude as caused the hearts of sinners to tremble within them. But no sooner did this first feeling of ecstasy subside than those young converts began to exhort their relatives and neighbors to turn to God and live.[3]

They had singing, impassioned sermons, and worshipers in the throes of religious ecstasy. All sorts of things went on at these meetings. In a world without television or the cinema, it was the best show in town. Similar meetings spread all over Kentucky, and from these seeds the Second Great Awakening began to grow. Within two years, the embers sparked by the McGee brothers burst out in full flame at Cane Ridge, the scene of the largest camp meeting yet held.[4] In the wake of Cane Ridge camp meetings sprang up almost everywhere across the Midwest, and within 15 years the number of Methodists in the United States mushroomed from a little over 60,000 to 200,000.[5] The demand for clergymen in the Midwest so far outstripped the supply that the Methodist Church found it necessary to set up a system of circuit-riding ministers. To qualify as a circuit rider, a candidate had to satisfy the church that (1) he was truly converted, (2) he knew and kept the laws of the church, (3) he could preach acceptably, and (4) he had a horse.[6] In addition to riding from place to place to preach in their assigned circuit, these clergymen organized and held periodic camp meetings.

Because so much planning and preparation went into camp meetings, all the circuit riders in a district collaborated on each individual camp meeting. They made sure that the event received good publicity and that the campground met certain strategic specifications. They strove to set up their campgrounds in shaded areas near an adequate supply of water and good pasture. They liked campgrounds near a main road close to the center of the district. The campgrounds had to measure approximately one acre in size on level ground to accommodate the hundreds of families attending. They would build a speaker's platform and an altar along with row upon row of bench seating that they segregated with men on one side and women on the other. When the attendees arrived, they circled their wagons and tents around the perimeter, and the camp would be ready for services.[7] Hucksters camped nearby to peddle food and other essentials to the attendees. Some of the hucksters fulfilled spiritual needs that could not be satisfied by worship services. The law of Illinois required these "whiskey camps" to be set up no closer than a mile from the campsite.[8]

Consumption of alcohol was not the only problem the organizers of a camp meeting faced. Worshipers repaired to the woods outside the campground to pray, but they did so for other reasons as well. One wag observed that more souls got conceived than converted at camp meetings. A more serious problem was people who came to the camp meeting with no intention of worshipping. These men would congregate at the whiskey camp to drink, gamble, fight, and engage in other types of mischief. This often took the form of disrupting the services with catcalls, tearing down tents, and otherwise harassing the worshipers. One manual for the organization of camp meetings recommended a police presence with one or more sworn law enforcement officers to maintain order.[9]

In August 1857 a young circuit rider named George D. Randle conducted a camp meeting in a 400-acre stand of trees known variously as Virgin's Grove, Walker's Grove, or Walnut Grove. Randle arranged to have the district elder, Peter Cartwright, serve as the featured speaker. Cartwright, a fiery preacher who had converted to Christianity at a camp meeting,[10] enjoyed fame in both religious and political circles in Illinois. As a prominent Illinois Democrat, Cartwright's life intersected Lincoln's on several occasions. They first clashed before the Black Hawk War when Cartwright was a well-dressed, well-fed presiding elder in the Methodist Church and Lincoln was still a common worker dressed in shabby clothes. Cartwright made a statement with which Lincoln disagreed, and they engaged in an animated debate.[11] It would not be their last. In 1832 Cartwright defeated Lincoln for a seat in the Illinois legislature. Lincoln learned from the experience he gained on this, his maiden voyage on the sea of electioneering, and the only popular vote that Lincoln ever lost came in his first race against Cartwright (he won the popular vote against Douglas but lost in the legislature due to gerrymandering).[12] When Lincoln faced Cartwright again in 1846 for a seat in Congress, he defeated the clergyman and served one term in the House of Representatives.[13] In the 1846 election Cartwright accused Lincoln of being a Deist, and in 1858 he supported Douglas in Lincoln's Senate campaign.[14] Although they confronted each other as adversaries in the political arena, they came together as allies shortly before Lincoln ran for president. Despite the fact that Cartwright once accused Lincoln of being "no Christian," Lincoln defended Cartwright's grandson on a charge of murder and got him acquitted.[15] The camp meeting at Walker's Grove would prove a minor intersection of the two men's lives. It was at the whiskey camp outside the meeting grounds that Preston Metzker was killed. George Randle later described the event in these words:

[M]any of the huckster and whiskey family also came, but we kept the whiskey-ites a mile off and made the hucksters show that they did not sell anything that would intoxicate and got along fine until Tuesday morning. The news came to camp meeting that a man was killed at the whiskey camp. This report proved true. This caused all the hucksters and whiskeyites to leave forthwith. Our meeting being under good way became more interesting than ever. Continued with great interest until the next Tuesday morning. There were some young men converted that have been preachers for years, and good acceptable men.[16]

The killing of James Preston Metzker, although important to victim and defendant and their families, was a rather pedestrian affair as murders go. Drunken patrons at a bar engage in mutual combat, and one of them dies. It is a common occurrence. Under the best of circumstances, it is difficult to determine what actually happened in one of these cases. The eyewitnesses have their ability to observe and recall impaired by alcohol. Partisans for the victim embellish their testimony to make the defendant look guilty, and partisans for the defendant embellish theirs to make the victim look deserving of death. It is a situation where, as a court reporter once told me, you can expect a teacup of truth for every gallon of testimony.

If we were setting out to write the history of a contemporary crime and its subsequent prosecution, we would of course personally interview as many witnesses as we could. We would also look to the back issues of newspapers, police reports, witness statements, and the transcript of the testimony at trial. We have almost none of these resources available for reconstructing the killing of Preston Metzker. All the witnesses have long since died. The newspaper reports are sparse. The *Daily Illinois State Journal* merely said, "The Menard Index reports that at the camp meeting recently held near Hiawatha, in Mason County, a man named Preston Metzker was killed in a fight with two bullies named Duff Armstrong and _____ Norris. Both have since been arrested."[17] We have neither police reports of the incident nor transcripts of the testimony given at the trials of Norris and Armstrong.[18] What, then, do we have other than the scores of biographies that mention the trial? We have the record of the trial, sparse as it is, and we have witness statements.

With the exception of the Western Republican and the Apolitical Observer, all of our witnesses gave their statements many years after the events they recounted. Unlike wine, a witness's testimony does not

improve with age. In addition to being far removed in time from the killing, most of the statements discuss the trial, not the killing. We must,
however, work with what we have or despair of ever knowing what happened. Oddly enough, the most complete statement we have comes from
a witness who did not testify at the trial—Duff Armstrong himself. In
Lincoln's day, Illinois law recognized a "well settled" rule that anyone
who had "some certain, legal and immediate interest in the result of [a
case]" was disqualified from testifying.[19] Since nobody has more certain,
legal, and immediate interest in the result of a criminal prosecution than
the defendant, Duff Armstrong could not testify in his own defense at
the trial.

Rather than one statement from Armstrong, we have several, all given
years after the killing. The most complete statement, which is reproduced
in Appendix A of this text, comes from an 1896 *New York Sun* news
article.[20] We have another somewhat less complete statement in
A Reporter's Lincoln by Walter B. Stevens[21] and snippets of statements
by Armstrong in other sources.[22] In addition to the statements by
Armstrong, we have access to numerous witness statements taken by
researchers working to gather information for use in biographies of
Lincoln. The research material collected by William H. Herndon provides
us with far and away the largest collection of these statements.[23] The collections of Ida N. Tarbell[24] and William E. Barton[25] add to our store of
information, and the pardon papers of James H. Norris,[26] Armstrong's
co-defendant, round out our array of primary sources. In addition to
these primary sources, we will refer to those early biographers who give
evidence of having engaged in serious efforts to uncover the facts of the
Almanac Trial.

The story of Pres Metzker's death begins with a Menard County farmer
named Nelson Watkins, a man who believed in always being prepared.
Watkins wanted a weapon that he could easily carry concealed but
that—in the hands of someone who knew how to use it—could inflict
grievous injury. He settled upon a slungshot as ideal for his purpose.
A small but heavy weight at the end of a leather cord fit into one's pants
pocket without making an obtrusive bulge and could be deployed in an
instant to smash an adversary's skull. It could be as deadly as the sling
David used to defeat Goliath. A slungshot lacked the range of a sling,
but the slungshot never needed to be reloaded. Watkins used an empty
eggshell as a mold, pouring a mixture of molten lead and zinc into it
and producing an ovoid lump. Next, he took a piece of calfskin cut from
a boot and, using an awl, he punched holes along the edges of the calfskin. He wrapped the calfskin around the lump and ran squirrel skin
string through the holes, sewing the leaden lump securely into the calfskin

pouch. Then he attached the pouch to a leather strip cut from the tanned hide of a groundhog. Finally, he put a loop in the end of the leather strip to fit around his wrist so that the weapon wouldn't slip out of his hand in the heat of battle.[27] His preparations made, Watkins loaded up in his wagon and set out on the trek to Walker's Grove. Because his interest ran to spiritual affairs of the liquid variety, he did not make his camp at the revival site, but at the whiskey camp. Some evidence suggests that he even parked his wagon next to the wagon of Duff Armstrong.[28] During the festivities at the whiskey camp, Watkins lost his slungshot. Someone found the slungshot on the ground not far from where Armstrong and Metzker had their encounter, and the slungshot eventually found its way to the Cass County Courthouse, in Beardstown, where the prosecution introduced it as evidence against Duff Armstrong, claiming it was the very weapon that Armstrong used to take Metzker's life. According to Watkins's account of how he lost the slungshot, it could not possibly have been the murder weapon. After drinking his fill on the fatal night, Watkins crawled under his wagon to sleep, but the slungshot in his pocket caused him discomfort. He took the slungshot out and placed it on the reach[29] of the wagon. Forgetting about the slungshot when he awoke the next morning, he got into the wagon and drove off, allowing the slungshot to fall to the ground.[30] Although he did not testify to this fact at trial, before he went to sleep he saw Armstrong and Metzker fighting and saw Armstrong use what looked like a wagon hammer to strike a terrible blow to Metzker's eye.[31] Watkins, of course, knew what a wagon hammer was, as did almost everyone living in the nineteenth century. Nowadays almost no one has any idea what a wagon hammer is. The 1929 edition of *Funk and Wagnalls New Standard Dictionary of the English Language* defines a wagon hammer as "An upright bolt with a head like a hammer, used for pivoting the doubletree to the tongue." The wagon hammer is also known by the more descriptive term of "hammer-headed doubletree pin." In layman's language, it is a bolt that attaches the horses' harness rigging to the wagon. It must be sturdy, and it could serve quite well as a makeshift club. Watkins was a friend of the Armstrongs, and he did not want to see Duff Armstrong hanged for the killing. He decided to keep quiet about what he saw. Watkins did not tell what he saw until months after Armstrong's acquittal, when he spoke to one of the Armstrong jurors. If Watkins spoke the truth, the slungshot rested in his pocket at the time of the fight, and Armstrong could not have used it to strike Metzker.

Unsurprisingly, we have two other versions of how the slungshot came to be found lying on the ground near the scene of the crime. The first alternative version comes from two books published in 1960, one by

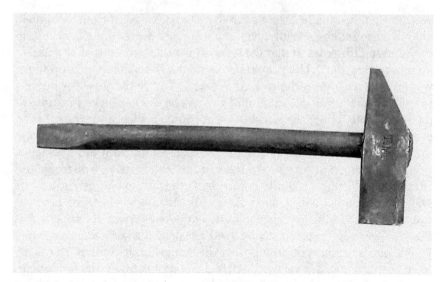

An old-fashioned wagon hammer. (Forged for George R. Dekle, Sr. by Terry Moore of Texas Wagon Works, Gonzales, Texas)

John J. Duff and the other by Reinhard H. Luthin. Both sources tell this alternate story in exactly the same words:

Watkins testified that the sling shot found near the scene of the alleged crime and produced by the State as the weapon with which Armstrong had struck Metzker, was in fact Watkins's own property, that he, Watkins, had it in his home on the night of the supposed murder, and that he had thrown it away, at the exact spot where it had been found, on the day following the alleged murder.[32]

Since Luthin cites Duff as a source for his account of the Almanac Trial,[33] it is reasonable to assume that Luthin copied Duff's words. Duff carefully noted his sources throughout his book, but the sources cited by Duff for his account of the Almanac Trial do not substantiate the story. Duff surely had a source for this claim, but he neglected to cite it. Duff's version apparently has been discounted by most later biographers. I found only one subsequent source that repeated the tale.[34] Between these two versions, we must prefer the first because it comes from John T. Brady, who not only served on the jury at Armstrong's trial, but also discussed the case with Nelson Watkins a few months after the trial.[35]

Our third story about the slungshot comes from another person intimately involved in the trial—J. Henry Shaw, who served as one of Armstrong's prosecutors. After the trial Lincoln gave Shaw the slungshot and said, "Here, Henry, I'll give you this to remember me by." Shaw kept the slungshot as a souvenir, and he still had it in 1866 when he wrote these words to William H. Herndon:

It was made by Armstrong for the occasion. He took a common bar of pig lead, pounded it round, about the size of a large hickory nut, then cut a piece of leather out of the top of one of his boots, and with a thread and needle he sewed it into the shape of a slungshot, and thus improvised in a few minutes a very fatal weapon.[36]

Shaw would not have said this unless he disbelieved Watkins, but he did not say why he believed this alternate version. Because nobody at the trial testified to seeing Armstrong make the slungshot, we can conclude that Shaw probably inferred this from the available evidence. In weighing the direct testimony of Watkins against the inference drawn by Shaw, we must accept Watkins's story as the true history of the slungshot.

Earlier on the afternoon of August 29, Duff Armstrong had amused himself by participating in the horse races at the camp. Armstrong had a horse that he entered in some of the races, but we have no record of how he fared. However, he didn't fare so poorly that he ran out of money to buy whiskey. Armstrong later recalled that at the time he fought Pres Metzker, he had weathered the worst effects of his drinking bout and had begun to sober up. We should doubt his claim; alcohol dulls not only the reflexes, it impairs judgment. Those under the influence of alcohol are oftentimes the ones least capable of assessing their degree of intoxication. According to Armstrong, the fight began around 10:00 that evening while Armstrong lay sleeping. Metzker came by and awakened Armstrong with a curse. Metzker yanked on Armstrong's leg, pulling him off his roost. Armstrong got back onto his makeshift bed, and Metzker pulled him off again. Armstrong said, "Let me alone, Pres, I am sleepy," and Metzker walked off. He didn't stay gone long, though. Metzker came back and pulled Armstrong off his roost a third time. Grabbing Armstrong's hat, Metzker threw it to the ground and stomped it. Metzker told Armstrong, "You have no business here. You ought to be home picking up chips for your ma." He meant this statement as an insult. Chips were the dried dung of cattle used for fuel.[37] Armstrong told Metzker to mind his own business. Armstrong then got up and walked over to one of the bars, where he ordered a drink of whiskey. As Armstrong lifted the glass to his mouth, Metzker grabbed his arm, spilling his whiskey. By this time Armstrong had reached his limit with Metzker. Armstrong put down his glass and, turning toward Metzker, warned him, "Pres, if you do that again, I will knock you down even if you are bigger than me. You have run this thing far enough." Metzker continued to harass Armstrong until the smaller man hit Metzker in the face. Armstrong said he struck hard enough to knock the skin from his knuckles. Watkins said that Armstrong picked up a wagon hammer lying on the bar and used it to strike Metzker.[38] By some versions of the story, Metzker went down from Armstrong's blow, but Armstrong maintained that Metzker reacted by clinching with him. A bigger, stronger man does well to clinch with a smaller man who knows how to use his fists. It brings the big man too close for the small man to punch effectively, and the bigger man can over-power the smaller, taking him to the ground and pummeling him. This was apparently Metzker's plan, but he failed to take Armstrong's skill as a wrestler into account. When Metzker tried to clench, Armstrong threw him. Both men hit the ground, but neither stayed there. Metzker, the first to regain his feet, charged Armstrong. "Then," Armstrong later recalled, "we fought like tigers." Apparently Armstrong gave a good account of himself, for the fight lasted some time. Inevitably, however, superior size and strength won out. Metzker grounded Armstrong and mounted him. Pinned to the ground and unable to properly defend him-self against Metzker's heavy blows, Armstrong risked serious injury. The onlookers intervened, pulling Metzker off of Armstrong. The fight ended with Metzker the apparent winner, and the two men walked to the bar. According to Armstrong, "We walked up to the bar and each get-ting a drink of whiskey, we bumped glasses and were friends again. But Pres had not got through with me. As we stood there, without warning he hit me a blow on the upper lip." When Metzker took his glass and prepared to hit Armstrong again, another man stepped up and said, "Stop that Pres, if you strike him with that glass I will kill you." Metzker then stole a quilt from a buggy nearby, wrapped himself in it, and walked off. Armstrong said this was the last he saw of Metzker until the next morning.[39] According to Armstrong's brother, A. P., Metzker initiated the fracas by spitting in Armstrong's face.[40] This claim finds no support from any statement Duff ever made and can be discounted. We have some evidence suggesting the fight did not go as described by Armstrong. Some sources have Armstrong giving Metzker a beating,[41] but given the dispar-ity in size this seems unlikely.

Caleb Dilworth, Armstrong's original attorney, would later write that the two men fought until separated by others, and during the fight Armstrong struck Metzker in the eye. Although Dilworth did not say Armstrong struck Metzker with a weapon, this should not be taken as evidence that Armstrong used only his fist. Dilworth was Armstrong's attorney, and we can expect him to downplay facts harmful to his client. According to Dilworth, the two men made up after the fight, and Metzker left the company of Armstrong. Dilworth wrote that as Metzker walked

A neck yoke. (Courtesy Hansen Wheel and Wagon Shop, Letcher, South Dakota)

across the camp, James Norris saw an opportunity to avenge himself for some previous wrong that Metzker had done him. Norris picked up a neck yoke and hid behind a tree. When Metzker walked by, Norris jumped out and hit the back of Metzker's head with the neck yoke. Norris then fled the scene.[42] A neck yoke is a part of a draft horse's harness. It consists of a stick of wood some three feet long, tapered on the ends. It can make a formidable club.

Dilworth and Armstrong differ on what happened next. According to Dilworth, Metzker got on his horse and left camp shortly after being struck by Norris. Armstrong claimed that the next morning he saw Metzker buy a drink at the bar, bathe his swollen eye with a glass of whiskey, mount his horse, and ride off headed toward home. He fell off his horse a number of times on the way home. When he got home, he took to his bed and languished for three days before dying.

Chapter 9

The Prosecution

The county coroner, upon receiving word of Metzker's death, immediately convened a coroner's jury of 12 men. Once the jurors had assembled in the presence of Metzker's body, the coroner chose one of the 12 and swore him as the foreman of the jury.[1] The coroner then swore the other members of the jury, and the inquest began. We have no record of the witnesses called before the coroner's jury, but we can infer that many of the men who later testified before the grand jury also testified before the coroner's jury. Dr. Benjamin F. Stephenson, the doctor who examined Metzker's body and determined cause of death, almost certainly testified before the coroner's jury, as did Charles Allen, the house painter from Pittsburgh who claimed to have seen the murder. Stephenson would have testified that Metzker died of blunt force trauma to the right eye and the back of the head, either blow being sufficient to cause death. According to Stephenson, the skull was broken around Metzker's eye, and part of the fractured bone had been driven into his brain.[2] Allen would have identified Norris as the man who struck the back of Metzker's head with a neck yoke and Armstrong as the one who struck Metzker in the eye with the slungshot. The jury made a presentment finding that Metzker died as a result of the criminal acts of James H. Norris and William Duff Armstrong. The two men were arrested and placed in jail to await the next term of circuit court.

On October 26, 1857, the Honorable James Harriott, circuit judge of the Twenty-First Judicial Circuit of Illinois, convened the October term of the Mason County Circuit Court at Havana, Illinois.[3] Each county of the circuit held two terms of circuit court per year, once in the fall and once in the spring. These terms ran from one to two weeks, depending upon how many cases had accumulated since the previous term. The terms were staggered so that the judge, the state's attorney, and the lawyers appearing before the court could ride the circuit and attend terms of court in all the counties of the circuit. The first order of business would have been to impanel a grand jury to consider criminal charges brought since the last term of court. The grand jury was to be impaneled from a group of 23 men chosen by the county commissioners of Mason County. A few weeks before the term began, the county commission chose the men and summoned them to appear on the first day of the October term.[4] The proceedings immediately hit a snag when too few men appeared to make out the full complement of 23 grand jurors. Judge Harriott, not for the last time that term, ordered the sheriff to go out and find a sufficient number of prospective jurors to bring the total number of grand jurors to 23. The sheriff went out and rounded up five men to serve, including David Ott, a man who would later be the occasion for an attack on the legal sufficiency of the indictment.[5] Judge Harriott appointed John H. Havinghorst foreman of the jury. Havinghorst took the oath of the foreman,[6] the remaining grand jurors were sworn, and the grand jury retired to secret session. Hugh Fullerton, the recently elected state's attorney for the Twenty-First Judicial Circuit, guided their investigations.[7] Fullerton began practicing law in 1845, but when the United States declared war on Mexico in 1846, he received a commission as a second lieutenant in Company I of the Sixth Regiment, Illinois Volunteer Infantry. After the war he resumed the practice of law in Mason County. When the Civil War broke out, he personally raised Company C of the Second Regiment of Illinois Cavalry and received a commission as captain of the company. By war's end, he was a major. After the war, he once again returned to the practice of law and was still in active practice in 1882.[8]

After four days of hearing cases, the grand jury returned several indictments, among them an indictment of Norris and Armstrong for the murder of Metzker. On the following day, October 30, the two men appeared before Judge Harriott for arraignment on the charges. Judge Harriott appointed William Walker as attorney for Norris, but Hannah Armstrong had scraped together enough money to hire Caleb Dilworth as attorney for her son.[9] Walker, a respected attorney and a native of the Walker's Grove area, began practicing law in 1844. He had a junior partner by the name of Lyman Lacey and maintained his offices in Havana. After the Civil War, he moved to Lexington, Missouri, where he became a judge.[10] Dilworth had not practiced as long as Walker, but he was a man to be reckoned with. When the Civil War broke out, he recruited for the Eighty-Fifth Illinois Volunteer Infantry (Duff Armstrong's regiment) and was elected lieutenant colonel. Eventually command of the regiment devolved upon him, and he received a commission as a full colonel. He saw action at Chickamauga and Kennesaw Mountain, where he became brigade commander by virtue of the fact that all the officers above him were killed in action. While commanding the brigade at the siege of Atlanta, he got shot in the throat. After recovering from that wound, he returned to service and by the war's end he was a brevet brigadier general.[11] After the war, he moved to Nebraska, where he served as attorney general.[12] All these distinctions were in his future, however; in 1857 he was merely a young lawyer who charged modest fees. He immediately had Armstrong file an affidavit asking for a change of venue. The affidavit read:

William Armstrong one of the defendants in this cause first being duly sworn according to law deposes and says that he fears that he will not receive a fair and impartial trial in this court, on account of the minds of the inhabitants of said Mason County being prejudiced against him. He therefore petitions the Court that a change of venue in this case be awarded to him. . . .[13]

Norris did not ask for a change of venue, and this fact has led to unjustified criticism of his attorney, William Walker.[14] A change of venue would have caused a delay of the trial for several months. Armstrong moved for his change of venue in October 1857 and did not stand trial until May of the following year. Norris wanted to get out of jail as quickly as possible, and he directed his lawyer to go ahead and try the case immediately.[15] He made a capital mistake. Of the two defendants, Norris was the one most in need a change of venue. Just a year before he had stood trial for another killing and won an acquittal on a plea of self-defense.[16] This fact, which would have been common knowledge, made Norris's prospects before a Mason County jury even bleaker than Armstrong's. This gross error, however, was not Walker's fault. Although some criminal defense lawyers portray themselves as being in charge, the defendant has the authority to make major decisions about the course of the defense. Defense attorneys can advise their clients as to the wisest course of action, but they cannot lawfully command the client to agree with them. As one old lawyer of my acquaintance used to say, "You can lead your clients to knowledge, but you can't make them think." Walker not only did what his client told him to do, he never gave up on Norris. Despite the fact that Norris later made unflattering comments about him,[17] Walker continued to advocate for Norris until 1863, when he finally won a pardon for the man.[18]

Norris opted for a speedy trial, but before he could be tried, his defense did some legal maneuvering. Both Walker and Dilworth asked that the indictment be quashed (dismissed), but Judge Harriott overruled their motion.[19] At this point in the court record it becomes difficult to interpret precisely what was going on, and our problem is aggravated because the October 29 indictment has disappeared from the court records. A careful study of the available documents, however, allows us to reconstruct a plausible course of events.

When the grand jury returned the indictment against Norris and Armstrong on October 29, their lawyers immediately sat down and scribbled out a motion alleging 10 reasons that the indictment should be quashed:

1st. There was no proper order made by the County Court of Mason County to authorize the Clerk to issue the venire upon which the grand jury were summoned.

2nd. There was no proper venire issued.

3rd. The grand jury was improperly summoned.

4th. There is a variance between the return of the sheriff and the record in relation to summoning and returning the grand jury into court.

5th. One or more of the grand jurors who served upon the grand jury and who assisted in finding the indictment in the above cause is disqualified from serving as grand juror according to law and was not a body legally assembled to find said indictment.

6th. The indictment is defective upon its face.

7th. The indictment does not sufficiently describe the wound.

8th. The indictment does not state that the defendants acted in concert.

9th. The indictment states two different assaults to have been made and does not state which caused the death of the deceased.

10th. The indictment is in other respects informal and insufficient.[20]

When the motion came up for hearing on October 31, Dilworth and Walker lost. They believed they had a winning issue, however, and decided to come back the next week to ask for a rehearing of the motion. They actually did have a winning issue. Their fifth allegation claimed that someone on the jury was not qualified to serve, and they were right. They supported that allegation with an affidavit from David Ott stating that he was 77 years of age.[21] Under Illinois law, only free white male taxable citizens between the ages of 21 and 60 could serve on juries,[22] but Ott's affidavit was insufficient to persuade Judge Harriott to quash the indictment. When court reconvened on November 5, the defense had more ammunition. They had a second affidavit in support of their motion to quash: grand juror James McCowan's affidavit stated that he was 71 years old.[23] David Ott's affidavit was also redated to show that it had been sworn to on November 5. Faced with mounting proof that he had a flawed indictment, Fullerton did what any prosecutor should do. He entered a *nolle prosequi* (dismissal) of the indictment,[24] marched back into the grand jury room, and got another indictment,[25] this time without the assistance of McCowan and Ott. Removing McCowan and Ott from the panel did not prevent the grand jury from acting because Illinois law provided that the grand jury could act with as few as 16 members.[26] Walker and Dilworth immediately took their old motion to dismiss, marked out the date of October 30, interlined the date of November 5, and pressed it upon the court again. Dilworth also renewed Armstrong's motion for change of venue. Judge Harriott again overruled the motion to dismiss, but he took the motion for change of venue under advisement.

Legal reform has made the pleading of court documents much simpler than it was during the nineteenth century. Where a modern pleader could charge the murder of Pres Metzker in a one-count indictment and squeeze all the allegations onto one letter-sized page, Fullerton's indictment covered eight pages of legal paper and contained three counts. Shorn of most of its excess verbiage, the first count read:

The grand jurors ... in and for the County of Mason ... present that James H. Norris and William Armstrong ... on the twenty-ninth day of August in the year of Our Lord one thousand eight hundred and fifty-seven ... within the County of Mason and State of Illinois, in and upon one James Preston Metzker ..., unlawfully, feloniously, willfully, and of their malice aforethought did make an assault. And the said James H. Norris with a certain piece of wood about three feet long ... in and upon the back part of the head of ... James Preston Metzker then and there unlawfully, feloniously, willfully, and of his malice aforethought, did strike, giving to the said James Preston Metzker then and there with the stick of wood aforesaid in and upon the said back part of the head of him the said James Preston Metzker, one mortal bruise and the said William Armstrong with a certain hard metallic substance called a slung-shot ..., in and upon the right eye of him the said James Preston Metzker then and there unlawfully, feloniously, willfully and of his malice aforethought did strike, giving to the said James Preston Metzker then and there with a slung-shot aforesaid in and upon the said right eye of him the said James Preston Metzker one other mortal bruise, of which said mortal bruises the said James Preston Metzker from the said 29th day of August in the year aforesaid until the 1st day of September in the year aforesaid at the County of Mason and State of Illinois aforesaid did languish, and languishing did live on which said first day of September in the year aforesaid the said James Preston Metzker ... died; and so the jurors aforesaid upon their oaths aforesaid do say that the said James H. Norris and William Armstrong the said

James Preston Metzker ... unlawfully, feloniously, and of their malice afore-thought did kill and murder contrary to the form of the statute in such cases made and provided and against the peace and dignity of the same People of the State of Illinois.[27]

Counts two and three contained substantially the same language, but count two alleged that Norris and Armstrong both hit Metzker behind the head with the club, and count three alleged that they both hit him in the eye with the slungshot. Remarkably, the indictment tracked the lan-guage of an indictment set out in the appendix to the fourth volume of the 1779 edition of Blackstone's *Commentaries on the Laws of England*.[28] As required by Illinois law, the names of the witnesses who testified before the grand jury were endorsed on the indictment under the signature of the foreman.[29]

You will have noticed that although the indictment specifically described Armstrong's weapon as a "slungshot," it described Norris's weapon as a "stick of wood" rather than as a "neck yoke." This gives evidence that Fullerton was a careful pleader. Nineteenth-century rules of pleading were much more stringent than they are today, and any "variance" between the pleading and the proof could lose the case. Ambrose Bierce parodied these strict rules of pleading with his definition of "Technicality" in *The Devil's Dictionary*. Bierce wrote that the charge "Sir Thomas Holt hath taken a cleaver and stricken his cook upon the head, so that one side fell upon one shoulder and the other side upon the other shoulder," failed to properly charge murder because it "did not affirm the death of the cook, that being only an inference."[30] Fullerton felt no fear of pleading that Armstrong used a slungshot because he had the slungshot to put into evidence. Not having the neck yoke, he described it as broadly as possible so as not to have a variance between pleading and proof.

Some modern readers might be puzzled that the indictment uses the term "malice aforethought" and does not mention premeditation. Antebellum Illinois law did not divide murder into degrees, and a mur-derer could receive the death penalty even though he did not intend to kill. The prosecution needed to prove only "malice aforethought," which existed when the accused acted with a "deliberate intention unlawfully to take away the life of a fellow creature" or "when all the circumstances of the killing show[ed] an abandoned and malignant heart."[31]

Having dealt with the motion to quash the indictment, the next order of business was to arraign the defendants. They were given copies of the indictment, a list of the witnesses called before the grand jury, and a list of the grand jurors, and this was the sum total of the discovery allowed at that time. Both defendants entered pleas of not guilty, and Armstrong

The Almanac Trial courthouse. (Photograph by George R. Dekle, Sr.)

renewed his motion for change of venue. Norris, on the other hand, announced that he was ready for trial when he "put himself upon the country."[32] Fullerton likewise announced ready for trial, and jury selection began. When the county commission chose 23 men to serve as jurors for the October term of court, they also chose 48 men to serve as petit jurors. Twenty-four men reported to court on the first Monday of the term to serve as the jury panel for the first week of trials. The second group of 24 men appeared in court on the second Monday and served as the jury panel for the second week.[33] Voir dire examination of the jury began with Hugh Fullerton, assisted by L. W. Ross and John Collier, representing the people. William Walker, possibly assisted by his partner Lyman Lacey, represented Norris.[34] At this point the prosecution hit a second snag. Because of the public outcry against Norris and Armstrong, most of the men on the jury panel freely admitted they could not sit as fair and impartial jurors. When the lawyers finished exercising challenges on the first panel of 24, they had too few jurors for a full complement of 12. Judge Harriott ordered the sheriff to go out and recruit 24 more prospective jurors. When they exhausted the new panel without selecting a full jury, Harriott sent the sheriff out for 24 more prospective jurors. When those 24 were exhausted without getting a jury, Harriott sent the sheriff out to recruit 24 more men. He had to send the sheriff out one more time before they could seat a jury. This was no quick and easy process; the trial began on November 5, but the jury returned its verdict on November 7. The verdict read: "We the Jury agree to find the defendant guilty of manslaughter and as penalty eight years service in the State Penitentiary." All 12 jurors signed the verdict.[35] Judge Harriott then granted Armstrong's motion for change of venue,[36] moving the trial of the case to Cass County.

The sheriff had to take Norris to the state penitentiary in Alton,[37] and he had to transport Armstrong to the Cass County jail in Beardstown. Because all three towns lay on the Illinois River, the sheriff took his two prisoners by steamboat. Although he handcuffed the men together for the trip, apparently he otherwise gave them the run of the boat. Norris wanted to take full advantage of this freedom to walk about the boat. Armstrong refused to leave his seat, pleading fatigue as an excuse. Armstrong later told his friends that he feared Norris would try to escape and drag him overboard.[38]

At this point we may pause to ask, "Where was Lincoln while all this was going on?" Some biographers have mistakenly claimed that Lincoln actually moved for the change of venue on Armstrong's behalf,[39] while others write that he merely counseled it.[40] Although he may have advised moving for a change of venue, we know that he was in Danville, Illinois, on October 26 attending the October term of the Vermillion County Circuit Court.[41] The next week he divided his time between Danville and his home in Springfield. On Monday, November 2, he was still in Danville attending court, and when court adjourned for the day, he rode back to Springfield, arriving early enough to cast his ballot in a local election. Saturday, November 7, found him back in Danville working on a pardon petition for George High, who had received a sentence to prison for horse theft.[42] Given that Danville is approximately 120 miles east of Springfield and Havana is approximately 48 miles northwest of Springfield, Lincoln could hardly have been in Havana on November 5 to argue Armstrong's motion for change of venue.

Lincoln came into the case only after Norris's conviction. As with almost every detail of Lincoln's life, we have multiple versions of how he became involved. The most heartwarming version originated with the Western Republican.[43] According to the Western Republican, when Lincoln heard that the son of his old friend Jack Armstrong was in trouble, he immediately sat down and wrote a letter to Hannah Armstrong volunteering his services in the boy's defense. Two of Lincoln's official campaign biographies quoted the Western Republican as saying Lincoln volunteered,[44] and many early Lincoln biographers readily accepted the story.[45] The full text of the supposed letter even found its way into print:

Springfield, Ohio, September 18, [1857]

Dear Mrs. Armstrong:—I have just heard of your deep affliction, and the arrest of your son for murder. I can hardly believe that he can be guilty of the crime alleged against him. It does not seem possible. I am anxious that he should have a fair trial, at any rate; and gratitude for your long continued kindness to me in adverse circumstances prompts me to offer my humble services gratuitously in his behalf. It will afford me an opportunity to requite, in a small degree, the favors I received at your hand, and that of your lamented husband, when your roof afforded me grateful shelter without money and without price.

Yours truly,

Abraham Lincoln[46]

The story of Lincoln volunteering to defend Duff Armstrong received tacit support from Armstrong's younger brother, John, at the 1912 meeting of the Lincoln Centennial Association. Armstrong, who had been invited to speak to the Association, was introduced by Judge J. Otis Humphreys in the following words:

On page 280 of the little souvenir volume which lies before you will be found a letter which Mr. Lincoln wrote, in September, 1857, to a distressed widow, tendering gratuitously his services in defense of her son, who had been indicted for murder. The circumstance is one familiar to many, perhaps all, of you. It was the Armstrong case. What most of you do not know is that we have here, as one of our guests tonight, a brother of the young man who was then defended by Mr. Lincoln. I am going to call upon Mr. John Armstrong to give briefly his recollection of that stirring event.[47]

In his speech Armstrong never said a word against the letter.[48] Away from a large audience, however, Armstrong expressed doubts about the letter's authenticity. When Alonzo Rothschild sent an investigator to interview Armstrong for his 1917 biography of Lincoln, the investigator reported back that Armstrong (who was only nine years old at the time of the trial) had no memory of his mother ever receiving such a letter from Lincoln, and he was sure that if Lincoln had sent such a letter, he would remember it.[49] Modern historians deem the letter a forgery,[50] saying it lacks Lincoln's phrasing and style.[51] The fact that it purports to come from Springfield, Ohio, also casts doubt on its authenticity.

As John Armstrong remembered, his mother recruited Lincoln,[52] and it apparently took some persuading to get him to accept the case. Hannah Armstrong later recalled that she first wrote him asking for assistance and he wrote her back, but she lost the letter. Apparently she wasn't satisfied with the answer she got, because she went to see him in Springfield to ask his help.[53] Hannah even went as far as sending Thomas S. Edwards, one of the old Clary's Grove Boys, to Springfield to plead her case.[54] According to Ida Tarbell, Hannah met with Lincoln when he was in Beardstown attending the May 1858 term of court (the term in which Duff stood trial), and only then did she finally persuade him to take the case.[55]

Edgar Lee Masters (1931) suggested that Lincoln did not want to take the case because he did not appreciate what Hannah had done for him in his early years.[56] This allegation fails in light of the history of Lincoln's relationship with Hannah—he always stood ready to do anything he could for her, even to the point of discharging her son from the army. His affection for Hannah was so great that Jack Armstrong used to jokingly accuse him of being the real father of one of Duff's younger brothers.[57] After his election as president, Hannah made a trip to Springfield to say goodbye to the man who had been so kind to her. Some of "the boys," probably the Clary's Grove Boys, teased her that she was going to Springfield to sleep with Lincoln one last time. Hannah reminisced that she shut them up by telling them that "it was not every woman who had the good fortune and high honor to sleep with a President."[58] A more plausible reason has been advanced that Lincoln tried to beg off because of his relative inexperience in the trial of murder cases.[59] As the fictional Old Bailey barrister Horace Rumpole once said, "[M]urder is nothing more than common assault, with unfortunate consequences."[60] This aphorism doesn't hold true for "whodunit" murders, but the killing of Pres Metzker really did amount to little more than a common assault with unfortunate consequences. A lawyer who spent as much time in court as Abraham Lincoln did would have no problem defending such a case.

Some have suggested that Lincoln had little talent for homicide cases because he "lost" more cases than he won, but this is not the case. Although most of his clients got convicted, only one got convicted as charged of murder.[61] The majority of his "losses" consisted of manslaughter convictions. A criminal prosecution is not a zero sum game, where—absent a tie—you have a clear winner and a clear loser. Both sides can win a criminal prosecution, and both sides can lose. Many a defendant facing the death penalty will count it a fabulous victory if the jury returns a verdict for manslaughter. This would especially be true in antebellum Illinois, where manslaughter carried a maximum penalty of eight years. I once defended two men charged with life felonies who thought I had done a wonderful job when I got them convicted of a crime carrying a five-year maximum. By this yardstick, Lincoln had great success defending homicide cases. As a matter of fact, Lincoln pulled off one of the most spectacular wins imaginable in one murder case—he got his clients acquitted by proving that the supposed murder victim was still alive. Lincoln himself thought the win so remarkable that he wrote an anonymous newspaper article describing the case.[62]

Lincoln's reluctance likely stemmed from his natural desire not to ruin a lifelong friendship. Experienced lawyers know that when you try a case so highly charged with such personal attachments as Lincoln had in the Almanac Trial, you are hampered by those attachments, and you are always cognizant of the possibility that a loss of the case means the loss of a friend. It is far better to sit on the sidelines and encourage your friends as someone else handles the case. What probably decided Lincoln upon taking up the case was another belief that most experienced trial lawyers would have had in a similar situation—the firm belief that if he took up the case, he would give Duff Armstrong the best chance for acquittal.

Chapter 10

The Trial Begins

Jonathan Gill had a problem. He believed his wife had committed adultery and that she carried another man's child in her womb. Deciding on a geographical solution for his problem, he returned his wife to her father and left Illinois for the Minnesota Territory, taking with him the two children already born into the marriage. Mrs. Gill did nothing for a number of years, but eventually she took legal action. Desertion was recognized as a ground for divorce in antebellum Illinois, and the law required significant alimony of any husband who abandoned his wife.[1] Mrs. Gill filed a bill of divorce in Cass County Circuit Court.[2] In the Minnesota Territory Gill was effectively beyond the jurisdiction of the court and could have ignored the bill of divorce except for one small detail—he still owned land in Illinois. He hired J. Henry Shaw, the most prominent attorney in Beardstown, to represent him. Shaw had Gill file an answer alleging adultery as a defense to the bill of divorce,[3] and the matter came up to be tried during the November 1857 term of court.

Shaw expected a busy time for that term of court—he had the hotly contested divorce, and the Metzkers had retained him to assist Hugh Fullerton in the prosecution of Duff Armstrong.[4] If John T. Brady can be believed, Shaw was not the Metzkers' first choice for a lawyer. According to Brady, the Metzkers first tried to hire a prominent attorney from Springfield, a tall, thin lawyer by the name of Abraham Lincoln. Lincoln would work as a prosecutor from time to time, but when he heard the name of the defendant, he flatly refused to take the case.[5] Shaw felt that he needed help with his divorce case, and he knew where he could get it.

He wrote Lincoln, asking him to come to Beardstown and assist him in the divorce proceeding. Lincoln readily agreed. Shaw likely reached out to Lincoln for help because he saw in Lincoln a kindred spirit. They had both traveled the same sort of path to enter into the practice of law. Shaw grew up on a farm where he learned to use his hands just as Lincoln had done. Like Lincoln, Shaw had little formal education. He went to school for three weeks and learned the rudiments of literacy. Apparently those three weeks awakened in Shaw a voracious appetite for learning. The boy read everything he could get his hands on and practiced his letters on any scraps of paper he could find. His contemporaries said he would never amount to anything unless he got his nose out of the books and pursued a serious career. Shaw kept his nose in the books and began reading law at the age of 21. Just as Lincoln had done, Shaw begged and borrowed law books to read. Shaw read law from the age of 21 until the age of 25—often propping his law book onto the handle of his plow as he plowed the fields. With one hand on the law book and one hand on the plow handle, he followed the mule back and forth across the field as the plow cut furrows in the ground. We have no record of how straight he cut furrows plowing by this method. At age 25 he left his plow and went to Springfield to take the bar examination before the Supreme Court of Illinois. He passed and thus began a distinguished career as both a practicing lawyer and a state legislator.[6]

After Lincoln's death, Shaw corresponded with Lincoln biographer William Henry Herndon, and we have Shaw's description of Lincoln's involvement in both the Gill case and the Armstrong case. When Lincoln arrived in Beardstown for the November term, Shaw had no suspicion that Lincoln had come for any other reason than to tend to the divorce case. They tried the divorce case to a jury, and on November 20, 1857, the jury found for Ruth Gill. She won on the issue of custody, but Judge Harriott put the question of alimony off until the May 1858 term of court. The next day Lincoln argued a bond motion on behalf of Duff Armstrong and lost. Writing to Herndon, Shaw expressed no concern about Lincoln's arguing the bond motion. Shaw went on to say that when Lincoln came back for the May term to help him with the divorce, he was surprised when Lincoln also appeared for Armstrong and helped to try the case. Some biographers fault Lincoln for ambushing Shaw and offer this incident as evidence of unethical conduct.[7]

Lincoln arrived in Beardstown on May 6 and met with Shaw on that date. They had two cases to deal with, the alimony issue for the Gill case (which they lost) and a property dispute between two of their clients. Of that second matter, Shaw had this to say:

At the May term I expected Mr. Lincoln down to assist in the alimony case again, and he came in due time, called at my office, and said I had "been suing some of his clients, and he had come down to attend to it." He then had reference to a new chancery case entitled "George Morre vs. Christina Moore and the heirs of Peter Moore" for a specific performance, the defendants all living near Springfield. I explained the case to him, and showed him my proofs. He seemed surprised that I should deal so frankly with him, and said that he should be as frank with me, that my client was justly entitled to a decree, and he should so represent it to the court, that it was against his principle to contest a clear matter of right. So my client got a deed for a farm, which, had another lawyer been in Mr. Lincoln's place, would have been litigated for years, with a big pile of costs, and the results probably the same. Mr. Lincoln's character for professional honor stood very high. He never vexed an opponent, but frequently threw him off his guard by his irresistible good humor. But I digress—I still thought that Mr. Lincoln had come to our court more particularly to attend to the Gill and Morre cases and was very much surprised afterwards to see the immense interest he took in the Armstrong case.[8]

It is hard to see how Shaw could say he was surprised that Lincoln represented Armstrong in May 1858 when he had already seen Lincoln appear for Armstrong in the previous term of court. We have a conflict between Shaw's testimony and established fact. In resolving this conflict, we should keep in mind an ancient legal principle of evidentiary analysis—we should try to resolve conflicts without attributing untruthfulness to anyone. Only if the conflict cannot be resolved should we reject testimony as untruthful.[9] If we carefully review both the language of Shaw's letter and the court record, we can solve the mystery without attributing mendacity to Shaw or unethical behavior to Lincoln.

Let us trace the course of events in the Armstrong case during the November 1857 term of Cass County Circuit Court. On Monday, November 16, Fullerton petitioned the court to issue a writ of certiorari to the Mason County Circuit Court ordering a transcript of the proceedings against Armstrong that had taken place at the beginning of the month.[10] The writ issued the next day,[11] but the transcript did not arrive in Cass County until April of the following year.[12] The case could not go forward until the transcript arrived. Fullerton could do nothing except make a *pro forma* motion to continue the case until the May 1858 term of court. Caleb Dilworth did not need to be present for such a routine, uncontested matter. He either knew the case could not be tried in November and did not go to Cass County, or he learned of Fullerton's inability to go forward and returned to Mason County—all that can really be said with certainty is that he was not in court when Fullerton called the motion up for hearing. The court minutes for the hearing on the motion for continuance clearly state that Armstrong appeared "in proper person"—without counsel.[13] Instead of hearing just the motion to continue, the court heard a second motion made by the defendant without benefit of counsel. Armstrong wanted out of jail, so he asked to be admitted to bail. Judge Harriott denied Armstrong's motion for bail and granted Fullerton's motion for continuance.[14] Lawyers, and especially defense lawyers, hate to see defendants come before the court without the aid of counsel. Often a lawyer in such a situation will volunteer (or even be asked by the judge) to make a limited appearance on behalf of the unrepresented defendant for the purpose of helping at that hearing. We are now in the realm of speculation, but Lincoln could well have seen the son of his old friend appearing before the court in proper person, felt sorry for him, and stepped in to handle the bond hearing. If the course of events ran this way, Shaw and everyone else would have assumed Lincoln acted in a limited capacity, and Shaw could very well have been surprised that Lincoln came back and assisted in the trial of the case the next May. Whatever happened to cause Lincoln to appear on Armstrong's behalf during the November term, he did. On Saturday, November 21, Lincoln called the matter of bond back up for hearing and made a spirited argument to Judge Harriott for Armstrong's release but with as little success as Armstrong had when he asked in proper person.

It may be that Lincoln's limited appearance in November was the occasion for Shaw's surprise the following May. If, however, we read Shaw's words carefully, we will see that he was less surprised by Lincoln's appearance on Armstrong's behalf than he was by Lincoln's "immense interest" in the case. Shaw could tell that Lincoln saw this as more than just another case. Shaw had probably never heard of Lincoln's close personal connection to the Armstrong family, but by the end of the trial he (and the jury) would know full well the bonds of affection between Lincoln and the Armstrongs.

At some time during the day of May 6, in addition to meeting with Shaw, Lincoln also met with Caleb Dilworth. Dilworth later recalled that Lincoln said Hannah Armstrong had approached him and asked him to join in Duff Armstrong's defense. Lincoln then volunteered his services to help Dilworth in the defense. Dilworth described the meeting in a letter to J. McCan Davis, who investigated the trial for Ida Tarbell, in the following words:

When we reached Beardstown, I found Mr. Lincoln there on other business, and during the day he came to me and said that "Mrs. Armstrong had come to him and asked him to assist in the trial of the case, and that if it would come off while he was there he would do so if I was willing." Of course I was glad to have him try the case.[15]

It appears from Dilworth's account that Lincoln's final decision to take an active part in the trial of Duff Armstrong came only after he arrived in Beardstown and met with Hannah Armstrong on May 6. This fact could also account for why Lincoln made no mention of his involvement in the case to Shaw. When he met with Shaw, Hannah had not yet persuaded him to take the case. Lincoln then checked into the Dunbaugh House[16] and undoubtedly met with the other members of Armstrong's legal team. Strangely enough, William Walker was also there to lend a hand. Much is made of the fact that Lincoln represented Duff Armstrong without charging a fee; few have commented on the fact that Walker also charged no fee. Although Walker never mentioned the fact in his immense correspondence on the trial, his partner Lyman Lacey did. In a letter to Lincoln biographer J. T. Hobson, Lacey (who stayed in Havana to mind the office while Walker went to Beardstown for the trial) said:

I was well acquainted with Hannah Armstrong, mother of "Duff," with whom Lincoln had boarded in Menard County, which also joins Mason, when he was a young man, and before he was a lawyer. That was the reason Lincoln would not charge anything for defending her son. Our firm, Walker and Lacey, did not charge her anything for our services. "Duff" could not pay.[17]

Lacey did not expressly say so, but it seems that he was somewhat put off by the fact that lavish praise had been heaped upon Lincoln for defending Armstrong without pay while his and Walker's generosity went virtually unnoticed. We can fully understand why Lincoln was in Beardstown offering free legal services to Armstrong, but why was Walker there? What motivated him? I believe we can find his reason, but we will have to leave the realm of recorded fact and enter the realm of inference to do so. He may simply have been motivated by a desire to help the relatively inexperienced Dilworth, or as an act of benevolence toward Hannah Armstrong, or for both reasons. Human beings usually engage in complex behavior for a multitude of reasons. The evidence supports another inference. As we learned in a previous chapter, Judge Harriott had appointed Walker to represent Norris, and Illinois law had compelled Walker to do so without compensation. We also learned that, despite the fact he never earned a cent from the representation of Norris, he never gave up on his client and eventually got Norris pardoned. Armstrong's acquittal figured large in Norris's pardon. Given these facts, we can reasonably infer that Walker went to Beardstown to help get Armstrong acquitted so that he could argue the acquittal as grounds for Norris's pardon. Of course, none of the three reasons we have advanced can pass our test of proof by clear and convincing evidence. As we shall see later, although the acquittal of Armstrong was a factor in Norris's pardon, Armstrong's acquittal had no logical relevance as an argument supporting the proposition that Norris deserved a pardon. Armstrong's defense team was busy that evening at the Dunbaugh House. Although Dilworth and Walker knew the facts of the case, Lincoln did not. He had to digest Walker's notes taken at the trial of Norris,[18] to interview witnesses, and to discuss strategy with Dilworth and Walker. No competent modern attorney would walk into a capital murder case on Thursday and try it on Friday, but Dilworth himself attested that this is exactly what Lincoln did:

He not being acquainted with the facts, that night we met in a room with the witnesses and he examined them. The next morning the trial commenced.[19]

There is a possibility that Lincoln made his offer of help to Dilworth during the November 1857 term; and Dilworth, who wrote his letter almost 40 years after the trial, merged the memory of Lincoln's November 1857 offer with the memory of Lincoln's involvement in the May 1858 trial. The psychological literature recognizes that our memories sometimes merge our recollection of separate similar events into a single remembered event.[20] If this is the case, Lincoln had a few months to prepare rather than a single evening. There is, however, one fact that strongly indicates that Lincoln did not finally decide to become involved in the trial until May 6, and that is the timing of the witness subpoenas for the prosecution witnesses. Fullerton had issued his subpoenas for the prosecution witnesses well in advance of the trial, and he had specified that the witnesses should appear before the court on the first Monday in May (May 3),[21] the start date for the May term of Cass County Circuit Court. Thus, we see that the trial was set to begin on May 3, and most of Fullerton's witnesses appeared on May 3, having arrived in town on the evening of May 2.[22] Had it not been for the failure to appear of two essential witnesses, the trial would have ended well before Lincoln's May 6 arrival in Beardstown. If Lincoln had intended to try the case, he would have arrived in Beardstown on May 2 as did almost everyone else involved in the trial. One witness gives evidence against this reconstruction: John T. Brady reports that Nelson Watkins said he went to Lincoln's offices in Springfield to discuss his testimony.[23] This evidence was provided decades after the event and comes to us through multiple layers of hearsay. We may reasonably assume that Watkins told of meeting Lincoln in the hotel room on May 6, and Brady misremembered the location of the interview when he repeated the story decades later.

The conversation Watkins reported having with Lincoln sounds more like a conversation that would be had on the eve of trial, not some weeks or months before.[24]

The nonappearance of the two witnesses presented Fullerton with a monumental problem. The essential elements of a murder are (1) the death of the victim (2) by the criminal act or agency (3) of the defendant (4) acting with malice aforethought. Fullerton intended to prove the first two elements with the testimony of Dr. Benjamin F. Stephenson and the second two elements with the testimony of Charles Allen. Neither man answered his subpoena. Without them, Fullerton could not possibly prove his case. On Tuesday Fullerton issued an instanter subpoena for them.[25] When a subpoena is issued "instanter," that means the recipient must immediately come to court to testify. By the time Lincoln arrived in Beardstown the witnesses had still not appeared, and Fullerton took his efforts to the next level by seeking to have them arrested. At the common law, when a witness failed to appear, the court did not issue a warrant for the witness's arrest, it issued a writ of attachment. The only significant difference between a warrant and a writ of attachment is that they have different titles; the effect is the same, if the witness can be found, he gets arrested and hauled into court. At Fullerton's request, the court duly issued a writ of attachment.[26]

Obtaining Stephenson's presence would not prove a difficult task. It appears that Stephenson had done what some professionals do from time to time—ignored his subpoena. Sometimes those who occupy positions of power and prestige in a small community believe they are above such mundane duties as responding to court process. When this occurs, all that need be done is to make the professional understand that he can come to court in one of two ways—of his own free will or in handcuffs. What probably happened with Stephenson was that they sent a message to his medical offices informing him of the issuance of the writ and the options he faced, and he came to court posthaste.

Allen presented another problem. He hadn't ignored his subpoena, he had evaded it. Allen was apparently a friend of the Armstrongs and had come to regret having implicated Duff in the murder. He agreed with them that he would go into hiding until the trial was over, and they made arrangements for him to hide out in the nearby town of Virginia. This ploy was doomed to failure unless Allen agreed to disappear from Illinois permanently. Had Fullerton been unable to procure the presence of Allen in court for the May term, he would have gotten a continuance to the November term. Unless Allen fled the jurisdiction, he would surely be arrested in the interim, placed in jail, and held until the November term. Fullerton might be able to get several such continuances, and Armstrong would rot in jail in the interim. There was no speedy trial rule in the nine-teenth century.

What happened next has been the subject of much discussion. When Lincoln found out that the Armstrongs had hidden Allen away, he insisted that Allen be brought to court. There is some dispute as to pre-cisely how Allen got back to Beardstown. The oral history has two of Duff's cousins hitching up a wagon and going to get Allen,[27] but the court records show that Deputy Sheriff John Husted arrested Allen and traveled 60 miles to bring him back to court.[28] How Husted managed to log 60 miles between Beardstown and Virginia is something of a mystery in itself, given that the two towns were only 13 miles apart.[29] The fact that he received travel expenses of $0.05 per mile suggests that he padded his expense account. Husted would later claim that he traveled to Clary's Grove, a distance of approximately 30 miles, where he arrested Allen at midnight and brought him back to court.[30] For reasons that will become apparent in Chapter 12, we discount his story. What likely happened is that Lincoln sent for Allen, the Armstrongs produced Allen in court on May 7, and Husted served the writ of attachment on him in the court-room. This is a common scenario for such situations. Dr. Stephenson appeared the same day but did not get arrested. Dr. Stephenson's higher social status explains, but does not justify, the difference in treatment between the two wayward witnesses.

Apparently Fullerton had been stung by his partial loss of the Norris case and was determined to achieve a better result against Armstrong. He summoned more witnesses than for the Norris case, and he enlisted the aid of John S. Bailey, the elected state's attorney for the Fifth Judicial Circuit.[31] Fullerton could not have been happy when he walked into court on the morning of May 7 with his two assisting attorneys and saw that he was confronted by not simply Caleb Dilworth, but also by two of the most prominent attorneys in that part of Illinois. His displeasure could only be heightened by the fact that one of those prominent attor-neys was Abraham Lincoln. Fullerton and Lincoln had contested a mur-der trial the previous year, and that case had ended badly for Fullerton.

The year before, in Woodford County, Illinois, Fullerton had pros-ecuted a woman named Melissa Goings for killing her husband. Although Goings's claim of self-defense seemed plausible in light of her husband's reputation for abusiveness, Fullerton indicted her for the capital offense of murder. At first she was released on bond, but at a pretrial hearing the judge revoked her bond. Lincoln, who had just been retained in the case, asked for time to speak with his client and prepare the case. The judge granted a recess, and when court reconvened, Mrs. Goings was nowhere to be found. The bailiff accused Lincoln of advising his client

Oldest known photograph of the Almanac Trial courtroom, taken in 1937.
(Library of Congress)

to flee, and Lincoln vehemently denied the accusation. Legend has it that
when Lincoln denied counseling his client to flee, he qualified the denial
by saying "She asked me where she could get a drink of water, and I told
her there was some mighty good water in Tennessee."[32] Lincoln had
practiced law long enough to know the utter foolishness of saying any
such thing in open court before a judge who would not have appreciated
the humor. Given his reputation as a jokester, it is likely that he did make
such a statement after court recessed, and the two separate incidents
became fused in popular memory.

The lawyers for both sides were ready for trial, the witnesses had been
gathered in and stood ready to testify, 24 veniremen stood ready to serve
as jurors. The judge took his place upon the bench, and then something
remarkable happened. The prosecutor called up a riot case against
two men named William McCrudden and Joseph Whitaker, and
announced ready for trial. In a scenario reminiscent of Norris's trial the
previous year, Whitaker's lawyer moved for a change of venue and only
McCrudden stood trial that day. All those assembled for the Armstrong
trial had to wait patiently while Fullerton selected a jury and tried
McCrudden. The trial of Armstrong could not commence until the jury
in the McCrudden case came back with a verdict. They couldn't finish

jury selection because half of the 24 jurors summoned for jury duty that day were deliberating upon the McCrudden verdict. Three jurors from the McCrudden case wound up serving on Armstrong's case. One of those jurors was John T. Brady, whose reminiscences would later serve as material for countless Lincoln biographers.[33]

While Fullerton tried the riot case Armstrong's lawyers sat in the courtroom waiting. Abram Bergen, the inexperienced young lawyer who had come to court to see what he could learn from the trial of the case, studied Lincoln during this time. He would later reminisce:

> In the courtroom, while waiting for the Armstrong case to be called for trial, I watched and studied his face for full two hours. . . . He sat among the lawyers for these two hours with his head thrown back, his steady gaze apparently fixed on one spot of the blank ceiling, without the least change in the direction of his dull, expressionless eyes, and without noticing anything transpiring around him, and without any variation of feature or movement of any muscle of his face. I suppose he was thinking of his coming case.[34]

When the McCrudden jury retired to deliberate on its verdict, they probably began the voir dire of the 12 available jurors, but after excusing three prospective jurors from the panel, they had to await the McCrudden verdict to finish voir dire with the jurors from that trial. Finally the jury returned its verdict in the first case, they completed jury selection, and the Almanac Trial got under way. Probably the most important part of a jury trial occurs at the very beginning—jury selection. If you have the wrong jury, it matters little how good a case you have. All trial lawyers have their superstitions about the types of jurors they want on a jury, and apparently Lincoln was no exception. John J. Duff (1960) tells us that he didn't like blond haired, blue eyed men—they were too prosecution oriented; nor did he want men with high foreheads—their minds were already made up; he liked fat men, thinking they made ideal jurors; and he preferred young men to old.[35] Much ink has been spilled repeating the story that Lincoln conducted a very careful voir dire examination and selected only young men because such men would be more sympathetic to the defense.[36] It would seem that if he sought young men it was because he had a natural preference for young men in all cases, not as a special strategy for the Armstrong case. This legend apparently originated with Ida Tarbell, who is the earliest biographer to discuss the matter.[37] Tarbell seems to have gotten this idea from one of the witnesses at the trial, William Douglas, who remembered that "Lincoln was smart enough to get a jury of young men. They averaged about twenty-three years of age."[38] William H. Weaver, another witness to the trial, came away with a very different description of Lincoln's strategy. "I watched him when they impaneled that jury and on some excuse or other he always cast out the decidedly dark, coarse-haired brunette or the very blond thin-skinned applicant. Every one of those twelve men were types of medium coloring in hair and eyes. ..."[39] Tarbell's investigator, J. McCan Davis, tried to substantiate Douglas's story with Dilworth and Walker. Dilworth replied, "I cannot tell now as to the age of the jurors. I don't think there was any point made as to that part of the case. Of course we endeavored to get those that would be as favorable to our side of the case as we could."[40] This is a less than ringing endorsement of the idea that procuring a jury of young men played any significant part in the trial strategy. Walker recalled that the jury was composed of old, gray haired men.[41] As we shall soon see, he was wrong, but he could hardly have had such an erroneous recollection if a major strategy of the voir dire was to seat as young a jury as possible. We thus have a witness at the trial saying that Lincoln tried to get a young jury and the two lawyers who tried the case with Lincoln denying that assertion. It seems reasonable to believe Dilworth and Walker against Douglas, especially in light of other evidence supporting the lawyers. When we consider the fact that the life expectancy of Americans in the 1850s was 35,[42] we must ask how young was "young" in 1858? Ida Tarbell gives us an indication when she tells us that the average age of the jurors was under 23.[43] The 10 jurors whose age could be determined from census records had an average age of 28, and only Milton Logan, the foreman, was over 35.[44] When we factor in one final consideration, we must conclude that the average age of the jurors was determined more by chance than by any design on Lincoln's part. Due to the trial of the riot case, we can infer that the Almanac Trial probably started no earlier than 10:00 a.m. We know the jury returned its verdict before 7:02 p.m. because that is when the sun set in Beardstown on May 7, 1858.[45] This means that if no time were taken off for lunch, the trial went from voir dire to verdict in nine hours. During that time, the court had to conduct voir dire examination of the jury, take the testimony of no fewer than 16 witnesses,[46] have an instruction conference to consider proposed instructions for the jury, give both sides the opportunity to make final arguments, instruct the jury on the law, and allow the jury time to deliberate. The jury is said to have deliberated for 30 minutes, reducing the time to eight and one half hours. We have no precise figures for the time consumed by the other portions of the trial, so we must estimate. A reasonable estimate of the time would be 30 minutes per witness, a total of four hours and 40 minutes; 30 minutes for the instructions conference; two hours total for both prosecution and defense final arguments; and 30 minutes for instructing the jury on the law. After we have subtracted all these times from the time available, we have 50 minutes remaining for the lawyers to question the jurors on voir dire. Early in my career I tried several murder cases that lasted only a day. None of the voir dire examinations in those cases lasted longer than an hour and a half. Lincoln's voir dire would have gone no longer. Fifty to 90 minutes is not enough time to conduct anything more than the most superficial voir dire examination. We must relegate Lincoln's careful voir dire strategy to the realm of myth.

As for the course of the testimony for the prosecution, we have very little evidence beyond what we have already said about the facts of the case, but we can flesh out the outline with a few more details. All the witnesses agreed that Metzker provoked Armstrong to the point that Armstrong retaliated by striking Metzker a vicious blow to the eye. When Metzker finally got the smaller man to the ground, two men pulled him off of Armstrong. William Douglas, the first witness called by Fullerton, had this to say about the fight: "George Dowell and I parted them. We could not tell how badly Metzker was hit. His eye was fearfully blackened and we washed him. I said 'George, his skull is cracked.' "[47] After the fight Metzker and Armstrong parted company, and as he walked through the camp, Metzker was ambushed by someone wielding a neck yoke. From the conflicting testimony of the eyewitnesses to the fight, Fullerton sought to paint a picture of Armstrong and Norris as two aggrieved men who plotted together to waylay Metzker. Dr. Benjamin F. Stevenson, who later gained fame as one of the founders of the Grand Army of the Republic,[48] repeated the testimony he had previously given before the coroner's jury, the grand jury, and at the Norris trial. Except for Allen, none of the prosecution witnesses could tell the jury whether Armstrong used a weapon. This is not unusual for witnesses to a drunken brawl. Armstrong probably used some sort of weapon. One man could conceivably fracture another's skull with his bare fist, but the fist will usually fracture before the skull. Mike Tyson, one of the heaviest punching boxers of all time, fractured his fist rather than Mitch "Blood" Green's skull when they had their 1988 street fight.[49]

J. McCan Davis described the trial in the following words:

The testimony was of a most conflicting character. Apparently no two persons had observed precisely the same incidents of the fight. Most of Armstrong's witnesses (he had twenty-five in all) were sure he had no weapon in his hand when he struck Metzker; some acknowledged the night too dark to see the affray with distinctness. Witnesses varied widely as to the precise hour of the encounter. Some said it was as early as nine o'clock; others, as late as eleven; while most of them fixed it between ten and eleven o'clock. So much uncertainty was favorable to the defense. Yet there were circumstances pointing strongly to Armstrong's guilt. A sling-shot found on the grounds near the scene of the fight was produced;

it was picked to pieces by the man who made it and fully identified by him. Yet it was not traced to Armstrong's hands by any positive evidence. But now came a witness who seemed not to have participated in the general spree of the fateful night, and who was able to recall with great distinctness and particularity all that happened. His name was Charles Allen, and he was the most formidable witness produced by the prosecution.

He had, according to his story, stood by and watched the fight; he had seen Armstrong strike Metzker with the terrible sling-shot, "because" he declared, "the moon was shining brightly." ... Allen was corroborated to some extent by other witnesses, who swore that it was a bright, moonlight night, though none were ... so positive as Allen, nor so circumstantial in his description of the fight. ... Of nothing was Allen more positive than that the moon was full and high in the heavens. ... With Allen's testimony unimpeached, conviction seemed certain.[50]

When Fullerton finished his direct examination and tendered Allen, Lincoln rose to his feet and began his questioning. Little did he know he was embarking upon the most celebrated cross-examination in the history of American jurisprudence. We have now come to the point where we must determine if it is justly celebrated.

Chapter 11

The Famous Cross-Examination

The Western Republican characterized Charles Allen as a vile perjurer who tried to swear an innocent man onto the gallows, and that picture has seemingly colored all subsequent interpretation of the trial. Generations of lawyers have admired the supreme talent Lincoln displayed by dramatically confronting Allen with the almanac's irrefutable proof of his falsehood. Is the admiration justified? No one should doubt that Lincoln performed the cross-examination maneuver sometimes called commit and contradict. The dispute arises over when Lincoln did his contradicting. Did he commit Allen and immediately confront him with the contradiction by using the almanac during cross-examination as Allen sat in the witness stand, or did he commit on cross-examination and delay his contradiction until final argument as Allen sat in the audience? We cannot deny that waiting until final argument would be the safer course of action. When confronted with a contradiction, a witness may very well come up with a plausible explanation, and the cross-examination will fall flat. If the point on which the witness is contradicted goes to the heart of the case, then the case may well be lost when the witness explains. Even on lesser contradictions the lawyer can do severe damage to his case by confronting the witness and thereby giving the witness an opportunity to explain away the apparent contradiction. On the other hand, although saving the contradiction for final argument prevents the witness from explaining, the drama of the contradiction is lost. Cross-examiners in American courts daily face the dilemma of when to contradict. Cross-examiners in other common law jurisdictions have no such dilemma—they must commit and confront. Lord Herschell clearly stated this rule in the old English case of *Browne v. Dunn:*[1]

My Lords, I have always understood that if you intend to impeach a witness you are bound, whilst he is in the box, to give him an opportunity of making any explanation which is open to him; and, as it seems to me, that is not only a rule of professional practice in the conduct of a case, but is essential to fair play and fair dealing with witnesses.[2]

In jurisdictions that recognize the rule in *Browne v. Dunn,* if the witness is not given the opportunity to respond to a contradiction, then the judge can remedy the situation in one of three ways. She can (1) require that the witness be recalled for further examination and confronted with the evidence, (2) refuse to allow the offending party to argue the contradictory fact to the jury, or (3) instruct the jury that:

The [defense] gave evidence that [the almanac showed the moon near setting at the time of the incident]. That proposition was not put to the [witness Charles Allen]. In other words, he was not asked to comment on whether that was the case. The result is that he has not had the opportunity to respond to the suggestion [that he perjured himself when he said the moon was high overhead and shining brightly], and you do not have the benefit of the evidence he might have given had he been asked.[3]

Almost all lawyers and most modern biographers writing on the subject of the Almanac Trial tell us that Lincoln committed and confronted on cross-examination in conformity with the rule in *Browne v. Dunn.* Most of the early writers mention no dramatic confrontation of Allen and have Lincoln taking the safer course of committing and contradicting in final argument. The easiest way to settle the matter definitively would be to look at the transcript of testimony, but there were hardly any court reporters in Illinois before the Civil War. Consequently, the record of the Armstrong case contains no official transcript of testimony. There are, however, numerous variant transcripts of Lincoln's cross. Where did they come from? Is any one of them authentic?

We have already demolished the Wellman-Donovan transcript as coming from the imagination of a novelist. We must now look at the other transcripts and see what to make of them. Some transcripts we can immediately reject as inauthentic because the authors readily admit that they have invented the transcripts and offer them only as examples of what likely happened.[4] Historians have been putting words in the mouths of their subjects at least since the time of the great Greek historian Thucydides, who frankly admitted making up dialog:

As to the speeches which were made either before or during the war, it was hard for me, and for others who reported them to me, to recollect the exact words. I have therefore put into the mouth of each speaker the sentiments proper to the occasion, expressed as I thought he would be likely to express them, while at the same time I endeavored, as nearly as I could, to give the general purport of what was actually said.[5]

Although invented dialog has a long and honorable pedigree in historiography, it does not get us any closer to what actually happened, especially when the authors are not as careful as Thucydides in making the reader aware that the dialog is invented. In addition to Donovan's discredited transcript, we have at least five additional candidate transcripts that may get us close to the facts of Lincoln's famous cross-examination. For convenience of reference, we will call each transcript by the name of the man most closely associated with it. The first is a transcript that was popularized by the late Professor Irving Younger,[6] who lectured to lawyers all over the nation about his Ten Commandments of Cross-Examination; the second comes from William Makepeace Thayer's biography of Lincoln;[7] the third from Charles Carlton Coffin's biography;[8] the fourth from Wayne Whipple's biography;[9] and the fifth from Milton Logan, one of the jurors at the trial.

We can quickly eliminate Coffin's transcript as spurious for a number of reasons. First, Coffin has Metzker being killed with a knife and second, Coffin's transcript has Lincoln confront Allen with the almanac but doesn't have Lincoln asking him any questions about it. Instead, Lincoln turns and makes a speech to the jury. Lincoln declares: "Gentlemen, either this witness is wrong or this almanac is wrong, for it says there was no moon that night. Which will you believe?"[10] This is excellent theater but improper trial procedure. During the examination of a witness, the lawyers simply ask questions of the witness without making asides to the jury. Beyond the implausibility of Lincoln's perpetrating such a breach of courtroom protocol, to credit Coffin we must accept that Lincoln faked the almanac. Coffin says the almanac showed that there was no moon at the time of the killing.

Thayer gives an account of the trial so contrary to the known facts that we can hardly credit his rendition of the transcript. He has Lincoln writing Hannah that he will take the case, moving for a continuance, and conducting a lengthy investigation.[11]

Whipple seems to be of two minds about the cross-examination. He gives us two versions, one of which has Lincoln confronting Allen with a calendar,[12] and the other has him saving the almanac for final argument.[13] The transcript he gives us has no dramatic confrontation, meaning that Lincoln would have had to contradict Allen during final argument. Where did Whipple get his transcript? He got it from Thayer. Table 11.1 shows the two transcripts (along with Coffin's) set out side by side in a synopsis similar to those done by Burton H. Throckmorton,[14] Kurt Aland,[15] and many others for the Gospels. Identical and nearly identical wording is underlined. The table shows that Whipple felt free to both omit and amend Thayer, as well as to add new material.

Let us now turn to Younger's transcript. Younger reports the cross examination as going like this:

Q: Did you actually see the fight?

A: Yes.

Q: And you stood very near to them?

A: No, it was one hundred and fifty feet or more.

Q: In the open field?

A: No, in the timber.

Q: What kind of timber?

A: Beech timber.

Q: Leaves are rather thick in August?

A: It looks like it.

Q: What time did all this occur?

A: Eleven o'clock at night.

Q: Did you have a candle there?

A: No, what would I want a candle for?

Q: How could you see from a distance of one hundred and fifty feet or more without a candle, at eleven o'clock at night?

A: The moon was shining real bright.

Q: Full moon?

A: Yes, a full moon.
   [Lincoln produces the almanac.]

Q: Does not the almanac say that on August 29 the moon was barely past the first quarter instead of being full?

A: (No answer).

Q: Does not the almanac also say that the moon had disappeared by eleven o'clock?

A: (No answer).

Q: Is it not a fact that it was too dark to see anything from fifty feet, let alone one hundred and fifty feet?

A: (No answer).[16]

Table 11.1.   Spurious Transcripts of Lincoln's Cross-Examination

Coffin (1892)	Thayer (1882)	Whipple (1908)
	Q: Could there be no mistake in regard to the person who struck the blow? A: None at all: I am confident of that.	Q: Couldn't you be mistaken about this? . . .
	Q: What time in the evening was it? A: Between ten and eleven o'clock.	. . . What time did you see it? A: Between nine and ten o'clock that night.
	Q: Well, about how far between? Was it quarter-past ten or half-past ten o'clock, or still later? Be more exact, if you please. A: I should think it might have been about half-past ten o'clock	
		Q: Then you say there was a moon and it was not dark. A: Yes, it was light enough for me to see him hit Metzker on the head.
Q: You say that you saw him strike the fatal blow? Q: Yes.	Q: And you are confident that you saw the prisoner at the bar give the blow? Be particular in your testimony, and remember that you are under oath.	Q: Are you certain that you saw the prisoner strike the blow?—Be careful— remember—you are under oath!
	A: I am; there can be no mistake about it.	A: I am sure. There is no doubt about it.
Q: What time was it? A: About eleven o'clock in the evening.		
	Q: Was it not dark? A: Yes; but the moon was shining brightly.	Q: But wasn't it dark at that hour? A: No, the moon was shining bright.

(*continued*)

Table 11.1. (Continued)

Coffin (1892)	Thayer (1882)	Whipple (1908)
Q: Was it a bright night? A: Yes, the moon was nearly full.	Q: Then it was not very dark, as there was a moon? A: No; the moon made it light enough for me to see the whole affair.	
Q: What was its position in the sky? A: It was just about the position of the sun at ten o'clock in the forenoon.		
Q: You say that the moon was nearly full, and shining so bright that you could see Bill strike the blow. A: Yes.	Q: Be particular on this point. Do I understand you to say that the murder was committed about half-past ten o'clock, and that the moon was shining brightly at the time?	Q: Now I want you to be very careful. I understand you to say the murder was committed about half past nine o'clock, and there was a bright moon at the time?
	A: Yes, that is what I testify. [By Mr. Lincoln:] Very well. That is all.	A: Yes, sir. [By Mr. Lincoln:] Very well. That is all.
[Lincoln takes an almanac from his pocket and shows it to the jury. Lincoln addresses the jury:] Gentlemen, either this witness is wrong or this almanac is wrong, for it says there was **no moon** that night. Which will you believe?	[Lincoln does not produce the almanac until after the prosecution rests. In final argument he accuses the witness of fabrication because the almanac shows **no moon** at the time of the killing.]	[Lincoln does not produce the almanac until after the prosecution rests. In final argument he accuses the witness of fabrication because the almanac shows **no moon** at the time of the killing.]

This transcript seems to be the most often quoted by those who write on the Almanac Trial, while Coffin, Thayer, and Whipple have been ignored by subsequent biographers. Where did Younger's transcript originate? We will find it instructive to compare Younger's transcript to Donovan's. Although we know Donovan's to be spurious, it has some remarkable similarities to Younger's transcript. For example, both transcripts speak of the murder occurring in a stand of beech trees. This is noteworthy for a murder that occurred in a place known as Walnut Grove. Upon close examination of the transcripts, we find much common wording between Younger and Donovan. Our comparison of Donovan and Younger impels us toward the conclusion that Younger's transcript is a revision of Donovan's. There are, however, details in Younger's transcript that do not appear in Donovan's. Where did the Younger transcript pick up these additional details? Younger's transcript first appears in print during the twentieth century. It cannot be found in any book predating 1936. This is so because the second source of Younger's transcript first saw publication in 1936 in Albert Woldman's *Lawyer Lincoln*. In discussing the Almanac Trial, Woldman gives a conjectural reconstruction of the cross-examination. He makes it plain that he is not giving a verbatim transcript of the cross-examination by setting the cross out in paragraph form with no quotation marks:

Did you actually see the fight? Yes. Well, where were you standing at the time? About one hundred fifty feet away from the combatants. Describe this weapon again. The sling-shot was pictured in detail. And what time did you say all this occurred? Eleven o'clock at night. How could you see from a distance of one hundred and fifty feet, at eleven o'clock at night? The moon was shining real bright. A full moon? Yes, a full moon, and as high in the heavens as the sun would be at ten o'clock in the morning. He was positive about that. [Lincoln produces the almanac and has Allen read it.]

Did not the almanac specifically say that the moon on that night was barely past the first quarter instead of being full? And wasn't it a fact that the almanac also revealed that instead of the moon being high in the heavens in the position of the morning sun, it had actually disappeared by eleven o'clock? And wasn't it a further fact that it was actually so dark at the time that it was impossible to see distinctly from a distance of fifty feet, let alone one hundred and fifty feet?[17]

This language should sound familiar. It is obvious that some enterprising person took Woldman's conjectural reconstruction and worked it into Donovan's transcript. In Table 11.2 we have set Donovan's and Younger's transcripts in a synopsis with Woldman's reconstruction. For clarity, we have formatted Woldman's reconstruction as though it were a transcript. Wherever there is an identity of words between Woldman

Table 11.2. Synopsis of Younger's Transcript with the Transcripts of Donovan and Woldman

Woldman (1936)	Younger (1975)	Donovan (1898)
[Q] Did you actually see the fight? *[A] Yes.*	*Q: Did you actually see the fight?* *A: Yes.*	Q: And you were with Lockwood just before and saw the shooting? A: Yes.
[Q] Well, where were you standing at the time? [A] *About one hundred fifty feet away* from the combatants.	Q: And you stood near <u>them?</u> A: <u>No,</u> *it was a hundred and fifty feet or more.*	Q: And you stood very <u>near to them?</u> A: <u>No,</u> about twenty feet away.
. . .	Q: In the open field? A: No, in the timber.	. . . Q: In the open field? A: No, in the timber.
	Q: What kind of timber? A: Beech.	Q: What kind of timber? A: Beech timber.
	Q: Leaves on it rather thick in August? A: Yes.	Q: Leaves on it are rather thick in August? A: Rather.
[Q] And what time did you say all this occurred? *[A] Eleven o'clock at night.*	*Q: What time did all this occur?* *A: Eleven O'clock at night.*	. . .
	Q: Did you have a candle?	Q: Did you not see a candle there, with Lockwood or Grayson?
	A: No, what would I want a candle for?	A: No. What would we want a candle for?
[Q] How could you see from a distance of one hundred and fifty feet, at eleven o'clock at night?	*Q: How could you see from a distance of a hundred and fifty feet or more* without a candle *at eleven o'clock at night?*	Q: How, then, did you see the shooting?
[A] The moon was shining real bright.	*A: The moon was shining real bright.*	A: By moonlight!

(continued)

Table 11.2.   (Continued)

Woldman (1936)	Younger (1975)	Donovan (1898)
[Q] A full moon? *[A] Yes, a full moon,* and as high in the heavens as the sun would be at ten o'clock in the morning.	*Q: A full moon?* *A: Yes, a full moon.*	
[Lincoln produces the almanac and has Allen read it.]	[Lincoln produces the almanac and has the judge take judicial notice of it.]	[Lincoln confronts the witness with an almanac and moves for his arrest.]
[Q] Did not the almanac specifically say that the moon on that night was barely past the first quarter instead of being full?	*Q: Does the almanac not say that on August twenty-ninth,* the moon had disappeared, *the moon was barely past the first quarter instead of being full?* A: No answer.	
[Q] And wasn't it a fact that the almanac also revealed that instead of the moon being high in the heavens in the position of the morning sun, *it had actually disappeared by eleven o'clock?*	*Q: Does not the almanac also say that the moon had disappeared by eleven o'clock?* A: No answer.	
[Q] And wasn't it a further fact that it was actually so dark at the time that it was impossible to see distinctly from a distance of fifty feet, let alone one hundred and fifty feet?	*Q: Is it not a fact that it was too dark to see anything from fifty feet, let alone one hundred and fifty feet?* A: No answer.	

and Younger, the text is italicized. Wherever Younger and Donovan coincide, the text is underlined. The conclusion is inescapable. Younger's transcript is an amalgamation of Woldman's and Donovan's.

Our final transcript comes from Milton Logan, the foreman of the Armstrong jury. As Logan recalled, the cross examination went like this:

Q: Did you see Armstrong strike Metzker?

A: Yes.

Q: About how far were you from where the affair took place?

A: About forty feet. I was standing on a knoll or hill looking down at them.

Q: Was it a light night?

A: Yes it was.

Q: Any moon that night?

A: Yes, the moon was shining almost as bright as day.

Q: About how high was the moon?

A: About where the sun would be at 1 o'clock in the day.

Q: Are you quite certain there was a moon that night?

A: Yes sir, I am certain.

Q: You are sure you are not mistaken about the moon shining as brightly as you represent.

A: No sir, I am not mistaken.

Q: Did you see Armstrong strike Metzker by the light of the moon, and did you see Metzker fall?

A: I did.

Q: What did Armstrong strike him with?

A: With a sling shot.

Q: Where did he strike Metzker?

A: On the side of the head.

Q: About what time did you say this happened?

A: About 10 o'clock at night.[18]

The thing that most immediately catches our attention is that the transcript sounds more like a direct examination than it does a cross-examination. It seems friendly and has no dramatic confrontation. Indeed, Logan remembered that Lincoln did not "cross question" Allen. By this he certainly meant that Lincoln did not conduct an aggressive, combative cross-examination. Some biographers who have reproduced the Logan transcript append a description of Lincoln confronting Allen,[19] but this has to be borrowed from the legend of the cross. The odds that Logan gives us a verbatim transcript of the cross-examination are vanishingly small. The transcript comes from an interview he gave in 1906, almost a half century after the trial. We have good reason beyond the passage of time to question the accuracy of Logan's transcript. In his interview he remembered a lot of things that just didn't happen: the regular panel was exhausted and 50 more jurors were brought in; the trial lasted two days; Lincoln spoke on final argument for five or six hours. As time passes our memory of detail fades, but thematic memory, the memory of the most important aspects of an event, can last forever. Logan remembered that Lincoln performed a friendly cross-examination and a significant final argument.

The legend of the confrontation has no support from reliable historical sources. One item of reliable evidence and one item alone can be mustered to support the accuracy of the confrontation legend—the recollection of J. Henry Shaw that after the trial several jurors told him the almanac "floored" the witness.[20] This is a slender thread from which to hang the theory that Lincoln confronted Allen. The recollection is just as consistent with the theory that Allen was in the audience for the final argument and reacted strongly to Lincoln's production of the almanac.

Some support for the commit and confront scenario can be found in John T. Brady's recollection of the cross-examination:

The prosecuting witness, Allen, testified in the trial that the reason he could see a slung-shot that Armstrong had in his hand, with which he struck Metzker, was that the moon was shining very bright, about where the sun would be, at one o'clock in the afternoon. Mr. Lincoln was very particular to have him repeat himself a dozen or more times during the trial about where the moon was located, and my recollection is now, *that the almanac was not introduced until Mr. Lincoln came to that part of Allen's testimony telling the Court where the moon was located.* Mr. Lincoln was very careful not to cross Mr. Allen in anything, and when Allen lacked words to express himself, Lincoln loaned them to him.[21] [emphasis added]

The italicized portion of Brady's statement can be read as support for the confrontation theory, but it adds slight weight to the theory because it was given years after the fact, and Brady's recollection had grown so dim that he said the prosecution called Allen as their only witness.[22] Further, the statement is just as consistent with the interpretation that Brady was speaking of Lincoln using the almanac during final argument when he discussed Allen's testimony.

It seems that when Donovan borrowed Eggleston's fictional cross-examination and presented it as factual, the popular imagination became captivated by the picture of Lincoln dramatically confronting the witness. This picture took such hold that the subsequent discrediting of Donovan's transcript could not erase it. Readers and biographers ever after have come to the Almanac Trial with the preconception that Lincoln used the almanac on cross-examination, and that preconception has caused them to overlook the evidence that he did no such thing.

Having discredited the evidence indicating that Lincoln confronted Allen with the almanac, we should be through with our analysis—the proponent of a theory should bear the burden of proof, and no proponent of the commit and confront scenario can possibly carry the burden of proof. We will nevertheless undertake to disprove the theory. Conventional wisdom teaches that it is impossible to prove a negative, but it can be done if we can prove a positive fact that conclusively refutes the fact we are seeking to negate.

The complete absence of a commit and confront scenario from the Lincoln literature prior to Donovan's appropriation of the Eggleston transcript goes far to prove that Lincoln committed the witness and then contradicted him in final argument, but there is more proof than that. William Douglas, the first witness to testify for the prosecution, remained in the courtroom after testifying. He heard the testimony of all the witnesses and was certain that Lincoln did not confront Allen with the almanac. He told J. McCan Davis, "I remember distinctly about Lincoln using the almanac. He didn't produce it until he got up to make his talk."[23] Except for the one ambiguous sentence in Brady's statement, both he and Logan describe Lincoln as conducting a very friendly, nonconfrontational cross-examination.

The easygoing manner of cross-examination described by Logan and Brady seems to show that Lincoln was well aware of the maxim that when you cross-examine, you need not examine crossly. Lincoln's contemporaries thought that as a cross-examiner "he had no equal. ... If any obstinate witness appeared and was determined to conceal facts which Lincoln desired brought out, Lincoln would neither show resentment nor attempt to coerce the witness but would go after him in a nice, friendly way, questioning about things which were foreign to the point desired, thus placing him at ease, making him forget his antagonistic ideas, and, before he was aware of the harm he was doing his side, the whole story would be laid bare. ... "[24] In the impeachment of a witness, Lincoln seems to have preferred gentle humor to vitriol. Nothing illustrates this point better than a story that Lincoln told about a cross-examination he conducted in a relatively unimportant case:

I was retained in the defense of a man charged before a justice of the peace with assault and battery. It was in the country, and when I got to the place of trial

I found the whole neighborhood excited, and the feeling was strong against my client. I saw the only way was to get up a laugh and get the people in good humor. It turned out that the prosecuting witness was talkative; he described the fight at great length; how they had fought over a field, now by the barn, again down to the creek, and over it, and so on. I asked him on cross-examination how large that field was; he said it was ten acres; he knew it was, for he and someone else had stepped it off with a pole. "Well, then," I inquired, "was not that the smallest crop of a fight you have ever seen raised off of ten acres?" The hit took. The laughter was uproarious, and in half an hour the prosecuting witness was retreating amid the jeers of the crowd.[25]

In addition, we can argue that Lincoln did not confront Allen with the almanac for the simple reason that when he examined Allen he did not have the almanac. In speaking of when the almanac was obtained, Caleb Dilworth said, "When this testimony was given, we procured the almanac, I think now from one of the public officers of the court. We examined it, and when the defense commenced, Mr. Lincoln offered it into evidence."[26] John Armstrong agreed with Dilworth that "When the evidence was all in Mr. Lincoln asked for an almanac and a Mr. Jacob Jones left the court room, went to a nearby drug store and returned with an almanac for the year 1857, which Mr. Lincoln showed to the jury. . . ."[27] Duff Armstrong himself recalled that Lincoln sent Jones to look for the almanac on the morning of the trial and that after Allen testified everyone thought he was going to be convicted.[28] If Lincoln had used the almanac to impeach Allen with the electrifying results of the legend, nobody would have thought Armstrong was going to get convicted.

The recollections of Dilworth and John Armstrong suggest that when Lincoln examined Allen, he had no idea where the moon might have been and was just shooting in the dark hoping he might hit something. If that is the case, then Lincoln's cross-examination of Armstrong was not a carefully planned deployment of the commit and contradict method. If, as it seems, Lincoln did not become involved in the case until May 6, when Hannah Armstrong petitioned him one last time, that fact increases the probability that Lincoln had no grand scheme of contradicting Allen on the position of the moon because he knew little or nothing about the case before meeting with the defense witnesses later that evening. Instead of being a careful planner, Lincoln seems to have done a good job of being quick-witted, thinking on his feet, and deciding to look up the position of the moon on the fly during the heat of battle.

Some modern lawyers might protest that this reconstruction makes Lincoln look incredibly haphazard in his cross-examination of Allen, but they will say that against the backdrop of the extensive present-day discovery available in criminal cases. For example, in some modern jurisdictions the defendant can demand a list of the state's witnesses and then depose them before the trial.[29] Mid-nineteenth-century criminal courts had almost no discovery, and criminal prosecutions could fairly be characterized as "trial by ambush." In such an environment, preparation was difficult, and quick-wittedness was an indispensable asset.

We have now traced out the course of the cross-examination and have decided that Lincoln most likely used the commit and contradict technique rather than commit and confront. We now must turn to the question of the precise nature of the contradiction Lincoln found in the almanac.

Chapter 12

The Misplaced Moon

Charles Allen testified that he saw the fight by the light of a brightly shining moon high overhead. Other witnesses attested to the brightness of the moon, while some witnesses declared it was too dark to see clearly. Lincoln adduced an almanac showing that the moon was not high overhead, but precisely where was the moon supposed to be at the time of the fight? Memories vary. Some say Lincoln proved it had already set;[1] others that it had not yet risen;[2] others simply that Lincoln showed there was no moon at all that night.[3] If any one of these sources correctly state what Lincoln showed with his almanac, then Lincoln was a fraud and a con artist. As has been shown time and time again, the moon was in the sky at the time of the fight, but it was close to setting. The moon has been figured to have set as early as 11:57[4] and as late as five minutes after midnight.[5] The U.S. Naval Observatory's records show that the moon reached its first quarter on August 27, 1857; that on August 29 it was waxing gibbous with 70 percent of its surface showing; and that on the night of August 29, 1857, the moon set in Mason County, Illinois, at four minutes after midnight.[6] Ward H. Lamon looked at the conflict between the testimony of the witnesses and the evidence of the astronomers and pronounced Lincoln a fraud. Where there is conflict in testimony, somebody must be lying, right? Wrong. It is axiomatic that conflict in testimony does not mean that either version of the testimony is a lie.[7] This axiom forms the bedrock for the rule of evidentiary analysis that posits that before you call anyone a liar, you should try to resolve conflicts in testimony without attributing untruthfulness to any witness.[8]

Eighth Month.		AUGUST, 1857.									31 Days.
Moon's Phases. D. H. M. Full Moon, ... 5 1 21 E. Last Quarter, ... 12 0 34 E. New Moon, ... 19 11 18 M. First Quarter, ... 27 9 56 M.			Moon's place.		CALENDAR For Boston, N. Y. State, N. England, Wisconsin, Michigan, Iowa, Oregon, and the Canadas.			Sun slow.	CALENDAR For N. York City, N. Jersey, Penn., Conn., Ohio, Indiana, Illinois, Nebraska, and Utah.		
D. M.	D. W.	Miscellaneous Phenomena.	S.	D.	Sun rises. H. M.	Sun sets. H. M.	Moon sets. H. M	M.	Sun rises. H. M.	Sun sets. H. M.	Moon sets. H. M.
1	Sat	5th. Bat. of Brownston, '12.	♐	21	4 53	7 19	0 21	6	4 57	7 15	0 29
31)		8th Sunday after Trinity.			Venus in Gemini.				Day's length. 14h. 16m.		
2	*Su*	☽ farthest south. *Oppres-*	♑	5	4 54	7 18	1 9	6	4 58	7 14	1 18
3	Mo	♅ S., 6h. 58m. morn. *sively*	♑	18	4 55	7 16	2 7	6	4 59	7 13	2 15
4	Tu	♂ S., 10h. 59m. morn. *hot*	♒	1	4 56	7 15	rises	6	5 0	7 12	rises
5	We	○ 5th. *and dry.*	♒	15	4 57	7 14	7 36	6	5 1	7 10	7 32
6	Th	9th. Abd. of Santa Anna, '55.	♒	28	4 58	7 13	8 1	6	5 2	7 9	7 58
7	Fri	♃ 90° from ☉. *The want of*	♓	12	4 59	7 11	8 23	5	5 2	7 8	8 22
8	Sat	Nep. ☌ ☾. *rain is felt.*	♓	25	5 0	7 10	8 43	5	5 3	7 7	8 44
32)		9th Sunday after Trinity.			Mars in Leo.				Day's length. 14h. 1m.		
9	*Su*	16th. Bat. of Camden, 1780.	♈	9	5 1	7 9	9 4	5	5 4	7 5	9 6
10	Mo	Greenwich Obs. foun'd, 1675.	♈	22	5 2	7 7	9 27	5	5 5	7 4	9 31
11	Tu	☿ south. 11h. 1m. eve.	♉	5	5 3	7 6	9 54	5	5 6	7 3	9 59
12	We	☾ 12th. ♃ ☌ ☾. *Still contin-*	♉	19	5 4	7 4	10 27	5	5 7	7 1	10 33
13	Th	♅ near ☾. *ues dry.*	♊	2	5 5	7 3	11 10	5	5 8	7 0	11 18
14	Fri	12th. ☾ in perigee.	♊	16	5 6	7 2	morn	4	5 9	6 59	morn
15	Sat	♀ near ☾. *Wells in places*	♋	0	5 7	7 0	0 3	4	5 10	6 57	0 12
33)		10th Sunday after Trinity.			Jupiter in Taurus.				Day's length. 13h. 45m.		
16	*Su*	♄ near ☾. *give out.*	♋	13	5 8	6 59	1 9	4	5 11	6 56	1 17
17	Mo	♂ near ☾.	♋	27	5 10	6 57	2 23	4	5 12	6 54	2 30
18	Tu	☾ south, 11h. 19m. morn.	♌	11	5 11	6 56	3 38	4	5 13	6 53	3 44
19	We	● 19th. ☿ in ☋. *A little*	♌	25	5 12	6 54	sets	4	5 14	6 51	sets
20	Th	Guerriere taken, 1812.	♍	9	5 13	6 53	7 32	3	5 15	6 50	7 30
21	Fri	☿ near ☾. *cooler.*	♍	23	5 14	6 51	7 51	3	5 16	6 48	7 51
22	Sat	♅ 90° from ☉.	♎	6	5 15	6 50	8 9	2	5 17	6 47	8 9
34)		11th Sunday after Trinity.			Saturn in Cancer.				Day's length. 13h. 27m.		
23	*Su*	Dr. Herschell died, 1823.	♎	18	5 16	6 48	8 27	2	5 18	6 45	8 30
24	Mo	27th. Bat. Long Island, '76.	♏	0	5 17	6 46	8 47	2	5 19	6 44	8 51
25	Tu	Nep. south. 1h. 18m. morn.	♏	12	5 18	6 45	9 10	2	5 20	6 42	9 16
26	We	Moon in apogee.	♏	24	5 19	6 43	9 49	2	5 21	6 41	9 56
27	Th	☽ 27th. *Rainy appear-*	♐	6	5 20	6 41	10 13	1	5 22	6 39	10 21
28	Fri	♀ near ♄. *ances.*	♐	18	5 21	6 40	10 58	1	5 23	6 38	11 7
29	Sat	☿ in aphelion.	♑	0	5 22	6 38	11 52	1	5 24	6 36	morn
35)		12th Sunday after Trinity.			Uranus in Taurus.				Day's length. 13h. 10m.		
30	*Su*	27th. Louis Philippe d., '50.	♑	12	5 23	6 37	morn	0	5 25	6 35	0 1
31	Mo	♀ south. 9h. 15m. morn.	♑	24	5 24	6 35	0 57	0	5 26	6 33	1 5

ON MATRIMONY.

Tom praised his friend, who changed his state,
For binding fast himself and Kate
In union so divine.
"Wedlock's the end of life," he cried;
"Too true, alas!" said Jack, and sighed,
"'Twill be the end of mine."

Why is a lean dog like the very wise? Because he is a thin cur.

An editor, whose subscribers complained he did not give them news enough, told them to read the Bible, which would doubtless be news to most of them.

Joseph's brethren cast him into the pit, because they thought it a good opening for the young man.

There is the same difference between the real and the ideal, that there is between a castle in Ayrshire and a castle in the air.

Almanac entry for August 29, 1857. (George R. Dekle, Sr.'s library)

We will reserve the question of whether Lincoln used a fake almanac until later. For now we are going to assume that he was innocent of fraud and that Allen was giving honest, but not necessarily accurate, testimony. Although most of our sources claim that the almanac showed there was no moon in the sky on the night of the killing, a significant minority report that Lincoln's almanac showed that the moon was near setting when Armstrong struck Metzker. We have good reason to credit the minority report and discount the majority opinion. Abram Bergen remembered that when Lincoln produced the almanac, it caused a flurry of activity on the part of the prosecutors. First, they examined it. Not satisfied with what the almanac said, they sent for another almanac for comparison purposes. This delayed the trial somewhat because an almanac for the previous year was hard to find. Finally, the prosecutors found a suitable almanac and compared it to Lincoln's. Bergen recalls that they at first made an objection about some slight difference.[9] John T. Brady remembered the objection the prosecutors made. After the examination one of the prosecutors said, "Mr. Lincoln, you are mistaken, the moon was just coming up instead of going down at that time." Lincoln replied, "It serves my purpose just as well, just coming up, or just going down, as you admit it was not over head as Mr. Allen swore it was."[10]

If, as the almanac said, the moon was in the sky at the time of the fight, where did the myth of the almanac's moonless night originate? It may have come from one of two sources. The first source could be the characteristic of human memory that gave rise to the cliché of the boasting fisherman. Just as the one that got away gets bigger and bigger with each retelling, every time the witnesses retold the story of the almanac, the moon sank lower and lower on the horizon until it disappeared completely. This "boasting fisherman" syndrome has been recognized at least since the eighth century BCE, when Homer sang of the aged Nestor telling Achilles and Agamemnon that the heroes of his youth were much more heroic than the heroes besieging Troy.[11] We will address the second possible source later in this chapter.

To evaluate the accuracy of Allen's report, we need to know where the moon was in the sky and what time the fight occurred. We immediately run into problems because nobody really knew what time the fight occurred. Everyone was drunk and wristwatches were not yet invented. The best the witnesses could do would be to estimate the time. This is why Caleb Dilworth discounted the materiality of the almanac, saying, "In relation to the almanac or the condition of the moon at that time, we did not put much stress on that part of the case, because it was so uncertain at what time of the night the affray occurred."[12] Estimates ranged from as early as 9:00 to as late as 11:00.[13] For the purpose of discussion we will take 11:00 as the hour of the fight because that is the time given in most accounts. The moon would then be within one hour of setting. How high above the horizon could it have been?

In 1999 Donald W. Olson and Russell Doescher, professors in the Department of Physics at Southwest Texas State University, decided to investigate the Almanac Trial. They were intrigued by the discrepancy between what the almanac showed and what the people of Mason County remembered about the position of the moon on the night of the killing. It seems almost everyone remembered that August 29 was a bright moonlit night. Their investigation revealed some interesting facts. First, the moon was "running low" on August 29. This means that the moon never got very high above the horizon. When the moon crosses the meridian we would expect it to be 90 degrees above the horizon. On August 29 it was only 20 degrees above the horizon when it crossed the meridian at 7:44 p.m. Second, the moon set extremely fast that night. You would expect a moon on the meridian to take six hours to set. That night the moon set in four hours and 20 minutes. It set so quickly because it goes through an 18-year cycle of "running low" to "running high," and in 1857 the moon was at the stage of the cycle when it ran the lowest.[14] Olson and Doescher think this fact explains the discrepancy between the popular memory of a moonlit night and what the almanac said. I have a simpler explanation that we will discuss in due course.

According to Olson and Doescher's calculations, at 11:00 p.m. on the night of the murder the moon was only 8 degrees above the horizon, which means the moon would have been invisible at the whiskey camp. Unless they were bonsai trees, the stand of trees in Virgin's Grove would have certainly blocked the moon almost completely at 8 degrees above the horizon. Furthermore, that night the moon would never have been as high as Allen said it was. If we're going to believe Allen was an honest witness, we're going to have to find a light source for Allen to see by, and we're going to have to find an explanation for why he said the moon was overhead. We can easily find Allen's true light source. We can also find an explanation for Allen's misplaced moon.

First, for the light source: According to Duff Armstrong, Allen had plenty of light to see by. In his 1896 newspaper interview Armstrong said, "The truth is there was no moon that night. If there was, it was hidden by clouds. But it was light enough for everybody to see the fight. The fight took place in front of one of the bars and each bar had two or three candles on it."[15] Armstrong was, of course, mistaken about the moon, but he certainly wasn't mistaken about the light coming from the bars.

Now the misplaced moon: Allen was one of many witnesses who attested to the brightly shining moon, but he was the witness who was most emphatic.[16] We must take all the witnesses' assertions about where the moon was with a grain of salt. If this fight followed the pattern of the scores of bar fights that I have prosecuted and defended, the witnesses were all under the influence of alcohol. This fact alone ought to be enough to draw the inference that Allen didn't know where the light was coming from and just assumed it was coming from the moon high overhead. But we have more. The psychological literature recognizes a phenomenon known as the "light from above bias" or the "light from above prior." Whenever we look at anything, unless we particularly notice the light source, we assume the light comes from above. We not only assume it comes from above, we assume that the light source is over-head and slightly to our left.[17] There are optical illusions that rely on the light from above prior. Are the rows of figures dents or bumps? The light from above prior predisposes you in one way or another depending on how the picture is oriented.[18]

For all the previously mentioned reasons, Lincoln's almanac might have impeached Allen in the eyes of the jury, but it really does nothing to make us think that Allen committed perjury. Allen testified he saw Armstrong hit Metzker in the eye; Armstrong admitted he hit Metzker in the eye. Allen testified he had enough light to see clearly; Armstrong admitted Allen had enough light to see clearly. Allen testified he saw Armstrong use a deadly weapon (a slungshot); Nelson Watkins confirms that Armstrong used a deadly weapon (a wagon hammer). The only indication we have that Allen was anything more than mistaken comes from people who impugn Allen's integrity. One early biography, which suppressed Allen's name, described him as a "disreputable man."[19] Thompson McNeely, a noted attorney from Allen's hometown said, "Allen would swear to anything in a trial and would work on either side of the case very nicely."[20] In my experience as a trial lawyer, negative character evidence of this type is near worthless. We must also ask ourselves the chicken-and-egg question: Which came first, Allen's testimony at trial or his repu-tation for untruthfulness? The publication of the Western Republican's purple prose about exposure of Allen's "perjury" ruined whatever repu-tation for honesty he may have had. We should also remember that Allen had so little animus toward the Armstrongs he agreed to hide out in Virginia to evade his trial subpoena. When he went onto the stand, he was under arrest for trying to help the Armstrongs. If he had been the type of witness to "work on either side of the case very nicely," all he had to do was to testify that after due reflection, he wasn't so sure about what, if anything, Armstrong had in his hand. I have tried a number of cases where witnesses friendly to the defendant repented their initial statement and became so "unsure" of what they saw or heard that they won acquittals for their friend.

The conclusion that Allen was an honest but mistaken witness raises the question of whether Lincoln did anything wrong by impeaching him. The short answer to that question is "No." We have no evidence that Lincoln knew anything at all about the light from the bars. Remember, he had just come into the case. As Caleb Dilworth remembered, on the afternoon of May 6 Lincoln knew next to nothing about the killing and spent the entire evening in Dilworth's room interviewing witnesses and trying to get a handle on the facts of the case.[21] The odds that Lincoln was aware of the alternative light source are very small. Even if Lincoln knew, it would be proper to show that Allen was mistaken about the light source to discredit him. According to modern tenets of legal ethics, a criminal defense attorney is not prevented from cross-examining a witness simply because the lawyer believes the witness is telling the truth.[22] Only if Lincoln used a faked almanac could we say he behaved improperly in impeaching Allen. We are now ready to dispose of the issue of the faked almanac.

As we have seen, the story first arose during Lincoln's presidential campaign as a sort of antidote to the news article "Thrilling Episode from the Life of Abe Lincoln," in which the Western Republican describes the Almanac Trial.[23] Ward H. Lamon accepted the story of the fake almanac uncritically, and it persists to this day.[24] Many biographers have tried to scotch the story by simply referring to the fact that Lincoln was known as "Honest Abe." This is a weak defense to the charge of forgery, and I think we can find a better one. The only evidence that makes it creditable is the fact that many witnesses to the trial remembered the almanac showing no moon at all. We have already accounted for this fact by the natural tendency of reminiscences to embellish the drama of an event. Others remember the moon being near the horizon, and almanacs for 1857 showed the moon on the horizon. Why forge an almanac when an authentic one will serve just as well?

Two men helped to perpetuate the story of the fake almanac. These two men were Dr. Charles E. Parker, who testified at the trial, and John Husted, the deputy sheriff who swore he traveled 60 miles to arrest Charles Allen after the Armstrongs delivered him to the courtroom. The stories of these two men came decades apart, but they fit together well enough for an uncritical investigator to accept. What follows is the story as told by the two men.

On the night of May 6 Lincoln came into Parker's offices and asked whether Parker had an almanac for 1857. Parker said he didn't. Lincoln told him that if he couldn't find an almanac to refute the testimony of the prosecution witnesses, his client would hang. After Lincoln left Parker decided to assist him by "doctoring" an almanac. He had an almanac for 1853 that showed no moon on August 29. Parker took the almanac to a print shop and asked the printers to change the date of the almanac to 1857. They agreed. The next morning, when he came to court to testify, he gave Lincoln the doctored almanac. What most people miss from this story is that Parker claimed Lincoln was just as much a victim of fraud as the judge and jury. Parker, a renowned practical joker, started telling this story around the time that the supposed forgery of the almanac became a campaign issue. His contemporaries took the story with a large grain of salt, believing it likely that Parker's practical joke was not forging the almanac but claiming to have forged it.[25] Caleb Dilworth contradicts Parker's story in almost every detail. In writing about Parker's story, Dilworth said:

I am satisfied that the almanac affair is an entire hoax; and as to Lincoln seeing the doctor the day before, that I know is a mistake because Mr. Lincoln was at my room the night before the trial, and that is the first time that he had any idea of what the proof was to be. We had the witnesses present, and he and I interrogated them. They remained there until late in the night.[26]

John Husted surfaced several years later, when he claimed to have the genuine forged almanac in his possession. The almanac purportedly was found among the papers of J. Henry Shaw when Shaw died, and Husted kept the almanac for several years before he realized its significance. When he finally got around to examining the almanac, he noticed that everywhere the year 1853 had been printed in the almanac, the 3 had been erased and a 7 put in its place. He then recognized the almanac as the one Lincoln used in the Armstrong trial. According to Husted, the forgery was discovered in the following manner: On the Tuesday following the trial a lawyer with the unfortunate name of "Tubby" Smith wanted to compare a date in his notebook with an almanac for 1857. Husted went to the courtroom and retrieved the almanac Lincoln had used. Smith compared the dates and found that they did not coincide. A further search was made for another 1857 almanac, and it coincided with Smith's notes. According to Husted, Smith "let the cat out of the bag," and the discrepancy made somewhat of a sensation among the lawyers assembled for court. Shaw was present, and he immediately confiscated the almanac. Husted said he was certain that the almanac he found in 1888 was the same almanac as the one confiscated by Shaw 30 years earlier. Husted sold the almanac along with affidavits supporting its authenticity,[27] and the history of the travels of that almanac has already been recounted in Chapter 4. Shaw gives us further reason to question Husted's story. When writing Herndon about the trial, Shaw mentioned Lincoln giving him the slungshot but said nothing about having the forged almanac. Indeed, he defended Lincoln against the charge of trickery with the almanac. He would hardly have done so if he had possession of Husted's fake almanac.

Ida Tarbell had J. McCan Davis investigate the allegations of forgery, and Davis came away from the investigation highly skeptical of the tales told by Parker and Husted. In arriving at his conclusions, he relied in part on character evidence for Parker, who was dead, and his own assessment of the credibility of Husted, whom he questioned personally. He entitled his report "How the Almanac 'Forgery' was Discovered," being careful to set off the word "forgery" in quotation marks. Although he got the story of how the forgery was discovered directly from Husted, he strongly suspected that Husted knew nothing of the actual discovery of the forgery but was parroting a news article about the discovery in which a man by the name of H. B. De Sollar described the "Tubby" Smith incident using almost identical words to the ones used by Husted. The story had appeared in a newspaper entitled the *Star of the West*, and the editor of the paper assured Davis that De Sollar was a reliable source. De Sollar, however, was not recounting something that he had seen but something that he had been told by Dr. Parker.[28] This amounts to nothing more than gossip, and the ultimate source of the gossip is Dr. Parker, the renowned practical jokester. T. L. Mathews gives us further reason to discount the testimony of Husted:

At [the time of Shaw's death] I was cashier of the First State Bank of Beardstown, Illinois, Mr. Shaw's home town, and the administrator of his estate placed Shaw's books and papers in my custody for disposal, and I hired the man Husted, who was an auctioneer, to sell them at public auction. Before the sale we made an inventory and I did not find, see, nor hear, of the discussed almanac Husted claimed to have found among Shaw's effects. ... Not long after I saw [the newspaper article reporting Husted's claim] I was in Beardstown and I hunted up Husted and demanded the almanac. With seeming hesitation and embarrassment he said he had sold the almanac to a lawyer in Chicago but could not or would not give me his name and address.[29]

Let us ignore the character evidence against Parker and Husted and look at cold facts. John T. Brady heard the debate between Lincoln and the prosecutors about whether the moon was going up or coming down at the time of the murder. This means that Lincoln's almanac showed the moon was somewhere in the sky when the murder occurred. Husted's fake almanac showed no moon at all on August 29.[30] Husted's fake almanac could not possibly have been the almanac Lincoln used.

We have already suggested the boasting fisherman syndrome as an explanation for the story of the moonless night and the vile perjurer, but another syndrome probably accounts for the variance between the story of the trial and the facts of the case—the lying politician syndrome. What appears to have happened is that the story of the Almanac Trial got embellished for use as campaign propaganda. Having the moon on the horizon was not nearly as dramatic as having it completely out of sight, so the Western Republican made the moon disappear from the sky. Having Charles Allen mistaken about the moon's position was not nearly as dramatic as having him lie about it, so the Western Republican made Allen a perjurer. The anti-Lincoln forces could not let the "Thrilling Episode" story go unanswered, so they made up the story of the fake almanac. If Lincoln is to be criticized for anything he did in relation to the Almanac Trial, he should be criticized for allowing his partisans to shamelessly embellish the story of the trial. We have already remarked upon the fact that Lincoln, despite being a first-rate storyteller, seems never to have said anything about the trial. He probably refrained from speaking about it because he was ashamed of the Western Republican's wildly exaggerated account. The end result was the besmirching of the reputations of two men—Charles Allen and Abraham Lincoln. It is likely that those stains will never fully be erased. Historian after historian has refuted the fake almanac claim, yet still it persists. As far as I can tell, no work prior to this has ever even attempted to rescue the reputation of Allen. He will forever be remembered as something he was not—a perjurer.

Any believer in the fake almanac myth who investigates all the evidence with anything remotely resembling an open mind will do what Albert Beveridge did. Beveridge began his investigation convinced that Lincoln used a forged almanac. While writing his biography of Lincoln, he wrote to his friend Jacob M. Dickerson that "between you and me, it is reasonably certain that Lincoln knew exactly to what Allen would testify or else the almanac was 'doctored,' although I am not going to say that because I cannot *positively* prove it" [emphasis in original].[31] After a full investigation, he was satisfied that Lincoln's almanac correctly showed the moon on the horizon. He wrote in his biography, "It is hard to account for the origin of the gossip of the false almanac; hard to explain the vitality and persistence of the story." He settled upon the explanation that the story was invented as campaign rhetoric.[32]

Chapter 13

Winning the Almanac Trial

Having thoroughly investigated our sources for the Almanac Trial, we have teased out a probable course of events very different from the tales told in the first three chapters of the book. Duff Armstrong and Preston Metzker got into a fight. Armstrong later claimed that Metzker bullied him beyond endurance and that he responded by striking Metzker a mighty blow in the eye. Charles Allen said Armstrong used a slungshot, Nelson Watkins said it was a wagon hammer. Whatever it was, the blow caused such an injury that William Douglas thought Armstrong had cracked Metzker's skull. Metzker then bested Armstrong in the ensuing scuffle, and upon being pulled off the smaller man, went his way about the whiskey camp. Later that night someone—possibly James H. Norris, possibly someone else—hit Metzker behind the head with a neck yoke. Metzker succumbed to his wounds. After Metzker died, Allen came forward, Watkins held his peace. The Mason County grand jury indicted Norris and Armstrong, and Norris opted to go to trial immediately while Armstrong wisely moved for a change of venue. Norris went to prison for manslaughter, and Armstrong went to Beardstown for trial. His case came up in the November 1857 term of court in Beardstown, but neither the prosecution nor the defense was ready to go forward at that time—the prosecution because the court records had not been transferred to Beardstown and the defense because Armstrong's attorney was absent from that term of court. Lincoln happened to be in Beardstown attending court and stepped into the breach by making a limited appearance to argue for Armstrong's release on bond. Eventually Armstrong came to trial on

Monday, May 3, 1858. The trial was delayed due to the absence of two essential prosecution witnesses, and it wasn't until Friday, May 7, that the prosecution could go forward with its case. Lincoln happened to arrive in Beardstown for another case on May 6, and Hannah Armstrong, who had been lobbying him to defend her son, made one last plea. Lincoln asked Armstrong's attorneys if he could help with the case, they agreed, and he spent the evening of May 6 learning the facts of the case. The prosecution put on its case, and it was a strong one. Charles Allen testified as the last witness for the prosecution, and Lincoln's cross-examination did little to call his testimony into question. When the prosecution rested, the jurors believed Allen,[1] and Armstrong believed that the jury would convict him.[2] But Lincoln had committed Allen to a key fact about the moon and used an almanac to contradict him in final argument. Lincoln may have committed Allen to this fact by design, or he may have done so by accident. If he had the almanac at the beginning of the trial, he did it by design. If he sent for the almanac after Allen testified, the contradiction was more a product of quick thinking than careful planning. Whichever way it happened, the almanac probably assumed a greater role in the memory of the case than in the actual trial of the case.

It cannot be denied that the almanac played a role in Armstrong's acquittal, but the defense team did far more than simply produce an almanac to save Armstrong's life. The prosecution presented two alternative theories to the jury. In one theory Armstrong acted alone to strike a fatal blow to Metzker's eye. In the other theory Armstrong and Norris conspired to kill Metzker, making Armstrong just as responsible for the injury to the back of Metzker's head as if he had struck the blow himself. The second theory fell apart during the presentation of the evidence as it became clear that the prosecution could prove no such connection between Norris and Armstrong. One very good way to absolve a client of guilt is to suggest that someone else committed the crime. This maneuver is sometimes jokingly referred to as the "some other dude did it" defense, or the SODDI defense. The defense becomes even stronger if you can actually identify the other dude. The prosecution's second theory actually advanced a SODDI defense for Armstrong by naming Norris as the other dude.

To achieve a victory, the defense had to (1) disassociate Armstrong from Norris and (2) lay the blame completely at the feet of Norris. The collapse of the prosecution's second theory achieved the first objective. The second objective had to be established by (a) showing that Armstrong had no weapon in his hand when he struck Metzker in the eye and (b) providing the jury with another explanation for the injury to Metzker's eye. Proper handling of Allen's testimony was essential to laying the blame at Norris's feet. Allen was the only prosecution witness to see Norris strike Metzker with a weapon. In his letter to Governor Yates, Norris described Allen as "my sole and only prosecutor."[3] If Allen were completely discredited, then the proof of Norris's guilt would disappear, and Armstrong's blow to Metzker's eye would be the only candidate for causing the fatal wound. It was thus essential to show that Allen was mistaken rather than lying. In the sixth chapter we discussed the defense's attempt to confute Allen by proving he was somewhere else at the time of Metzker's fight with Armstrong. This was an ill-conceived stratagem that obviously failed.[4] They were fortunate it failed, and they were doubly fortunate to recognize its failure. The defense severely weakened Allen's testimony with the almanac and with Watkins's ownership of the slung-shot; in final argument they had to handle this weakening by arguing that it showed Allen mistaken rather than lying.

The Western Republican said that Lincoln handled this delicate issue by drawing "a picture of the perjurer so horrid and ghastly that [Allen] could sit under it no longer, but reeled and staggered from the courtroom ..."[5] and generations of subsequent biographers have echoed the accusation of perjury. This would have been the wrong way to handle Allen's testimony. Although Duff Armstrong himself maintained Lincoln called Allen's testimony "a pack of lies,"[6] we probably get a much more accurate description of Lincoln's argument from William Walker and John T. Brady. Walker later wrote that "Mr. L—in his speech may have alluded to the absence of a moon to show that in as much as the witness was mistaken in regard to one thing, the jury should receive all his testimony with caution."[7] Brady recalled that Lincoln proved Allen "badly mistaken" about the position of the moon.[8] Although Walker accused Allen of perjury when asking that Norris be pardoned in his letter to Governor Yates, Lincoln doesn't appear to have made such an accusation at the trial.[9] It is ironic that to acquit Armstrong, the defense had to blame Norris for the murder, and Armstrong's acquittal was later argued as a reason to pardon Norris.

Having undermined the evidence that Armstrong used a weapon, the defense had to give the jury an alternative explanation for the wound to Metzker's eye. Doctor Charles Parker re-enters our story at this point. On May 6 the defense issued an instanter subpoena for Parker.[10] Parker testified at the trial the next day, and his testimony seriously damaged the prosecution case. Using a skull as a demonstrative aid, Parker explained how Norris's blow to the back of the head could have caused the broken bones around Metzker's eye.[11] If the frontal injury were only a crack running around the back of the skull to the front, Parker's testimony would be plausible, but the injury to the face was a compressed fracture with "part of the skull being driven up into the brain."[12] It is difficult to imagine how a blow to the back of the head could have driven bone from the front of the head up into the brain. In light of Parker's involvement in the fake almanac hoax, we have reason to question his candor. The only way that such an injury to the face could be caused by a blow to the back of the head would be for the blow to knock the victim down so that the victim's face would strike an object on the ground, but common sense tells us this without the aid of a medical doctor. In addition to Dr. Parker's testimony, the defense offered Metzker's falls from his horse as possible causes of the facial fracture.

Lincoln had to make the jury understand that Armstrong should not be held responsible for the injury inflicted by Norris. To drive this point home to the jury, Lincoln wrote out two proposed jury instructions that Judge Harriott agreed to give.[13] The instructions read:

That if they have any reasonable doubt as to whether Metzker came to his death by the blow on the eye, or by the blow on the back of the head, they are to find the defendant "not guilty" unless they also believe from the evidence, beyond reasonable doubt, that Armstrong and Norris acted in concert, against Metzker, and that Norris struck the blow on the back of the head.

That if they believe from the evidence that Norris killed Metzker, they are to acquit Armstrong, unless they also believe beyond a reasonable doubt that Armstrong acted in concert with Norris in the killing, or purpose to kill or hurt Metzker.[14]

All these points had to be put together and explained, and Lincoln excelled at the art of persuasive speech. He was the greatest orator of his age, and possibly the greatest American orator of all time. The lawyers involved in the case had nothing but praise for Lincoln's masterful job of arguing the case to the jury. Caleb Dilworth later wrote, "Of course Mr. Lincoln made a strong argument; everybody expected it and he did it. ..."[15] J. Henry Shaw recalled that Lincoln's argument "took the jury by storm." William Walker wrote, "The last fifteen minutes of his speech was as eloquent as I ever heard. ..."[16]

What won the case? Opinions varied. Judge Harriott believed that Dr. Parker's testimony was the deciding factor.[17] Brady voted for the almanac as the key piece of evidence.[18] Lincoln told the Armstrongs that the testimony of Nelson Watkins was just as important as the almanac.[19] Shaw insisted, "I have said it a hundred times, that it was Lincoln's *speech* that saved that criminal from the gallows" [emphasis in original]. Dilworth maintained that "what the case turned upon was the instructions [written by Lincoln and] given by the court."[20] Milton Logan thought it was a combination of the almanac and Lincoln's argument.[21]

Like the witnesses in *Rashomon*, they argue for different interpretations based on the same basic facts. I think we must conclude that no one stratagem won the case. It was a combination of all factors that carried the day.

Although both the Apolitical Observer's libel of Lincoln and the myth of the fake almanac have been thoroughly discredited, writers on the Almanac Trial have continued to find fault with Lincoln's ethics in handling various aspects of the case. Rather than refute all the criticisms, we can let the two most serious allegations serve as proxies for all. They are (1) that Lincoln engaged in chicanery with the witness Nelson Watkins and (2) that Lincoln made an inflammatory and unethical final argument to the jury. We will deal with the issue of Lincoln's final argument first. We have already discussed how Lincoln, in the closing part of his argument, made reference to his relationship with the Armstrongs. He talked about how he rocked Duff Armstrong as a baby and otherwise played upon the emotions of the jury. William Walker, in describing the effects of Lincoln's concluding remarks, wrote, "[S]uch the power and earnestness with which he spoke, that the jury and all sat as if entranced, and when he was through found relief in a gush of tears. I have never seen such mastery exhibited over the feelings and emotions of men as on that occasion."[22] By modern standards, Lincoln's argument was objectionable on several grounds. It alluded to facts not in evidence, it was inflammatory, and it dealt with issues irrelevant to the question of the defendant's guilt. Lincoln aimed his argument at the jurors' sympathies as much as at their intellect, and he succeeded in rousing their emotions. Shaw gives us a better idea of the construction of Lincoln's argument. He wrote that Lincoln first analyzed, dissected, and demolished the prosecution case. After destroying the prosecution case by the use of logical argument, "he raised himself in his full power and shook the arguments of his opponent from him as though they were cobwebs. He took the jury by storm. There were tears in Mr. Lincoln's eyes while he spoke. But they were genuine."[23] From the descriptions given by Walker and Shaw, we can see that Lincoln constructed his argument along the lines taught by Classical rhetoricians, who recommended that advocates should first argue their case logically and then end with a powerful appeal to the sympathies and emotions of the jurors. "[W]hen the facts and their importance are clearly understood, you must excite your hearers' emotions."[24] Lincoln arranged his argument in a format taught for over 2,000 years. We have no business using a twenty-first-century yardstick to measure a nineteenth-century speech made according to ancient principles of argument. Another point: Three capable lawyers sat at the prosecution table. They knew how to make objections. They objected to the almanac. They did not object to Lincoln's argument. In fact, they may have done something that invited Lincoln to make such a plea to the jury. According to James T. Brady's sometimes inaccurate memory, Fullerton, in his argument, told the jury that the Metzkers had tried to hire Lincoln to assist him in the prosecution, but Lincoln refused.[25] If he made such a statement to the jury, he virtually invited Lincoln to make reference to his great affection for the Armstrongs. Regardless of whether Fullerton made such a comment, Lincoln did absolutely nothing wrong when he ended his speech with an emotional appeal.

The prosecution made another mistake in arguing the case. Fullerton had a chance to reply to Lincoln's argument, but he said nothing to mitigate the force of one key piece of evidence for the defense. Milton Logan remembered: "[T]he prosecuting attorney in the case never questioned the issue of the almanac, nor did he refer in any way to the moon shining, or attempt to answer Mr. Lincoln's undisputed argument on this point."[26] Fullerton had a ready answer available: "Allen obviously made a mistake about the moon's position, but that doesn't mean that the night was so dark he couldn't see. It just means he doesn't remember where the light came from." The argument might not have persuaded the jury, but Fullerton certainly should have made it.

Let us now examine the allegations concerning Nelson Watkins. As you recall, Watkins testified to the fact that he made the slungshot found at the scene of the crime, describing it in minute detail before Lincoln showed it to him on the witness stand. Brady tells us that Watkins did not want to testify to this exculpatory fact because he believed he knew a fact that would do his friend Duff Armstrong no good. He feared that a skillful cross-examination by the prosecution would ferret out that damning fact, and his testimony would consign Armstrong to the gallows. In his efforts to avoid testifying, he tried to tell Lincoln what he knew. Lincoln refused to listen, and he put Watkins on the stand not knowing the dreadful fact that Watkins knew. Of course, we already know the fact—that Armstrong struck Metzker with a wagon hammer. Although Lincoln didn't know the fact, he had enough courtroom experience to realize that Watkins saw something happen between Armstrong and Metzker that would make Armstrong look very guilty.

Not long after the trial, Watkins the witness met John T. Brady the juror in connection with the purchase of some cattle. Naturally, their business discussions got sidetracked onto the trial. Brady had thought that Charles Allen was telling the truth about seeing Armstrong strike Metzker but discounted his testimony because the almanac contradicted it. According to Brady, Watkins gave him a reason to discount the almanac. Watkins told Brady of his pretrial meeting with Lincoln and his reluctance to take the stand. He told Brady about trying to reveal the reason for his reluctance and about Lincoln's refusal to hear it, and Brady passed this information on to J. N. Gridley when Gridley wrote his study of the trial.[27]

Critics suggest that Lincoln did something wrong by refusing to hear the awful fact that Nelson Watkins tried to tell him. Some defenders of Lincoln's virtue discount the story of Watkins and the wagon hammer because it comes from a single source, Brady, and Brady has proved unreliable on numerous details about the case. Upon first reading Watkins's story, in the account given by Gridley, I discounted it. After reading Brady's letter to J. McCan Davis, I came to credit it. My reasons for crediting the story are as follows. (1) Brady gave the story to Davis as an afterthought. It seemed that he was reluctant to say something that would reflect ill on Lincoln but decided at last to share what he knew. Brady's doing this tends to weakly validate the story. (2) Brady's report of the conversation between Watkins and Lincoln rings true in that it has the sound of a conversation that a lawyer would have with a witness before putting on the witness's testimony. This tends to offer somewhat stronger validation than the first point because Brady would have no experience with such conversations, and the odds that he would accidentally give an account with such verisimilitude are low. (3) Brady reports that Lincoln gave Watkins an explanation of the legal principle that redirect examination cannot exceed the scope of cross-examination. Brady himself stated that principle in the following words: "Mr. Lincoln assured him he would only be cross-questioned about the questions he put to him, and so he confined his questions to the slung-shot and Wadkins got off easy." The odds are vanishingly small that either Watkins or Brady, both laymen, would know this rule of law unless Lincoln explained it to Watkins and Watkins repeated the explanation to Brady.

We cannot save Lincoln's honor by dismissing Brady's report of Watkins's statement, so we must address the question of whether Lincoln did something unethical when he refused to hear Watkins's story of the wagon hammer. I believe he did something extremely risky, but I do not believe that he did anything unethical. Had he been a prosecutor rather than a defense attorney, twentieth-century rules of legal ethics would require him to find out the fact, and if it proved exculpatory, to disclose it to the defense. The U.S. Supreme Court promulgated this requirement in *Brady v. Maryland*,[28] but it applies only to prosecutors, and it wasn't decided until more than a century after the trial of Duff Armstrong. In 1857 neither the prosecution nor the defense had a duty to give evidence harmful to their case to the other side. With very limited exceptions, a criminal defense attorney has never been required to turn over such evidence to the prosecution.

Had I been defending Armstrong, I would have wanted to know what Watkins had to say. I believe such knowledge would be essential to assessing the risk of calling Watkins as a witness. Lincoln obviously would have disagreed with me. He knew Watkins was a two-edged sword, and he knew he could damage his case if the prosecution managed to wheedle the information out of Watkins. He decided to risk the damage without knowing its precise nature. His reason for doing so is obvious. Sometimes a defense attorney can know too much, and this knowledge can impair the attorney's effectiveness. Knowing beyond peradventure that your client is guilty can impair your ability to adequately evaluate the strength of the prosecution case. It always looks stronger than it actually is if you know your client is guilty. Sure knowledge of your client's guilt can also impede your ability to argue your case effectively. Lincoln had this very problem in another murder case. In *People v. Patterson*, a case he defended in Champaign County, certain knowledge of his client's guilt led him to make an ineffective final argument that lost the case.[29]

Lincoln knew Watkins had harmful knowledge of an undetermined nature and that calling him to the witness stand might lead to its discovery when the prosecution cross-examined. He told Watkins not to worry, that he would see to it that Watkins was not asked about the issue. His doing this has also been criticized as somehow underhanded and unethical. Notice, however, what Lincoln did not say. He did not say, "If you're asked about that fact, lie." Lincoln made Watkins understand that he would try to prevent questioning on the subject, but the two men also understood that if the prosecutor asked, Watkins would have to answer truthfully.

Could Lincoln be certain that he could prevent Watkins being asked the question? The examination of witnesses proceeds according to fixed rules, and one of those rules is the one Lincoln explained to Watkins and Watkins reported to Brady.[30] The cross-examiner, when asking questions of an opposing witness, "should not go beyond the subject matter of the direct examination and matters affecting the witness's credibility."[31] In questioning Watkins, Lincoln would limit his questioning to the identification of the slungshot. By asking nothing about the fight itself, he limited the prosecution to questioning on the issue of the slungshot alone. Some have questioned whether this rule applied in antebellum Illinois, as a search of the Illinois case law discloses no opinions specifically stating this rule prior to 1929,[32] but it is an ancient rule. In 1840 the U.S. Supreme Court recognized the "well established" principle that "a party has no right to cross-examine any witness except as to facts and circumstances connected with the matters stated in his direct examination. If he wishes to examine him to other matters, he must do so by making the witness his own, and calling him, as such, in the subsequent progress of the cause."[33] Despite his assurances to Watkins, Lincoln could not prevent the prosecution from asking questions that would elicit testimony about the wagon hammer, he could only impede the prosecution's asking the questions. If the prosecution asked and an objection was sustained, they had the right to call Watkins in rebuttal and ask him. Lincoln was probably depending on two things. First, that the prosecution would adhere to the old maxim of cross-examination not to ask a question when you don't know the answer. Second, that the prosecution would suspect a trap. There is an old trick that lawyers sometimes play—don't ask about a particularly damning piece of evidence and let the other side bring it out on cross-examination. Evidence that might harm the other side on direct examination can often destroy the other side if it is brought out on cross-examination instead. The prosecution, probably because they feared the trap, did not ask the question on cross-examination. What the prosecution should have done was, when Watkins was excused, ask him to wait outside the courtroom until a recess and then ask him the question. If they had done so, Watkins would have told them about the wagon hammer, and they would have called him in rebuttal. The prosecution fumbled, and Lincoln maneuvered them into fumbling. Did he do anything wrong? No. It's not up to him to see to it that the prosecution brings out evidence harmful to his client. He took a huge risk, but it paid off.

As Lincoln returned to his hotel after the trial, Abraham Byers, a photographer, asked him to pose for a picture. Lincoln agreed and went with Byers to his studio, which happened to be in Lincoln's hotel. There in Byers's studio, Lincoln patiently sat motionless for the 30 seconds necessary to take an ambrotype picture. Byers kept that photograph until his dying day. After his death, the photograph found its way to the University of Nebraska, where it still resides.[34]

We have thoroughly examined the litigation of the Almanac Trial, and we are now prepared to state whether Donovan, the Western Republican, or the Apolitical Observer gave us the true version of the Almanac Trial. We must say none of them and all of them. They all have elements of truth, and they all have their share of falsehood. Lincoln did perform an excellent cross-examination of Allen but not the dramatic display of courtroom fireworks depicted by Donovan. Lincoln did make an excellent final argument, but he didn't expose a perjurer as claimed by the Western Republican. The Apolitical Observer was correct that Lincoln was not lead counsel for the defense, but he was wrong to accuse Lincoln of misconduct.

Unretouched ambrotype of Abraham Lincoln taken on the afternoon of the trial. (As with all ambrotypes, the image is reversed.) (Archives & Special Collections, University of Nebraska-Lincoln Libraries)

Our investigation has punctured some revered myths about Lincoln's performance in the Almanac Trial. Admirers of Lincoln will probably be disappointed to learn that the dramatic cross-examination is a myth. When discussing my findings with a colleague, he reminded me of a line from *The Man Who Shot Liberty Valance*, "When the legend becomes fact, print the legend." I can only respond with a line attributed to Lincoln himself, "History is not history unless it's true."[35] The truth may not be as entertaining, but it shows Lincoln to be a capable, honorable trial lawyer who repaid a debt of gratitude by taking up the cause of a widowed mother and delivering her son from the gallows.

Chapter 14

Was Armstrong Guilty?

Did Duff Armstrong kill Pres Metzker? Did he commit murder? Should the jury have convicted him? Does Abraham Lincoln deserve censure for freeing a murderer? In this final chapter we will attempt to answer each of these questions. Let us begin our inquiry by tabulating the evidence that Armstrong struck a fatal blow to Metzker's head. Set forth below in outline form is the evidence that Armstrong struck such a blow, accompanied by supporting quotations. Paraphrases are set out in italics, direct quotes in quotation marks. No supporting quotations are provided for Charles Allen's evidence.

1. Duff Armstrong struck Preston Metzker.
   a. The testimony of Charles Allen.
   b. Armstrong's admission in the *New York Sun*: "I gave him a terrible blow, knocking the skin off my fist."[1]
   c. The testimony of Nelson Watkins: *[H]e saw Armstrong hit Metzker....*[2]
   d. The testimony of William Douglas: "George, his skull is cracked."[3]
2. Armstrong struck Metzker in the face.
   a. Armstrong's admission in the *New York Sun*: "His right eye was swollen shut."[4]
   b. The testimony of Nelson Watkins: *Armstrong [struck Metzker] in the eye....*[5]
   c. The testimony of William Douglas: "George, his skull is cracked."[6]

3. Armstrong used a deadly weapon.

    a. The testimony of Charles Allen.

    b. The testimony of Nelson Watkins: *Armstrong picked up an old-fashioned wagon hammer off the counter and struck Metzker with it.*[7]

4. Armstrong inflicted a grievous injury upon Metzker.

    a. The testimony of Charles Allen.

    b. The testimony of Nelson Watkins: *Armstrong killed Metzker by striking him in the eye with an old-fashioned wagon hammer.*[8]

    c. The testimony of William Douglas: "George, his skull is cracked."[9]

    d. The testimony of Dr. Benjamin F. Stephenson: *Upon the postmortem examination, it was found that there was a wound in the eye, part of the skull being driven up into the brains.*[10]

Against all this evidence we have: (1) Armstrong's assertion that he used only his fist, (2) the trial testimony of Armstrong's friends that he used only his fist, and (3) an almanac suggesting that the moon might not have given Allen enough light to see whether Armstrong had a weapon. Even if Armstrong struck Metzker with his bare fist, he still could have killed the man. When William Douglas saw Metzker's face immediately after Armstrong struck him, Douglas correctly thought that Metzker's skull was cracked.

If we revisit the standards of proof discussed in Chapter 1, we must conclude that Hugh Fullerton certainly had probable cause to believe that Armstrong inflicted a fatal wound upon Pres Metzker. Probable cause is all that is needed to commence a criminal prosecution. Fullerton was perfectly justified in bringing charges against Armstrong. Although reasonable people could disagree whether this evidence meets our self-imposed standard of clear and convincing evidence, we can certainly make a case for the proposition that it does.

Let us assume for the sake of argument that we do have clear and convincing evidence proving Armstrong struck a fatal blow to Metzker's head. That fact standing alone does not warrant the conviction of Armstrong. As we said in Chapter 10, to prove Duff Armstrong guilty of murder, Fullerton had to prove four elements: (1) the death of Metzker (2) by the criminal act or agency (3) of Armstrong (4) acting with malice aforethought. We have Metzker dead by the act or agency of Armstrong, but where is the proof that the act was criminal? Where is the proof that Armstrong acted with malice aforethought?

Under Illinois law in effect at the time of Metzker's death, Armstrong could very well have been responsible for Metzker's death but innocent of any crime. According to the Illinois Supreme Court, justifiable homicide was "the taking of human life in the necessary defense of one's person against violence. . . ."[11] We have evidence that Metzker, who had armed himself with a loaded whip, attacked Armstrong. If Armstrong struck the fatal blow while defending himself against an attack from a man armed with a deadly weapon, then he acted in justifiable self-defense.[12]

If Armstrong did not act in necessary self-defense, that still does not mean he was guilty of murder. The Illinois Supreme Court defined manslaughter as

[T]he unlawful killing of a human being, without malice express or implied, and without any mixture of deliberation whatever. It must be voluntary, upon a sudden heat of passion, caused by a provocation apparently sufficient to make the passion irresistible, or involuntary in the commission of an unlawful act, or a lawful act without due caution or circumspection.[13]

If Armstrong used excessive force in defending himself against Metzker, then he would be guilty of manslaughter. If Metzker provoked Armstrong beyond endurance and Armstrong lashed out at him with no intent to kill, then he would be guilty of manslaughter whether he used a deadly weapon or his bare fist. The evidence equally supports any of the three interpretations (justifiable homicide, manslaughter by use of excessive force in self-defense, or manslaughter upon provocation). When confronted with equally reasonable interpretations, one supporting guilt and the other innocence, the law requires that we accept the interpretation supporting innocence.[14]

What the evidence does not support, however, is an interpretation that makes Armstrong guilty of murder. According to Illinois law, murder was killing with malice aforethought, either express or implied. Express malice existed when the killer premeditated the murder. Implied malice existed when the killing was done without provocation and under circumstances that indicated the defendant acted with "an abandoned and malignant heart."[15] Express malice cannot be proven because we have no evidence of premeditation. Implied malice cannot be proven because we have sufficient evidence of provocation to negate any presumption that Armstrong acted with an abandoned and malignant heart.

Even if all the evidence taken together proves that Armstrong killed Metzker, even if it shows that Armstrong probably committed manslaughter, it does not establish Armstrong's guilt beyond a reasonable doubt. No matter how guilty Armstrong may have been, if the evidence does not establish his guilt beyond a reasonable doubt, our justice system requires that he be found not guilty. The jury returned the correct verdict at the trial, and even if they had heard the additional evidence we have unearthed, their verdict should still have been not guilty.

What of Lincoln? Assuming Armstrong killed Metzker, does Lincoln deserve censure for defending him? He does not. Although our society has long looked askance upon lawyers who defend guilty clients and get them acquitted, the probability that Armstrong was a killer should not take any of the luster off Lincoln's achievement in saving him from the gallows. Although the U.S. Supreme Court has declared that "the very nature of a trial [is] a search for truth,"[16] the statement does not fully describe a criminal trial. Although any court proceeding should rest firmly on the bedrock of truth, a properly conducted criminal trial is more a test of proof than a search for truth. It is the prosecutor's job to determine the truth and then go into court and try to establish that truth beyond a reasonable doubt. The defense attorney's job is to test that proof by subjecting it to rigid scrutiny. When the system works properly and the state proves a defendant guilty beyond a reasonable doubt, we can have a high degree of certainty that the defendant is truly guilty. Given the asymmetrical burdens of proof in a criminal trial (the defendant need not prove anything), we cannot say with any degree of certainty that someone who has been acquitted is truly innocent. To ensure as much as humanly possible that the innocent go free, we tolerate a system that often allows the guilty to escape punishment because of a failure of proof. When Lincoln performed his job of holding the prosecution to its burden of proof, he performed a noble and necessary task, regardless of whether he helped a criminal escape punishment. Lincoln subjected the state's evidence to rigid scrutiny, and the evidence failed to prove Armstrong guilty. He conducted his defense of Armstrong in conformity with the nineteenth century's highest standards of ethical conduct; and in doing so he showed himself to be a capable trial lawyer, a sagacious cross-examiner, and an excellent orator.

Appendix A

The Statements of the Major Participants

1A. WILLIAM DUFF ARMSTRONG: NEWSPAPER INTERVIEW, NOVEMBER 10, 1886[1]

Duff Armstrong said to the writer quite warmly: "It's all nonsense to talk about Mr. Lincoln having had that almanac made for the occasion. I recollect he called for an almanac, and there was none in the court-room. Then he sent my cousin Jake out to get one, and he went out and got the book that was shown to the jury. The almanac was all right."

1B. WILLIAM DUFF ARMSTRONG: NEWSPAPER INTERVIEW, JUNE 7, 1896[2]

It was a Saturday night, and camp meeting was over for the day. In the edge of the grove were three bars where liquor was sold. Here gathered all the men and boys who went to camp meeting to drink whiskey and have a good time, and a great many went for no other purpose. I had been at the meeting two or three days, and had been drinking much, but I was then becoming sober. It was probably 10 o'clock when I found a big goods box not far from the bars, and I stretched myself out for a night's sleep. Up to this time Pres Metzker and I had been good friends, but Pres had been drinking and was in an ugly mood. He came along, making a great deal of noise, and said to me, "D__n you, get up." Then he grabbed my legs and pulled me off. In a few minutes he jerked me down again. I said, "Let me alone, Pres, I am sleepy." He went away, but soon came back and pulled me off a third time, and took my hat, threw it upon the ground and stamped it. He said I had no business there that I ought to be at home stacking up chips for my box. I told him that was none of his business, and then I walked over to one of the bar counters and asked for a drink of whiskey. He followed, and just as I lifted the glass to my lips, he caught me by the arm, spilling my whiskey. I put down my glass and turned around to him and said "Pres, if you do that again, I will knock you down [even] if you are bigger than me. You have run this thing far enough." He had a loaded whip in his hand and was determined to have a fight with me. I gave him a terrible blow, knocking the skin from my knuckles. We clinched and Pres rather got the best of me. I was strong for my size and was able to catch him and throw him back over me. He got up first and came at me again. Then we fought like tigers. At last he got me under him. More than a hundred people stood by watching the fight, and when the boys saw Pres getting the better of me, they pulled him off. We walked up to the bar and each getting a drink of whiskey, we bumped glasses and were friends again. But Pres had not got through with me. As we stood there, without warning he hit me a blow on the upper lip. He was going to hit me with a glass when another man said "Stop that Pres, if you strike him with that glass I will kill you." Metzker stole a quilt from a buggy nearby, and wrapping it around him, walked off to bed. I saw nothing else of him until the next morning when he walked to the bar with the stolen quilt still around him. His right eye was swollen shut. He bathed it with a glass of whiskey, drank another glass, and then mounted his horse and rode away. Several days after that he died. Then the officers came and arrested me and put me in jail.

I had a preliminary trial at Havana and was held without bail. All the bad luck in the world seemed to come to me now. On this very day my father, Jack Armstrong, died. On his deathbed he said to my mother, "Hannah, sell everything to clear Duff." These were almost his last words. I was a kind of favorite with my ma and pa both. I always stayed at home with them.

After the change of venue to Beardstown Lincoln told my mother he would defend me. At the trial I had about twenty-five witnesses. The strongest witness against me was Charles Allen. He was the witness that swore about the moon. He swore it was a full moon and almost overhead. "Uncle Abe" asked him over and over about it, but he stuck to it. Then he said he saw me strike Metzker with a slungshot. "Uncle Abe" asked him to tell how it was done. He got up and went through the motion, struck an overhand blow just as he swore he saw me do by the light of the moon. "Uncle Abe" had him do it over again. After Allen's testimony, everybody thought I would be convicted. After "Uncle Abe" talked to the jury a while, he said: "Now I will show you that this man Allen's testimony is a pack of lies, that he did not witness this fight by the light of the full moon, for the moon was not in the heavens that night." And then "Uncle Abe" pulled out the almanac and showed the jury the truth about the moon. I do not remember exactly what it was—whether the moon had not risen or whether it had set; but whatever it was, it upset Allen's story completely. He passed the almanac to the jurors and they all inspected it. Then "Uncle Abe" talked about the fight, and showed that I had acted in self-defense and had used no weapon of any kind, but it seemed to me "Uncle Abe" did his best talking when he told the jury what true friends my father and mother had been to him in the early days, when he was a poor young man at New Salem. He told how he used to go out to Jack Armstrong's and stay for days, how kind mother was to him, and how, many a time, he had rocked me to sleep in the old cradle. He said he was not there pleading for me because he was paid for it; but he was there to help a good woman who had helped him when he needed help. Lawyer Walker made a good speech for me too, but "Uncle Abe's" beat anything I ever heard.

As "Uncle Abe" finished his speech he said "I hope this man will be a free man before sundown." The jury retired and nearly everybody went to supper. They left me there with the Sheriff, my brother Jim, and a parcel of boys. The jury was in a room nearby and it was not over five minutes after they went out when I heard them talking and laughing and my heart beat a little faster. As soon as the Judge and the lawyers got back from supper the jury was brought in. They had to pass me and I eyed them closely for some hopeful sign. One of them looked at me and winked. Then I knew it was alright, and when the foreman handed up the verdict of not guilty I was the happiest man in the world I reckon.

Now, my mother was not in the courtroom when the jury came in, and it is all stuff about her fainting and falling into my arms. She was away somewhere. I don't know just where. That night she went home with Jim Dick, the Sheriff. I went home with Dick Overton, and as we went down the courthouse steps he slipped a five dollar bill into my hand. "Uncle Abe" would not charge my mother a cent. He said her happiness over my freedom was his sufficient reward.

The almanac used by Lincoln was one which my cousin Jake Jones furnished him. On the morning of the trial I was taken outside the courtroom to talk to Lincoln. Jake Jones was with us. Lincoln said he wanted an almanac for 1857, Jake went right off and got one, and brought it to "Uncle Abe." It was an almanac for the proper year and there was no fraud about it. The truth is there was no moon that night. If there was, it was hidden by clouds. But it was light enough for everybody to see the fight. The fight took place in front of one of the bars and each bar had two or three candles on it. I had no slungshot. I never carried a weapon of any kind, never in my life. Metzker had a loaded whip, but he did not attempt to use it on me. It was only a fist fight, and if I killed Pres Metzker, I killed him with my naked fist.

1C. WILLIAM DUFF ARMSTRONG: NEWSPAPER INTERVIEW, N.D.[3]

"Armstrong," the reporter asked, "tell about the killing. Were you guilty?"

Duff looked down at the ground, stuck his knife in the sod two or three times and said with emphasis:

"No, I wasn't. Press pitched into me without any cause. I had had a drink or two but I knew what I was about. Press was getting the best of me when I gave it to him."

Then Duff told how Mr. Lincoln was brought into the case. His mother was known to the whole community as "Aunt Hanna." She had been kind to Lincoln when he lived in the Salem neighborhood. Local sentiment about the Metzgar affair was against Duff. The man who was indicted as an accessory to the killing had been given eight years in the penitentiary. In her distress, Aunt Hanna wrote to Mr. Lincoln who, at that time, had been living in Springfield a dozen or more years. Mr. Lincoln wrote back at once that he would defend Duff. He told the family to get a change of venue to Bardstown, on account of local prejudice. This was done. He told Aunt Hannah to rely upon him. Nobody knew what the defense was to be, Duff said. But when the case came to trial, Lincoln was there. He questioned the witnesses for the prosecution closely. There were two men who testified to the details of the fight. Lincoln had them describe the positions of the combatants when the slungshot was used; and they made the circumstances look bad for Duff. Then he pressed them to know how they could testify so accurately and led them into positive statements about the moonlight. They described the moon as being about the height of the sun at ten in the morning. Mr. Lincoln returned to this again and again, and asked the witnesses if they were sure they were not mistaken. As often as the question was put, so often they committed themselves. They insisted the moon shining down upon the combatants made every movement plain to them.

Then the almanac was produced. Duff said that Mr. Lincoln passed it to the jurors and asked them to see what kind of a night it was on which the fight took place and to judge the accuracy of such testimony as they had heard. The almanac was examined. It showed there was no moonlight such as the witnesses had sworn. Mr. Lincoln followed up this advantage with a speech in which he tore the testimony to pieces. He argued the theory that Armstrong had been attacked and that he had only exerted himself in self-defense. He told the jurors how he had held "little Duff" in his arms many a time at the Armstrong cabin while Aunt Hannah cooked the meals and he described the character of the little chap, as he had seen it forming. In such a way it seemed impossible to imagine him as making the assault described by these witnesses who had sworn there was a high moon when there was not. Duff was acquitted.

"He told mother that he wouldn't charge a cent for defending me, and he never did," said Armstrong as the narrative drew to a conclusion.

"But, Duff, what about the almanac?" was asked. "Where did Lincoln get it? Was it bogus?"

The gray eyes flashed. The jackknife was plunged into the grass roots as Armstrong blurted out in an indignant tone:

"It's all foolishness to talk about Lincoln having had that almanac fixed up for the trial. He didn't do anything of the kind. I recollect that after he had been asking the witnesses about the moonlight, he suddenly called for an almanac. There wasn't any in the courtroom of the year he wanted. So he sent my cousin Jake out to find one. Jake went out, and after a while he came back with the almanac. Lincoln turned to the night of the fight at the camp meeting and it showed there wasn't any moon at all that night. Then he showed it to the jury. That was all there was to the almanac story. The almanac was all right. I tell you he was a mighty smart man and a good one, too."

2. ABRAM BERGEN: LAW JOURNAL ARTICLE, 1897[4]

I have read all the descriptions of Lincoln's remarkable face, and examined all his portraits as they have appeared in magazines and elsewhere, but to my mind none of them conveys a perfect idea of the irregularity of his features. Studying his face directly from the side, the lowest part of his forehead projected beyond the eyes to a greater distance than I have ever observed in any other person. In the court room, while waiting for the celebrated Armstrong case to be called for trial, I looked at him closely for full two hours, and was so struck by this peculiarity of his profile that I remember to have estimated that his forehead protruded more than two inches, and then retreated about twenty-five degrees from the perpendicular until it reached a usual height in a straight line above his eyes.

During the two hours referred to Lincoln sat with his head thrown back, his steady gaze apparently fixed upon one spot of the blank ceiling, entirely oblivious to what was happening about him, and without a single variation of feature or noticeable movement of any muscle of his face. But when he began to talk his eyes brightened perceptibly, and every facial movement seemed to emphasize his feeling and add expression to his thoughts. Then vanished all consciousness of his uncouth appearance, his awkward manner, or even his high-keyed, unpleasant voice, and it required an extraordinary effort of the will to divert attention to the man, so concentrated was every mind upon what he was saying.

The trial occurred at the first term of court which I attended after my admission to the bar. I had an intense desire to learn how good lawyers examined witnesses, and especially to see and hear all of a trial conducted by counsel so eminent. Particularly was my closest attention directed to Mr. Lincoln and to every word and movement of his from the time he entered the court room until he took his departure. During the entire trial I was seated in the bar behind the attorneys for the State and those for the defendant, not more than four feet from any one of them, and noticed everything with the deepest interest, as any young lawyer naturally would.

During the introduction of the evidence Mr. Lincoln remarked to the judge that he supposed the court would take judicial notice of the almanac; but in order that there might be no question on that point he offered it as a part of the evidence for the defense, the court accepting it and remarking that any one might use the almanac in the progress of the argument. Lincoln, with his usual care, had brought with him from Springfield the almanac then regarded as the standard in that region. At a recess of the court he took it from his capacious hat and gave it to the sheriff, Dick, with the request that it should be returned to him when he called for it. In the succeeding campaign the Democrats induced Sheriff Dick to make an affidavit that he did not notice the year covered by the almanac, and this is taken by some as conclusive evidence that Lincoln intended to deceive. The only object was to break the monotony of his argument, and to fix the attention and memory of the jury on the fact proved.

When Lincoln finally called for the almanac he exhibited it to the opposing lawyers, read from it, and then caused it to be handed to members of the jury for their inspection. I heard two of the attorneys for the State, in whispered consultation, raise the question as to the correctness of the almanac, and they ended the conference by sending to the office of the clerk of the court for another. The messenger soon returned with the statement that there was no almanac of 1857 in the office. (It will be remembered that the trial occurred in 1858 for a transaction in 1857.) In the presidential campaign soon following it was even charged that Lincoln must have gone around and purloined all the almanacs in the court-house. However, I well remember that another almanac was procured from the office of Probate Judge Arenz, in the same building. It was brought to the prosecuting attorneys, who examined it, compared it with the one introduced by Mr. Lincoln, and found that they substantially agreed, although it was at first intimated by the State's attorneys that they had found some slight difference.

All this I personally saw and heard, and it is as distinct in my memory as if it had occurred but yesterday. No intimation was made, so far as I knew, that there was any fraud in the use of the almanac, until two years afterward, when Lincoln was the nominee of the Republican Party for the presidency. In that year, 1860, while in the mountains of Southern Oregon, I saw in a Democratic newspaper, published at St. Louis, an article personally abusive of Mr. Lincoln, stating that he was no statesman, and only a third-rate lawyer; and to prove the deceptive and dishonest nature of the candidate the same paper printed an indefinite affidavit of one of the jurors who had helped to acquit Armstrong to the effect that Mr. Lincoln had made fraudulent use of the almanac on the trial. For some inexplicable reason he failed to call this pretended knowledge to the attention of the other jurors at the time of the trial, but very promptly joined in the verdict of acquittal, and waited two years before giving publicity to what would at the proper time have been a very important piece of information.

Soon after this I saw an affidavit made by Milton Logan, the foreman of the jury, that he personally examined the almanac when it was delivered to the jury, and particularly noticed that it was for the year 1857, the year of the homicide. I had a better opportunity than any of the jurors to see and hear all that was publicly and privately done and said by the attorneys on both sides, and know that the almanacs of 1857 now preserved in historical and other public libraries sustain and prove to the minute all that was claimed by Mr. Lincoln on that trial as to the rising and setting of the moon, although my best recollection is that the hour of the crime was claimed to be about midnight instead of eleven o'clock, as stated in many of the books. I do not know that this calumny was ever called to Mr. Lincoln's attention, or if it was that he ever took the trouble to contradict it. He might well have pursued his regular habit of ignoring such things. If his public and private conduct and his reputation as a citizen and lawyer were not sufficient to refute the charge, his personal denial would have been of little more avail.

Ram on Facts and other books which publish what they pretend to be the truth as to this incident do not give the newspaper accounts as their authority, but all are based on a communication by J. Henry Shaw, a lawyer of Beardstown, a political opponent of Lincoln's, who was one of the prosecuting attorneys in the Armstrong case. His letter is printed in Lamon and in Arnold; and all other writers who have referred to the case cite that as their authority. Mr. Shaw says there were two almanacs at the trial, and that he believes Mr. Lincoln was entirely innocent of any deception in the matter. He farther states that the prevailing belief in Cass County was that the almanac was prepared for the occasion; and that Mr. Carter, a lawyer of Beardstown who was present at but not engaged in the Armstrong case, says he is satisfied that the almanac was of the year previous and thinks he examined it at the time.

This man Carter, who was Buchanan's village postmaster, had one case for jury trial at that term. Mr. Lincoln, for a $5 fee, had run Carter's worthless, litigious client out of court on a motion for security for costs. Of course, it was *easy* to satisfy Carter that Mr. Lincoln would do or had done almost anything diabolical, as it also was the maddened, unthinking camp-meeting people and the wicked, rough element, who alike had already condemned the accused, and who craved the rare spectacle of a hanging.

Other features of the Armstrong case were more interesting and more difficult of determination than this episode of the almanac. They called out the mental powers not only of Mr. Lincoln, but of his shrewd antagonists. In their solution Lincoln showed that he had mastered some technical questions in anatomy. The main witness testified that he saw Armstrong strike the deceased on the forehead with a slung-shot. The physicians testified that the blow on the forehead was inflicted by a man's fist. They further testified that death was caused by a blow with a club on the back of the head, which other evidence showed had been given by the man then in the penitentiary; and this evidence failed to prove that Armstrong was acting in concert with him. Lincoln's principal medical witness was Dr. Benjamin F. Stephenson, of Petersburg, Illinois, who afterward attained celebrity and honor as the founder and first organizer of the Grand Army of the Republic.

3A. JOHN T. BRADY: LETTER TO J. MCCAN DAVIS, MAY 23, 1896[5]

Dear Sir:

Yours of May 6th has been received, and in reply would say I remember the leading incidents of the Armstrong trial and especially Mr. Lincoln's cross-examination of the witness for the state, Mr. Allen, and his (Allen's) evidence that led to the use of the almanac. My remembrance is Allen swore it was about 9 p.m. Armstrong and Metzker had the fight, and that the moon was overhead, about where the sun would be about 1 p.m. When Lincoln cross-examined him, and by his questions made him say about a half a dozen times where the moon was, and he always insisted it was about where the sun would be at 1 p.m. Allen was on the stand for hours, and Lincoln was very good to him, encouraging him by supplying words as he hesitated for the and telling him not to get excited, but keep quiet and tell everything just as he saw it. My recollection is that when Lincoln opened the case for the defense he took off his coat and vest and removed his cravat (a large black silk handkerchief, worn over an old-fashioned stack) and unbuttoned his shirt collar. (The weather was very warm). He had on the table before him a great pile of notes written on foolscap paper, and for his assistant he had, I think, a lawyer from Havana, Illinois, named Walker, and as Mr. Lincoln proceeded Mr. Walker kept run of the notes; but Mr. Lincoln never once during his reviewing of the case, which took him something over a day, referred to the notes. When he came to Allen's testimony regarding the moon, my recollection is he picked the almanac up from the table that held his notes and papers. I do not remember what almanac it was, but have an impression it was Jayne's. The question as to the date of the almanac was never raised, and I believe it was a correct almanac (of 1857). When Lincoln introduced the almanac, the prosecuting attorney very strongly objected, and Judge Harriott asked to see it; and my recollection is that the judge examined it, and then passed it to the prosecuting attorney, and after he examined it Mr. Lincoln passed it to the foreman of the jury, and the jurors looked it over. The Judge ruled to admit the almanac. Then Mr. Lincoln made the point that "Allen must have been mistaken, as from the evidence of the almanac the moon was just going down." Then the prosecuting attorney made the remark "it was not going down, but just coming up," and Lincoln replied "it did not matter, for if it was just going down or just coming up, it was not overhead where the sun would be at 1 p.m., according to Allen's testimony."

The impression of the almanac evidence led the jury to the idea that if Allen could be so mistaken about the moon, he might have been mistaken about seeing Armstrong hit Metzker with a slung-shot, although Allen impressed me with the idea he was telling what he believed to be the truth.

My recollection is the jury was not out over half or three-quarters of an hour, just long enough to take one ballot, and as the jury retired I heard Mr. Lincoln say to Mrs. Armstrong, who was in the court room: "Your son will be a free man before the sun goes down." This was sometime during the afternoon. Mrs. Armstrong was in the court room when the jury returned, and was visibly affected by the verdict. Then Mr. Lincoln took the boy, young Armstrong, by the hand and gave him a good, sound talking to in regard to his wayward conduct, and told him how he should govern himself so as to honor his dead father's name and be a comfort to his mother. Mrs. Armstrong was weeping, and she turned to Mr. Lincoln and said: "Abe, I knew you would save my boy." She wore a calico dress and an old-fashioned slat sun-bonnet. During the trial the prosecuting attorney brought out the fact that the Metzkers tried to retain Lincoln for their attorney, and that when they told him who the accused murderer was, he refused to take the case, but sent word at once to Mrs. Armstrong he would defend her boy if she wanted him to. Lincoln made a speech which visibly affected everyone in the court room—judge, jury, lawyers, and people—relating what a debt of gratitude he was under to Mr. and Mrs. Armstrong for a home when he was homeless and in need, and that Mrs. Armstrong had been a mother to him, and he was only trying to partially repay a debt of gratitude in defending her son, and there was not enough in Illinois to have hired him to take a case against her.

About the slung-shot, I remember the evidence of the witness. Young Mr. Wadkins, who lived in the "barrens" northeast of Petersburg. He swore Armstrong never had the slung-shot, which was of lead and zinc. He swore that on the night of the fight he slept under a wagon, and in lying down the slung-shot was in his way and he took it out and laid it on the "reach" of the wagon above him and got up in the morning and forgot it. All this he swore to before the slung-shot was produced, and when it was produced it proved to be just as he had described it. Major Hugh Fullerton was prosecuting attorney, with J. H. Shaw assistant.

Respectfully,
J. T. Brady.

N.B. Some three months after the trial I was in the neighborhood where Wadkins lived buying cattle, and was with young Wadkins all of one day. (He was the slung-shot witness). He was a young man about my own age (about twenty-three) and he gave me a full account of the fight between Armstrong and Metzker, and what Armstrong struck Metzker with. The fight was at a camp meeting in Mason County around a huckster's wagon where they were selling whiskey, cider, and cigars. The men were drinking and got into a dispute, and Wadkins said Armstrong picked up an old-fashioned wagon hammer off the counter and struck Metzker with it, and he saw him do it. When Wadkins was summoned as a witness he was frightened for fear he would be obliged to tell *all* he knew, which he did not wish to do, as Armstrong was a cousin, or some relative. The other witnesses all swore Armstrong just struck Metzker with his fist. Wadkins told me they were all friends of Armstrong and wished to protect him. Wadkins told Lincoln he feared he would be cross-examined and would *have* to tell all he knew and he did not want to lie about it. Mr. Lincoln assured him he would only be cross-questioned about the questions he put to him, and so he confined his questions to the slung-shot and Wadkins got off easy. This item you may not wish to use, as you say the defendant is still alive, and so it might open an old wound and lead to controversy. You must use your own judgment. I only give it as given to me by Wadkins, and he positively told me he saw Armstrong hit Metzker with the wagon hammer. [Emphasis original].

J. T. Brady.

3B. JOHN T. BRADY: EXTRACT OF LETTER TO J. MCCAN DAVIS, MAY 23, 1896[6]

... My recollection is that Logan was the oldest man on the jury, and therefore we selected him as foreman. There might have been one man younger than myself, but my recollection is that I was about the youngest man on the jury, and that there were not more than three of the jury over thirty years of age. On the first ballot Armstrong was acquitted. We did not take a second ballot. The jury looked upon Allen as a truthful witness, but the almanac ruined his testimony.

The trial lasted over Sunday, and during Sunday, which was very warm, we were all lounging on the grass in the courthouse hard attended by a deputy sheriff. Mr. Lincoln and other lawyers were with us, and we talked and cracked jokes and killed time as best we could. I think the trial began on Thursday and ended on Tuesday.

3C. JOHN T. BRADY: INTERVIEW WITH JASON N. GRIDLEY, 1912[7]

The prosecuting witness, Allen, testified in the trial that the reason he could see a slung-shot that Armstrong had in his hand, with which he struck Metzker, was that the moon was shining very bright, about where the sun would be, at one o'clock in the afternoon. Mr. Lincoln was very particular to have him repeat himself a dozen or more times during the trial about where the moon was located, and my recollection is now, that the almanac was not introduced until Mr. Lincoln came to that part of Allen's testimony telling the Court where the moon was located. Mr. Lincoln was very careful not to cross Mr. Allen in anything, and when Allen lacked words to express himself, Lincoln loaned them to him. Allen was the only witness for the State, and there were eight or ten witnesses for the defense, and they all swore that Armstrong struck Metzker with his fist, and I am satisfied that the jury thought Allen was telling the truth. I know that he impressed me that way, but his evidence with reference to the moon was so far from the facts that it destroyed his evidence with the jury. The almanac that was produced was examined closely by the Court, and the attorneys for the State, and the almanac showed that the moon at that time was going out of sight; setting; and the almanac was allowed to be used as evidence by Judge Harriott.

There has never been a question in my mind about the genuineness of the almanac, that it was an up to date almanac; this I am sure of, as it was passed up to the Judge, jury and lawyers, who all examined it closely, and the State's Attorney said "Mr. Lincoln, you are mistaken, the moon was just coming up instead of going down at that time" and Mr. Lincoln retorted: "It serves my purpose just as well, just coming up, or just going down, as you admit it was not over head as Mr. Allen swore it was." As to the question of the validity of the almanac, Mr. Lincoln's long and honorable life is a distinct refutation of any such dishonorable action on his part.

My recollection of Mr. Lincoln's appearance as he addressed the jury is very vivid. The day was warm and sultry, and, as he rose to make his closing argument he removed his coat, vest, and later, his "stock," the old fashioned necktie worn by men in those days. His suspenders were home-made knitted ones, and finally, as he warmed up to his subject, one of them slipped from his shoulder, and he let it fall to his side, where it remained until he had finished speaking. In this "backwoodsy" appearance he was about as homely, and awkward appearing person as could be imagined; but all this was forgotten in listening to his fiery eloquence, his masterly argument, his tender and pathetic pleading for the life of the son of his old benefactor. Tears were plentifully shed by everyone present; the mother of Duff Armstrong, who was present, wore a huge sun-bonnet, her face was scarcely visible, but her feelings were plainly shown by her sobs.

As we were leaving the court room to pass into the jury room, I heard Mr. Lincoln tell Mrs. Armstrong that her boy would be cleared before sundown, which proved to be true. We were out less than an hour; only one ballot was taken, and that was unanimous for acquittal.

After we rendered our verdict, Mr. Lincoln shook hands with Duff Armstrong and then led him to his mother and gave him a short lecture on making a man of himself and being a comfort to his mother, telling him to care for her and try to make as good a man as his father had been.

One of the witnesses in the Duff Armstrong case was Will Watkins, whose father lived near Petersburg, in Menard County. About two months after the Armstrong trial, T. B. Collins and myself were in the Watkins neighborhood buying cattle; Mr. Watkins sent his son Will with us, to help look up cattle. I recognized him as being the witness that Mr. Lincoln used to prove that Duff Armstrong did not have the sling-shot which was exhibited at the trial, in his possession. It naturally followed that we talked of the trial. Will Watkins told me that Mr. Lincoln sent for him to come to Springfield; he questioned him about the sling shot, and asked how it happened to be lost, and then found near the spot where Metzker was killed. He said he told Mr. Lincoln that when he laid down that night under the wagon to go to sleep, that he laid the sling shot upon the reach of the wagon, and in the morning, forgot to get it, and when the wagon was driven away, it dropped off at the place where it was found. Watkins said that he told Mr. Lincoln that he (Lincoln) did not want to use him (Watkins) as a witness, as he knew too much, and he began to tell Lincoln what he knew, and Mr. Lincoln would not allow him to tell him anything and said to Watkins: "All I want to know is this: Did you make that sling-shot and did Duff Armstrong ever have it in his possession?" Watkins said he replied: "On cross-examination they may make me tell things I do not want to tell" and Mr. Lincoln assured him he would see to it that he was not questioned about anything but the slung-shot. Watkins told me that Duff Armstrong killed Metzker by striking him in the eye with an old fashioned wagon hammer and that he saw him do it. Watkins said that Douglass and all the other eight or ten witnesses for Armstrong who swore that Armstrong hit Metzker with his fist, all swore to a lie and they knew it, as they all knew he hit him with a wagon hammer. During the trial Allen testified that Duff Armstrong hit Metzker with a sling-shot and I felt he was telling the truth until Mr. Lincoln proved by the almanac that Allen was so badly mistaken about it being a bright moonlight night; then Allen's whole testimony was discredited. [emphasis in original]

4A. CALEB J. DILWORTH: LETTER TO J. MCCAN DAVIS, MAY 18, 1896[8]

Dear Sir:

Yours of the 13th has been forwarded to this place and just received. I recollect very well the trial of the State vs. Armstrong. The trouble originated near a camp meeting in Mason County Illinois. Armstrong, with some others, met at a whiskey wagon near the camp ground, and after some controversy Armstrong struck Metzker in the eye. The parties were separated, made up, and that part of the matter ended there.

Metzker then left Armstrong and his company and started through the camp grounds. One Norris, who had had a former difficulty with

Metzker, seeing Metzker coming, picked up a neck-yoke and stepped behind a tree. As Metzker passed, Norris stepped out and struck him (Metzker) on the back of the head with the neck-yoke, he (Norris) running away, and Metzker going home. Metzker lived about three days. Upon the post-mortem examination, it was found that there was a wound in the eye, part of the skull being driven up into the brains; also, there was a wound on the back part of the head, either of which wounds would have produced death. Both Armstrong and Norris were arrested and jointly indicted. I was employed by Armstrong and we took a change of venue in his case to Cass County. Norris was tried in Mason County, convicted and sent to the penitentiary. We afterwards went to Cass County to try Armstrong. When we reached Beardstown, I found Mr. Lincoln there on other business, and during the day he came to me and said that "Mrs. Armstrong had come to him and asked him to assist in the trial of the case, and that if it would come off while he was there was there he would do so if I was willing." Of course I was glad to have him try the case. He not being acquainted with the facts, that night we met in a room with the witnesses and he examined them. The next morning the trial commenced. The prosecution attempted to magnify the assault and wound on the eye, and claimed that the wound was made by a slung-shot. When this testimony was given we procured the almanac, I think now from one of the public officers of the court. We examined it, and when the defense commenced Mr. Lincoln offered the almanac in evidence. It was submitted to the attorneys of the other side and examined by them and objected to as being immaterial. It was admitted in testimony to the jury; I do not remember now whether it was passed from one juror to the other or not. The idea that it was "fixed up," as you call it, or "tampered with," is not correct. The almanac that was offered was the almanac covering the proper ground, and with no alteration or tampering with had in the case. I cannot tell now as to the age of the jurors. I don't think there was any point made as to that part of the case. Of course we endeavored to get those that would be as favorable to our side of the case as we could. In relation to the almanac or the condition of the moon at that time, we did not put much stress on that part of the case, because it was so uncertain as to what time of night the affray occurred. There was nothing peculiar about the trial from ordinary trials for murder until it came to that part of the case which we admitted as the turning point. Of course Mr. Lincoln made a strong argument; everybody expected it and he did it; but what the case turned upon was the instructions given by the court. There was no question but what the fight with Armstrong and Metzker was an individual affair, and Norris was not present and had nothing to do with it. The assault of Norris was also a separate and distinct affair, and Armstrong was not present and had nothing to do with the other matter. Norris had been convicted of the killing. Lincoln asked the court "to instruct the jury (as far as I can recollect now) that if they believe from the evidence that Norris had been tried and convicted for the murder of Metzker, and said conviction had not been set aside, then the jury might acquit Armstrong, unless the act of his was a part of the same transaction for which Norris had been convicted." The court gave this instruction, and of course the jury found for the defendant, as the testimony was clear and conclusive that Armstrong had nothing to do with the assault which Norris made. There was no scene or excitement when the jury came in, as everybody was satisfied, after hearing the instruction, what the verdict of the jury might be. My impression is Mrs. Armstrong was not present when the jury came in; but of this I cannot be certain.

During the evening of the day of the trial Mr. Lincoln did deliver an address in the court house. It was not a political address, and I recollect very well he commenced by saying that "he had often attempted to write a scientific lecture and had commenced several, but had never finished one, and on this occasion he proposed to put them all together and fire them off at one shot." It was an address discussing the progress and improvement of the world.

I do not recollect of Henry Shaw doing anything in the case except it might have been in selecting a jury; but my recollection is that Judge Bailey of Macomb assisted Mr. Fullerton in the prosecution, and I believe also William Walker of Havana was in the defense.

The above is the principal part that I recollect of the transaction.

4B. CALEB J. DILWORTH: LETTER TO J. MCCAN DAVIS, JUNE 5, 1896[9]

Dear Sir:

Yours of the 3d just received, and in answer I will say: I am satisfied that the almanac affair is an entire hoax; and as to Lincoln seeing the doctor the day before, that I know is a mistake because Mr. Lincoln was at my room the night before the trial commenced, and that is the first time that he had any idea of what the proof was to be. We had the witnesses present, and he and I interrogated them. They remained there until late in the night. The next morning early the case commenced, and he knew nothing about any theory of the slung-shot until it was presented during the trial. I never heard of the Tubby Smith affair. This, I believe is all I know about the affair.

5. WILLIAM A. DOUGLAS: EXTRACT OF INTERVIEW GIVEN TO J. MCCAN DAVIS, N.D.[10]

I remember distinctly about Lincoln using the almanac. He didn't produce it until he got up to make his talk. Then he got permission from the judge to let the almanac go to the jury.

Lincoln was smart enough to get a jury of young men. They averaged about twenty-three years of age.

I think the trouble between Armstrong and Metzker took place about 9 o'clock at night. Several witnesses swore that the moon was shining, but Allen was the most positive; he was sure it was a full moon. Lincoln proved by the almanac that it was in the dark of the moon.

After Lincoln's speech I felt sure of Armstrong's acquittal; so sure that I bet five dollars on the result, and won.

6. JAMES HARRIOTT: UNDATED INTERVIEW NOTES BY WILLIAM H. HERNDON[11]

Judge Harriott

... Lincoln came to Beardstown and defended the prisoner charged nothing—had an old almanac—Lincoln did not know it—no one noticed it—Lincoln believed that the principle witness was true—moon theory [didn't] saved the boy—There was no excitement—no furor—no enthusiasm: it was a common trial—Generally the article from beginning to end is a humbug—

Metzker was the killed. One man was sent to the penitentiary for the same offense 5 years—: This man struck Metzker with what was called a neck yoke—Year 1858—Armstrong tried—Armstrong got change of venue—Lincoln theory was that neck yoke killed Metzker and that it cracked the skull in front—where Armstrong is supposed to have struck—The almanac may have cut a figure—but it was Doctor Parker's testimony confirming Lincoln's theory—the Court Saw this—

7A. MILTON LOGAN: STATEMENT TAKEN BY S. G. GOLDTHWAITE FOR J. MCCAN DAVIS, MAY 12, 1896[12]

I was thirty-seven years old at the time of the trial. I think it was in September. During the trial Lincoln asked the prosecuting witness, "How far were you off from the scene of the tragedy? Could you see it plainly?" The answer was that the moon was shining, and witness thought it was about as high as the sun is when it is ten o'clock. It was a light night and he could see plainly. Lincoln then introduced an almanac which he picked up off of the table. He had, I suppose, gone down town somewhere and secured it. He then proved to the jury by the almanac that there was no moon at the time of the supposed murder. I think it was a Jayne's almanac, as they were much in use at that time. It was a large, square one, as I remember. John Husted of Beardstown has the almanac. Do not remember the color. Lincoln passed it to me first, I think, as I was sitting near him and all the jurors examined it. Neither the judge nor the prosecuting attorney looked at the almanac. Hugh Fullerton prosecuted the case. J. Henry Shaw did not assist him.

I do not think the almanac was altered by any one. If it had been, the prosecuting attorney, or some one of the jurors, would have been sharp enough to find it out.

(In regard to the Dr. Parker matter, Mr. Logan said he did not want the matter used in print. I will give it to you, however, and you can use it if you see fit. The old gentleman is peculiar and seems loth to quote anything which could in any way reflect on Lincoln's character. He said that Dr. Parker had told him that Lincoln fixed up the almanac to suit the case, not in so many words, but by intimations. Logan says that Dr. Parker was apt to jump at conclusions and make joking insinuations, and he did not take much stock in his statement.—S.G.G.)

I think the almanac owned by John Husted is the genuine almanac. Lincoln's sympathetic remarks to the jury particularly impressed me. One part I remember distinctly. He said, in words as near as I can remember: "Gentlemen of the jury, I defend this case without reward. Why? Because of the love I bear this boy['s] mother, who has washed my dirty shirts when I could not pay for it."

The slung-shot was found under the wagon next morning. Two or three boys slept under the wagon, and one of them took it out of his pocket because it was in his way, and put it on the "hound" of the wagon. It was not identified as Armstrong's.

Do not remember any doctors in the case. The jury was out five or six hours. They stood at first ten for acquittal and two for conviction. They all finally concluded that the guilt of Armstrong was not proved, and he ought to have the benefit of the doubt. Only one ballot was taken.

(Mr. Logan wanted to know if Allen was the prosecuting witness. If so, he remembered particularly the phrase he used, viz., that the moon was about as high as the sun would be at 10 o'clock a.m.—S.G.G.)

7B. MILTON LOGAN: NEWSPAPER INTERVIEW, JUNE 6, 1906[13]

Milton Logan, Sr., 90 years old, living, in Boonsboro, Boone County, was the foreman of the jury in the now famous Armstrong case in which

Abraham Lincoln defended young William or "Duff" Armstrong, as he was more commonly called, for murder in the spring of 1858. Mr. Logan is the only juror, if not the only survivor, of this now memorable trial. Mr. Logan is well preserved for a man of his years and takes pleasure in giving his reminiscences of Lincoln, and his murder case. Following is Mr. Logan's account of the trial and events leading up to it:

"Young William or Duff Armstrong lived near Petersburg, Illinois, and was fond of drink and went with a rough crowd. In August, 1857, Duff, and a number of his companions joined a crowd of ruffians, who had gathered near a camp meeting in Mason county, Illinois, Armstrong had been drinking for some days and finally in a drunken row on August 29 engaged in a fight with a comrade named Metzker. Later in the day Metzker was hit with an ox yoke by another drunken companion, Morris by name. Three days later Metzker died and Morris and Armstrong were promptly arrested, charged with his murder. Marks of two blows were found on the victim, either of which might have produced death. That Morris struck one blow was proven beyond a doubt, but did Armstrong deal the other? In the fight he claimed to have used nothing but his fists, but both the marks on Metzker's body showed them to have been made with some blunt instrument. Public sentiment was very strong against both the accused. It was generally believed that one blow was from a slung shot in the hands of Armstrong, and that he and Morris had acted together and deliberately planned to murder Metzker. Both were thrown into prison. Separate trials were secured for the prisoners. Morris was tried first, convicted and sentenced to eight years in the penitentiary for manslaughter, Armstrong remained in jail till trial and succeeded through his attorneys, who were from Havana, Illinois, in getting a chance of venue to Cass county, on the ground that the prejudice of the people in Mason county was so strong against him that he could, not secure a fair trial."

. . .

"I was then in my twenty-eighth year," continued Mr. Logan, "and was the oldest member of the jury, and Ben Ayr, who had but a month before reached his majority, being the youngest member. As I remember, I do believe the average age of the jury was not over 23 years. The examination of the witnesses on the part of the defense was conducted principally by Lincoln. A number of witnesses were from Clary's Grove and Lincoln had known their fathers and mothers early in life. William A. Douglas was the first witness called, William Killian the second."

. . .

As the trial progressed it became evident that there could have been no collision [collusion?] between Armstrong and Morris. The strongest evidence against the accused was that of a man named Allen, whose examination by Lincoln, as Mr. Logan remembers it, was about as follows:

Q: Did you see Armstrong strike Metzker?

A: Yes.

Q: About how far were you from where the affair took place?

A: About forty feet. I was standing on a knoll or hill looking down at them.

Q: Was it a light night?

A: Yes it was.

Q: Any moon that night?

A: Yes, the moon was shining almost as bright as day.

Q: About how high was the moon?

A: About where the sun would be at 1 o'clock in the day.

Q: Are you quite certain there was a moon that night?

A: Yes sir, I am certain.

Q: You are sure you are not mistaken about the moon shining as brightly as you represent.

A: No sir, I am not mistaken.

Q: Did you see. Armstrong strike Metzker by the light of the moon, and did you see Metzker fall?

A: I did.

Q: What did Armstrong strike him with?

A: With a sling shot.

Q: Where did he strike Metzker?

A: On the side of the head.

Q: About what time did you say this happened?

A: About 10 o'clock at night.

The prosecuting attorney in his examination of the witness, brought out the same testimony, and seemed well pleased with the results. Lincoln did not cross-question the witness. With this testimony unimpeached, conviction for Armstrong seemed certain.

The prosecuting attorney in a forceful address, asked for a conviction from the jury on the strength of the evidence given. Mr. Lincoln made the closing argument. After a careful review of the testimony, its inconsistency, contradictions, impossibilities, Mr. Lincoln asked permission to introduce an almanac of current issue in the trial. The judge ruled it could be introduced as evidence. The almanac showed, said Mr. Logan, that at the hour Mr. Allen, the prosecuting witness swore he saw the prisoner strike the fatal blow by the light of the moon, that there was no moon shining.

The almanac was submitted as evidence and was plainly confusing to the prosecution. Then commenced one of the most eloquent, pathetic and forceful appeals in behalf of the prisoner ever heard in a courtroom. "He spoke between five and six hours," continued Mr. Logan, "and commenced his address by saying he appeared before us without any expectation of reward; that the prisoner's mother, Hannah Armstrong, had washed and mended his worn shirts and clothes, and done for him, when he was too poor to pay her, and that he stood thereby to partially try and pay the debt of gratitude he owed her. He carried us with him as by storm, and before he had finished speaking, there were many wet eyes in the room. On retiring the jury on the first poll stood three for acquittal and none [nine?] for conviction. Myself, Desollers and one Hulstead, being those who favored acquittal."

"The force of Mr. Lincoln's argument however, remained with the jury, as did also the falsity of the testimony of Allen, the prosecuting witness. After being out some five or six hours, the entire jury were of one mind and brought in a verdict of acquittal and Armstrong was discharged."

"The story has been current," said Mr. Logan, "that the almanac introduced as evidence in the trial, and which threw the prosecution into confusion, and secured the acquittal of the prisoner, was a piece of trickery on the part of Mr. Lincoln, and that the almanac was not of the year 1857, when the murder was committed, but 1853, and that the three had cleverly been changed to a seven, and I have had a great many letters of inquiry from writers, and others in different parts of the country in regard to the same. I wish to say that this charge is not true, and I know the almanac used at the trial was published in 1857 and could not have been changed, as I had examined it very closely. Moreover, the prosecuting attorney in the case never questioned the issue of the almanac, nor did he refer in any way to the moon shining, or attempt to answer Mr. Lincoln's undisputed argument on this point. As a further proof that no trickery was used, or forgery committed in the trial, I would say the same would have been entirely unnecessary, as the skeptic has but to refer to the almanac for August, 1857, which shows that the moon was exactly in the position, as shown by Mr. Lincoln in the trial."

8. JAMES H. NORRIS: LETTER TO GOVERNOR R. YATES, FEBRUARY 22, 1863[14]

Sir:

It is with feelings of the most profound emotion that I venture to address you, feelings of such a nature that I scarce know in what terms to write you; my bests plan however will be to give your excellency a slight sketch of my case, and then you can judge whether I have been sufficiently punished or not:—In August "57" I together with a man named William Armstrong was charged with killing a man in Mason County, Illinois, of which offence I am as completely innocent as the babe unborn. I was placed in jail and at that time had a wife and 4 small children completely dependent upon me for support. I had no means whatsoever to fee counsel with, and under these circumstances was desirous of procuring a trial as quick as possible, the presiding judge (whose name was Harriet) appointed me as counsel a gentleman named William Walker, a young man inexperienced at the bar, and opposed to whom was Hugh Fullerton, L.W. Ross, and John Collier, gentlemen of wide experience and of great abilities, under these unfavorable circumstances it is no wonder that I was convicted of manslaughter and sentenced to state's prison for 8 years: —Armstrong procured a change of venue to Cass County and was there defended by our present President A. Lincoln and by him acquitted chiefly by breaking down the testimony of one Charles Allen. Said Allen being my sole and only prosecutor: —Now your excellency it looks very hard indeed that I should have to suffer 8 long years in a prison, on the oath of a man who was, afterwards proved to have given false testimony in the very same case but against a different party:

In November "61" a gentleman named William C. Pelham got up a petition in my favor and placed it on file in the Governor's office where I presume it still is. Pelham went to the war and got killed, and now I have got no one to attend to the case for me: under these circumstances I humbly beg and pray of your excellency to look into my case and if in your judgment I have been wronged to use your executive authority in my behalf and have me released from my imprisonment. If you require a letter of recommendation from this place, I can procure one, showing that I have conducted myself in a proper and becoming manner since my incarceration.

Will your excellency please answer this and let me know your determination.

9A. J. HENRY SHAW: LETTER TO WILLIAM HENRY HERNDON, AUGUST 22, 1866[15]

Dear Sir:

In the case of People vs. William Armstrong, I was assistant prosecuting counsel. The prevailing belief at that time, (and I may also say at the present) in Cass County was as follows. Mr. Lincoln, previous to trial,

handed an almanac of the year previous to the murder, to an officer of
court, stating that he might call for one during the trial, and if he did, to
send him that one. An important witness for the people had fixed the time
of the murder to be in the night, near a camp-meeting, that "the moon
was about in the same place that the sun would be at ten o'clock in the
morning and was nearly full," therefore he could see plainly etc. At the
proper time Mr. Lincoln called to the officer for an almanac and the one
prepared for the occasion was shown by Mr. Lincoln, he reading from it
that at the time referred to by the witness the moon *had already set*. That
in the roar of laughter following, the jury and opposing counsel neglected
to look at the date. Mr. Carter, a lawyer of this city who was present at,
but not engaged in the Armstrong case, says he is satisfied that the almanac was of the year previous, and thinks he examined it at the time. This
was the general impression in the court-room. I have called on the Sheriff
who officiated at that time, James A. Dick, who says that he saw a
"Goudy's" Almanac laying upon Mr. Lincoln's table during the trial,
and that Mr. Lincoln took it out of his own pocket. Mr. Dick does not
know the date of it. I have seen several of the petit juryman who sat upon
the case, who only recollect that the almanac *floored* the witness; but one
of the jury, the foreman, Mr. Milton Logan, says that the almanac was a
"Jayne's Almanac," that it was the one for the year in which the murder
was committed, and that there was no trick about it, that he is willing to
make an affidavit that he examined it as to its date and that it was the
almanac of the year of the murder. My own opinion is, that when an
almanac was called for by Mr. Lincoln, *two* were brought, one of the year
of the murder and the other of the year previous; that Mr. Lincoln was
entirely innocent of any deception in the matter. I the more think this,
from the fact that Armstrong was not cleared by any want of testimony
against him, but by the irresistible appeal of Mr. Lincoln in his favor.
He told the jury of his once being a poor, friendless boy; that Armstrong's
father took him into his house, fed and clothed him, and gave him a home
etc., the particulars of which were told so pathetically that the jury forgot
the guilt of the boy in their admiration of the father. [emphasis in original]

It was generally admitted that Lincoln's speech and personal appeal to
the jury saved Armstrong.

. . .

The murder occurred, I think, in 1857. He was indicted in Mason
County and a change of venue to this county. At the November Term
1857 of Cass Circuit Court, Mr. Lincoln labored hard to get Armstrong
admitted to bail, but his motion was overruled. The trial and acquittal
occurred at the May term 1858.

9B. J. HENRY SHAW: LETTER TO WILLIAM HENRY HERNDON, SEPTEMBER 5, 1866[16]

Dear Sir:

... My recollections of that trial are rather good, from the fact that I was with Mr. Lincoln a great deal of the time during both of the terms in which the Armstrong case was pending. My connection with him during those terms was as follows, Not knowing that he was intending to attend our November Term 1857, I wrote to him that I wished his assistance for defendant in the case of Ruth A. Gill vs. Jonathan Gill at that term, which was a suit for divorce, custody of child and alimony. He came down, as I then supposed, exclusively to attend to that case. The question of divorce was left for a jury, who brought in a verdict for complainant, who also go the custody of the child; but the question of alimony, the most important point in that case, was left open until the next term of court. At this term, November 1857, Mr. Lincoln argued the motion in the Armstrong case to admit to bail which was overruled. At the May term I expected Mr. Lincoln down to assist in the *alimony* case again, and he came in due time, called at my office, and said I had "been suing some of his clients, and he had come down to attend to it." He then had reference to a new chancery case entitled "George Morre vs. Christina Moore and the heirs of Peter Moore" for a specific performance, the defendants all living near Springfield. I explained the case to him, and showed him my proofs. He seemed surprised that I should deal so frankly with him, and said that he should be as frank with me, that my client was justly entitled to a decree, and he should so represent it to the court, that it was against his principle to contest a clear matter of right. So my client got a deed for a farm, which, had another lawyer been in Mr. Lincoln's place, would have been litigated for years, with a big pile of costs, and the results probably the same. Mr. Lincoln's character for professional honor stood very high. He never vexed an opponent, but frequently threw him off his guard by his irresistible good humor. But I digress—I still thought that Mr. Lincoln had come to our court more particularly to attend to the Gill and Morre cases and was very much surprised afterwards to see the immense interest he took in the Armstrong case. He went into it like a giant. The evidence bore heavily upon his client. [emphasis in original]

There were many witnesses, and each one seemed to add one more cord that seemed to bind him down, till Mr. Lincoln was something in the situation of Gulliver after his first sleep in Lilliput. But when he came to talk to the jury (that was always his forte) he resembled Gulliver again.

He skillfully untied here and there a knot and loosened here and there a peg, until, getting fairly warmed up, he raised himself in his full power and shook the arguments of his opponent from him as though they were cobwebs. He took the jury by storm. There were tears in Mr. Lincoln's eyes while he spoke. But they were genuine. His sympathies were fully enlisted in favor of the young man, and his terrible sincerity could not help but arouse the same passion in the jury. I have said it a hundred times, that it was Lincoln's *speech* that saved that criminal from the gallows, and neither money or fame inspired that speech, but it was incited by gratitude to the young man's father, who, as Mr. Lincoln said "was his only friend whcn he was a poor homeless boy." These are the only facts which I now recollect occurring at our court worthy of your notice concerning that case. ... [emphasis in original]

At the close of the trial of Armstrong in the Cass Circuit Court Mr. Lincoln had possession of the slungshot with which it was shown Armstrong killed Metzker.

He, Mr. Lincoln handed it to me, saying, "here, Henry, I'll give you this to remember me by."

I have that same slungshot now. It was made by Armstrong for the occasion. He took a common bar of pig lead, pounded it round, about the size of a large hickory nut, then cut a piece of leather out of the top of one of his boots, and with a thread and needle he sewed it into the shape of a slungshot, and thus improvised in a few minutes a very fatal weapon. If I can be of any other assistance to you in your worthy undertaking, shall be at your service.

10A. WILLIAM WALKER: LETTER TO GOVERNOR RICHARD YATES, JULY 10, 1863[17]

Dear Sir:

Enclosed please find letter from the warden of penitentiary in relation to the conduct of James H. Norris. I will give your excellency a brief statement of facts connected with the trial and conviction of Norris in our court. In the October term of our court Norris and one Armstrong were jointly indicted for the murder of a man by the name of Metzker. Norris was tried and Armstrong had a change of venue to Cass County. The testimony on the part of the people was that in the night at a camp meeting on Salt Creek the two defendant committed the deed one with a slungshot the other with a piece of wood resembling a neck yoke of a wagon. One witness alone so testified. The deceased lived several days, was under the influence of liquor at the time and never recovered his senses til death. I heard all the testimony and felt at the time that the conviction was wrong. Afterwards at a subsequent trial of the Cass Court about six months from the time of Norris conviction Armstrong was tried. His friends had time to prepare for the trial. Mr. Lincoln as an old friend of the Armstrongs. And on the last trial we proved by credible witnesses that the testimony of the witness who testified on the part of the people was absolutely false that the witness himself had said time and again that he was not at the place where the murder was committed at all. We proved that the witness was seen by different ones at other places during the whole of the night the offense was committed. This last trial and acquittal of Armstrong made everybody feel that Norris was wrongfully convicted. I have thought so all the time I was in each case and I feel sure that had we on the trial of Norris the same testimony that was had on the trial of Armstrong he would never been where he is. You may ask why something has not sooner been done for him. I can only answer by saying that Norris was a poor man and no one seemed willing to [illegible] in the matter.

I assure your excellency that the above statement is true and I further assure you that among those acquainted with the circumstances of the case there is not a doubt of his innocence and I hope in as much as almost six years has passed with the poor fellow suffering the pains of unmerited punishment that your excellency will pardon him and restore him to liberty.

10B. WILLIAM WALKER: LETTER TO WILLIAM HENRY HERNDON, JUNE 3, 1865[18]

Friend Herndon:

Your favor duly received. I am glad you have undertaken the task of writing the life of President Lincoln for publication. I did once know all about the case against Armstrong but no doubt many things occurred that have been forgotten. In the summer of 1857—at a camp meeting in the southeast portion of Mason County a man by the name of Metzker was murdered. Two men were charged with the offense. James H. Norris and William D. Armstrong both of whom were indicted at the fall term of our court of that year. Norris was tried and convicted of manslaughter. Sent to the penitentiary for eight years. Armstrong took a change of venue to Cass County and up to this time I had conducted the defense. In the spring of 1858 Armstrong at the Cass Court was put on his trial. Then Mr. Lincoln first appeared in the case. I had preserved the evidence adduced on the trial of Norris. This Mr. Lincoln scrutinized closely and very soon was fully posted in regard to the case. The testimony showed that the deceased together with a large number of others were off some distance, say half a mile from the place of worship where some wagons with provisions and liquors were stationed. At one of these wagons the difficulty occurred. The main witness swore that he saw Norris strike Metzker across the back of the head with some large stick, resembling a neck yoke of a wagon, and that Armstrong struck deceased with what appeared to be a slungshot, about the face, and that the parties clinched and fell to the ground. Metzker lived one or two days. The witness who testified to this stood off ten or fifteen paces from the parties in the night about eleven o'clock. On examination deceased showed fracture of the skull at the back and base of the brain, and also another fracture at or near the inner corner of the eye, which fracture occasion the most irritation. Either of which was shown would produce death. I examined the witnesses and when through Mr. Lincoln would tell me what to ask, having reference to some witness on the Norris trial. We made or showed numerous contradictions. Thus we showed by another witness that the man, who pretended to have seen all the difficulty, had not been on the ground at all that night. Mr. Lincoln made the closing argument for the defense. He spoke slow, and carefully reviewed the whole testimony, picked it all to pieces, and showed that the man though killed had not received his wounds at the place or time named by the witness, but afterwards and from the hands of someone else. He told of his kind feelings toward the mother of the prisoner, a widow, that she had been kind to him when he was young, lone, and without friends. The last fifteen minutes of his speech was as eloquent as I ever heard, and such the power and earnestness with which he spoke, that the jury and all sat as if entranced, and when he was through found relief in a gush of tears. I have never seen such mastery exhibited over the feelings and emotions of men as on that occasion. The boy was acquitted—none of that sickening thing occurred on his acquittal that some writer has mentioned. The old lady came to the parlor where Mr. Lincoln and the judge and some others were sitting and took Mr. Lincoln by the hand and with streaming eyes said God would bless him and his children, because he had been kind to the widow and orphan. The work he done was the result of his large kind heart, his reward the consciousness that he had done his duty. Should these facts be of any assistance—use them as you please.

10C. WILLIAM WALKER: LETTER TO WILLIAM HENRY HERNDON, AUGUST 27, 1865[19]

Dear Sir:

In regard to the trial of Armstrong in Beardstown, it was testified by the witness that the deed was done about eleven at night, and that there was a bright moon, and I think an almanac was brought in at my request for the year proper, from some of the clerk's offices below. The witness said he was some 30 yards distant and that he seen the blow struck with a slungshot. We showed by the almanac that at the hour of eleven at night no moon was visible, and by other witnesses that at the time of the trouble it was quite dark. Mr. Lincoln—in his speech may have alluded to the absence of a moon to show that in as much as the witness was mistaken in regard to one thing, the jury should receive all his testimony with caution. Mr. Lincoln's argument was that no jury ought ever to convict upon such testimony.

The jury acquitted, Mr. Lincoln's speech was in every sense honorable, high-toned, and professional. I think Judge Dummer was present during the trial and perhaps remembers the particulars of the trial as fully as I do. . . .

10D. WILLIAM WALKER: LETTER TO WILLIAM HENRY HERNDON, SEPTEMBER 15, 1866[20]

Friend Herndon

. . .

Mr. Lincoln only appeared the one time, and that on the trial, Mr. Lincoln closed the argument for the defense, in a speech of about one hour. It was a close and searching analysis of the testimony for about three fourths of the time, the remainder was an appeal to the jury and was the most eloquent and impressive I have ever heard. The feelings of the jury seemed to harmonize with the speaker, and he conveyed to them by his earnestness the conviction that Armstrong was innocent, not only to the jury but everyone else. The instructions given to the jury for the defense, will be found in Mr. Lincoln's own handwriting carefully prepared while the prosecution closed the argument. I believe I have answered all your questions. If not, keep on, I have but little to do and love to think about the greatest man that ever lived, and to curse in my soul the authors of his death.

Appendix B

Selected Documents from the Armstrong Court File

Court Minutes, October 29, 1857: This day comes the grand jury into open court and present the following Indictment, to wit: The People of the State of Illinois versus James H. Norris and William Armstrong: Indictment for Murder: Endorsed a true bill. John H. Havinghorst, foreman of the grand jury.[1]

Court Minutes, October 31, 1857: The People versus Norris and Armstrong: Now on this day comes the defendants by their attorneys and enters their motion to quash the indictment herein. Which motion is overruled by the court.

Affidavit, November 5, 1857: State of Illinois: Mason County: In the Mason County Circuit Court at the October Term, AD 1857: The People versus James H. Norris and William Armstrong: Indictment for Murder: William Armstrong one of the defendants in this cause first being duly sworn according to law deposes and says that he fears that he will not receive a fair and impartial trial in this court, on account of the minds of the inhabitants of said Mason County being prejudiced against him. He therefore petitions the Court that a change of venue in this case be awarded to him to some county where the [illegible] does not [illegible].

William Armstrong.

Subscribed and Sworn to before me this 30th 5th day of October November 1857.

R. Ritter, Clerk.

Judge's Docket, November 5, 1857: The People versus Norris and Armstrong: Indictment for Murder: Nol Pros [of the October 29 Indictment].

Indictment, November 5, 1857: State of Illinois: Mason County: Of the October Term of the Mason County Circuit Court in the year of Our Lord one thousand eight hundred and fifty-seven.

The Grand Jurors chosen selected and sworn in and for the County of Mason aforesaid in the name and by the authority of the People of the State of Illinois upon their oaths present that James H. Norris and William Armstrong late of the County of Mason and State of Illinois not having the fear of God before their eyes, but being moved and seduced by the instigation of the Devil, on the twenty-ninth day of August in the year of Our Lord one thousand eight hundred and fifty-seven with force and arms at and within the County of Mason and State of Illinois, in and upon one James Preston Metzker in the peace of the said People of the said State of Illinois then and there being, unlawfully, feloniously, willfully, and of their malice aforethought did make an assault. And the said James H. Norris with a certain piece of wood about three feet long which he the said James H. Norris in his right hand then and there held the said James Preston Metzker in and upon the back part of the head of him the said James Preston Metzker then and there unlawfully, feloniously, willfully, and of his malice aforethought, did strike, giving to the said James Preston Metzker then and there with the stick of wood aforesaid in and upon the said back part of the head of him the said James Preston Metzker, one mortal bruise and the said William Armstrong with a certain hard metallic substance called a slung-shot which he the said William Armstrong in his right hand then and there had and held, the said James Preston Metzker, in and upon the right eye of him the said James Preston Metzker then and there unlawfully, feloniously, willfully and of his malice aforethought did strike, giving to the said James Preston Metzker then and there with a slung-shot aforesaid in and upon the said right eye of him the said James Preston Metzker one other mortal bruise, of which said mortal bruises the said James Preston Metzker from the said 29th. day of August in the year aforesaid until the 1st day of September in the year aforesaid at the County of Mason and State of Illinois aforesaid did languish, and languishing did live on which said first day of September in the year aforesaid the said James Preston Metzker in the County and State aforesaid of the said mortal bruises died; and so the jurors aforesaid upon their oaths aforesaid do say that the said James H. Norris and William Armstrong the said James Preston Metzker in manner and form aforesaid unlawfully, feloniously, and of their malice aforethought did kill and murder contrary to the form of the statute in such cases made and provided and against the peace and dignity of the same People of the State of Illinois.

And the Grand Jurors aforesaid in the name and by the authority aforesaid upon their oaths aforesaid do further present James H. Norris and William Armstrong late of the County of Mason and State of Illinois not having the fear of God before their eyes but being moved and seduced by the instigation of the Devil, on the twenty-ninth day of August in the year of Our Lord one thousand eight hundred and fifty-seven with force and arms at and within the County of Mason and State of Illinois in and upon one James Preston Metzker in the peace of the said People of the said State of Illinois then and there being unlawfully feloniously, and willfully and of their malice aforethought did make an assault; and that the said James H. Norris and William Armstrong with a certain hard metallic substance commonly called a slung-shot which they the said James H. Norris and William Armstrong in both their right hands then and there had and held, the said James Preston Metzker in and upon the right eye of him the said James Preston Metzker then and there unlawfully, feloniously, willfully and of their malice aforethought did strike, beat and bruise, giving to the said James Preston Metzker then and there with the slung-shot aforesaid by striking, beating and bruising the said James Preston Metzker in and upon the right eye of him the said James Preston Metzker one other mortal bruise of which said mortal bruise the said James Preston Metzker from the said twenty-ninth day of August in the year of Our Lord one thousand eight hundred and fifty-seven aforesaid until the first day of September in the year aforesaid at the County of Mason and State of Illinois aforesaid did languish, and languishing did live on which first day of September in the year aforesaid the said James Preston Metzker in the County and State aforesaid of the said mortal bruise died. And so the jurors aforesaid upon their oaths aforesaid do say that the said James H. Norris and William Armstrong the said James Preston Metzker in manner and form aforesaid unlawfully, feloniously, willfully and of their malice aforethought did kill and murder contrary to the form of the statute in such cases made and provided and against the peace and dignity of the same People of the State of Illinois.

And the Grand Jurors aforesaid upon their oaths aforesaid in the name and by the authority of the People aforesaid do further present James H. Norris and William Armstrong late of the County of Mason and State of Illinois on the twenty-ninth day of August in the year of Our Lord one thousand eight hundred and fifty-seven not having the fear of God before their eyes, but being moved and seduced by the instigation of the Devil with force and arms at and within the County of Mason and State

of Illinois in and upon the said James Preston Metzker in the peace of the
People of the said State of Illinois then and there being, unlawfully, feloniously, willfully and of their malice aforethought did make an assault;
and that the said James H. Norris and William Armstrong with a certain
stick of wood three feet long and of the diameter of two inches which
they the said James H. Norris and William Armstrong in their right
hands then and there had and held the said James Preston Metzker in
and upon the back side of the head of him the said James Preston
Metzker then and there feloniously, willfully, unlawfully, and of their
malice aforethought did strike, beat and bruise, giving to the said James
Preston Metzker then and there with a stick of wood aforesaid in and
upon the said back side of the head of him the said James Preston
Metzker one other mortal bruise of which said mortal bruise the said
James Preston Metzker on the said twenty-ninth day of August in the
year aforesaid until the first day of September in the year aforesaid at
the County and State aforesaid did languish and languishing did live
on which said first day of September in the year aforesaid at the County
and State aforesaid of the said mortal bruise died; and so the jurors
aforesaid upon their oaths aforesaid do say that the said James H.
Norris and William Armstrong the said James Preston Metzker in manner and form aforesaid, unlawfully feloniously, willfully, and of their
malice aforethought did kill and murder; contrary to the form of the
statute in such cases made and provided and against the peace and dignity of the same People of the State of Illinois.

HUGH FULLERTON, state's attorney.
Endorsement: Filed November 5th 1857: The People of the State of
Illinois versus James H. Norris and William Armstrong: Indictment for
Murder: A True Bill: John H. Havinghorst, Foreman of the grand jury
   Witnesses Grigsby Z. Metzker, Charles Allen, James P. Walker,
William M. Hall, Joseph A. Douglas, William Douglas, B. F. Stephenson,
Hamilton Rogers, William Killion, Joseph Speltz, William Haines.

   Not bailable:
   James Harriott.

Motion to Quash Indictment, November 5, 1857: State of Illinois: Mason
County: Mason Circuit Court October Term: The People versus James H.
Norris and William Armstrong: Indictment for Murder: The said defendant comes and moves the court to quash the indictment in this cause for
the following reasons to wit:

1st. There was no proper order made by the County Court of Mason County to authorize the clerk to issue the venire upon which the grand jury were summoned.

2nd. There was no proper venire issued.

3rd. The grand jury was improperly summoned.

4th. There is a variance between the return of the sheriff and the record in relation to summoning and returning the grand jury into court.

5th. One or more of the grand jurors who served upon the grand jury and who assisted in finding the Indictment in the above cause is disqualified from serving as grand juror according to law and was not a body legally assembled to find said indictment.

6th. The indictment is defective upon its face.

7th. The indictment does not sufficiently describe the wound.

8th. The indictment does not state that the defendants acted in concert.

9th. The indictment states two different assaults to have been made and does not State which caused the death of the deceased.

10th. The indictment is in other respects informal and insufficient.

Dilworth and Campbell, Attorneys for Defendants.

Affidavit, November 5, 1857: In the October Term 1857 of the Mason County Circuit Court: State of Illinois, Mason County: The People versus James H. Norris and William Armstrong: Indictment for Murder: David Ott first being duly sworn according to law deposes and says that he is one of the acting grand jurors for this term of said court and was summoned by the sheriff of said county as such and affiant further says that he was seventy seven years of age on the 21st day of last January – and was present acting and assisting in finding the indictment in the above entitled cause and was sitting with the grand jury and acting as a grand juror in and for said county at the time the said indictment was found.

David Ott

Subscribed and Sworn to before this 30th 5th day of October November 1857.

R. Ritter, Clerk

Affidavit, November 5, 1857: In the October Term 1857 of the Mason County Circuit Court: State of Illinois, Mason County: The People versus James H. Norris and William Armstrong: Indictment for Murder: James McCowan first being duly sworn according to law deposes and says that he is one of the acting grand jurors for this term of said court – that he was chosen by the county court of said county at the September term 1857 as a grand juror in and for said county, and was summoned by the sheriff of said county as such – Affiant further says that he was seventy three years old last March – and he was present acting in finding the indictment in the above in titled cause – was sitting with the grand jury, and acting as a grand juror in and for said county at the time the said indictment was found.

James McCowan

Subscribed and Sworn to before me this 5th day of November AD 1857.

R. Ritter, Clerk

Judge's Docket, November 5, 1857: The People versus Norris and Armstrong: Motion to quash indictments and motion to discharge the prisoners. Motion to discharge withdrawn. Motion for change of venue for Armstrong. Motion to quash overruled. Prisoners arraigned. Plea Not Guilty. Venue for Armstrong changed to Cass County. Witnesses recognized in sum of $200 each to appear at Cass Circuit Court. Nov 6th. Jury empanelled in case of James H. Norris. Verdict guilty of manslaughter and fix penalty eight years' service in penitentiary. Motion for new trial and arrest of judgment overruled. Prisoner sentenced 8 years hard service in penitentiary.

Court Minutes, November 5, 1857: The People of the State of Illinois versus James H. Norris and William Armstrong: Indictment for Murder: Now on this day comes the People by their attorney and the court being fully satisfied that James H. Norris one of the defendants is unable to employ counsel and therefore appointed William Walker to defend the said defendant James H. Norris and thereupon come the said defendants by their attorneys and entered their motion to quash the indictment herein filed and the court after hearing the argument of the counsel and being fully advised of defendants' motion to quash the indictment filed herein, order that said motion be overruled and thereupon again comes the defendants by their attorneys and enter their motion to discharge the prisoners. James H. Norris and William Armstrong and thereupon again said defendants come and by leave of court withdraw their motion hereinbefore entered to discharge said prisoners James H. Norris and William Armstrong and thereupon came William Armstrong one of the prisoners by his attorneys and entered his motion for a change of venue as to him the said William Armstrong and [illegible] again comes as well the state's attorney on behalf of the People and [illegible] the defendants in proper person and by their attorneys and the defendants being furnished with a copy of the indictment, list of witnesses, and jurors say they are not guilty in manner and form as they are charged in the indictment filed herein. And James H. Norris one of the defendants herein for his trial puts himself upon the country and the People by their attorney do the like. And thereupon a jury was summoned to court to try the issue joined. And the regular panel of jurors being first exhausted, the court ordered the sheriff to summon twenty four jurors from among the bystanders to serve as jurors in the cause and thereupon the sheriff returned into court twenty four jurors as commanded. And the panel of jurors being returned into court as aforesaid by the sheriff being exhausted it was further ordered by the court that the sheriff be required to summon twenty four more jurors from among the bystanders to serve as jurors in this cause and the sheriff having thereupon returned into court twenty four jurors as last commanded and the said twenty four jurors last returned into court by the sheriff being also exhausted it was therefore further ordered by the court that the sheriff summon twenty four more jurors from among the bystanders to serve as jurors in the cause and the sheriff having returned into court twenty four jurors as last commanded therefore the following named persons were elected, to wit: John Davis, Isaiah Williams, J.P. Lipham, Robert Anderson, H W Kent; Jacob Head; J Patton, Wm Hartzell, C Riggs, LD Jones, Isaac N Ware, E.B. Switt [illegible]. Who being selected, tried, and sworn well and truly to try the issues joined upon their oath do say "We the jury agree to find the defendant guilty of manslaughter and as penalty eight years' service in the state penitentiary." It is therefore ordered and adjudged that the said defendant James H. Norris be sentenced to eight years imprisonment in the penitentiary of the State of Illinois. It is further ordered by the court that [illegible] Sheriff of Mason County execute this [illegible] by the adjournment of the court.

Jury Instruction, November 7, 1857: The Court instructed that on an indictment for murder the defendant may be acquitted of the charge of murder and found guilty on the same indictment for manslaughter. The jury are further instructed that if they should acquit the defendant of the charge of murder and from the evidence find him guilty of manslaughter they will fix the length of time the defendant shall serve in the penitentiary, in their verdict.

Jury Instruction, November 7, 1857: 8th. That if the People call out the admissions of the prisoner as evidence, then they will take admissions in his favor as well as against him. And if from such admissions they have a reasonable doubt as to the guilt of the prisoner, then they will find the prisoner not guilty.

Jury Verdict, November 7, 1857: We the jury agree to find the defendant guilty of manslaughter and as penalty eight years' service in the state penitentiary.

John Davis, Isaiah Williams, J.P. Lipham, Robert Anderson, H W Kent; Jacob Head; J Patton, Wm Hartzell, C Riggs, LD Jones, Isaac N Ware, E.B. Switt

Motion for New Trial, November 7, 1857: People of the State of Illinois versus James H. Norris et al.; Oct term of the Mason Circuit Court AD 1857: The defendant moves the court for a new trial and in arrest of judgment for the following reasons

First. [illegible] Because the indictment in this case is [illegible: vague?]

Second. Because the court [illegible] improper instructions to the jury

Third. The evidence did not support the verdict.

Fourth. Because the verdict is not such as the law authorizes in such cases.

Fifth. Because the grand jury was not impaneled in the manner as [illegible] by the statutes in such cases made and provided

Sixth. And for other good and sufficient causes appearing in the record.

Dilworth, Campbell, and Walker, Attorneys for Defendant

Court Minutes, November 16, 1857: The People versus William Armstrong: Venue from Mason County: And now on this day came the People of the State of Illinois by their attorney Hugh Fullerton Esquire and on his motion a writ of certiorari was ordered to be issued to the clerk of the Circuit Court of Mason County and leave was given him to withdraw the papers on file in this case for the purpose of getting them properly certified.

Writ of Certiorari, November 16, 1857: State of Illinois, Cass County: Of the October Term of the Mason Circuit Court AD 1857: The State of Illinois to Richard Ritter Clerk of the Circuit Court of Mason County,

Greeting: We being willing for certain causes to be certified of a certain indictment wherein the People of the State of Illinois are plaintiffs and James H. Norris and William Armstrong are defendants, now pending in the Cass County Circuit Court, we command you that you certify and send forthwith to this court a full true perfect and complete copy of all the records, and the originals of all papers filed in your office, with all things touching the same so full and entire as before you they remain, together with this write, before us at Beardstown at the County of Cass and State of Illinois at our said Circuit Court now holding, that we may further cause to be done therefore that which of right and according to our laws and constitution ought –

Witness James Taylor (Clerk of our said court) at Beardstown this Sixteenth of November AD 1857, the Seal of the said court being hereunto affixed.

James Taylor, Clerk.

Court Minutes, November 19, 1857: The People of the State of Illinois versus William Armstrong: Venue from Mason County: And now on this day come the People of the State of Illinois by their attorney Hugh Fullerton Esquire and the prisoner William Armstrong is brought to the bar in proper person a motion made by the prisoner to admit him to bail whereupon a motion was made on the part of the People for a continuance of this cause until the next term of this court which after due deliberation by the court was granted and the motion to admit to bail was overruled.

Court Minutes, November 21, 1857: The People versus William Armstrong: Venue from Mason: And now this day came the defendant by his counsel and entered his motion that the said defendant be admitted to bail which said motion was after hearing the arguments of counsel, upon due consideration overruled.

Transcript, April 15, 1858: At a Circuit Court begun and held at the court house in Havana in and for the County of Mason and State of Illinois on the fourth Monday in the Month of October AD 1857. Present the Hon. James Harriott Judge of the 21st Judicial Circuit of the State of Illinois, and Hugh Fullerton prosecuting attorney. J.P. West sheriff and Richard Ritter Clerk. Afterwards to wit: on the same day the sheriff of said county returned into court his venire of grand Jurors selected to serve this term of the said circuit court, who being called the following persons answered to their names, to wit: C.D. Loveland, James McCowen, Silas Cheek, William Atwater, John H. Havinghorst, William Colwell, John Rogers, William Ainsworth, Joseph Adkins, R C. Blunt, G. S. Town, George Vaughn, G.W. Phelps, Mathew Tomlin, George H. Short, Lorenzo R. Hastings, James N. Combs, and the panel not being full the court ordered the sheriff to summon from among the bystanders 5 persons to fill said panel and the sheriff returned the following named persons, to wit: William Falkner, Daniel Ott, Wm. Holton. John Allen, James Quick, and W. T. Ewers. The court then excused from serving on said grand jury John D. Cory, James M. [illegible]gles, Daniel Elam, and Joseph Statten. The Court then appointed John H. Havinghorst foreman of said grand jury and the said jury being duly sworn and charged by the state's attorney retired to consider of presentments. Be it remembered that afterwards, to wit: on the 5th day of November AD 1857 the grand jury in and for the county and state aforesaid came into open court the following indictment to wit:

The People of the State of Illinois versus James H. Norris and William Armstrong: Indictment for Murder: Endorsed A True Bill John H. Havinghorst foreman of the grand jury. And afterwards to wit: on the same day the following proceedings were had and entered of Record.

The People of the State of Illinois versus James H. Norris and William Armstrong: Indictment for Murder: Now on this day comes the People by their attorney and the court being fully satisfied that James H. Norris one of the defendants is unable to employ counsel thereupon appointed William Walker to defend the said defendant James H. Norris and thereupon came the said defendants by their attorneys and enter their motion to quash the indictment herein filed, and the Court after hearing the argument of the counsel and being fully advised of defendants motion to quash the indictment filed herein order that the said motion be overruled. And thereupon again comes the defendants by their attorneys and enter their motion to discharge the prisoners James H. Norris and William Armstrong and thereupon again said defendants come and by leave of court withdraw their motion hereinbefore entered to discharge said prisoners James H. Norris and William Armstrong and thereupon came William Armstrong one of the prisoners by his attorneys and enters his motion for a change of venue as to him the said William Armstrong. And now again comes as well the state's attorney on behalf of the People as the said defendants in proper person and by their attorneys and the said defendants being furnished with a copy of the indictment, list of witnesses and Jurors for plea herein say they are not guilty in manner and form as they are charged in the indictment filed here, and James H. Norris one of the defendants herein for his trial puts himself upon the country and the People by their attorneys do the like and thereupon a jury was commanded to come to try the issue joined and the regular panel of Jurors being first exhausted the court ordered the sheriff to summons twenty four Jurors from among the bystanders to serve as jurors in this cause and thereupon the sheriff returned into court twenty four jurors as commanded. And the panel of jurors returned into court by the sheriff as aforesaid being also exhausted It was further ordered by the court that the sheriff be required to summons twenty four more jurors from among the bystanders to serve as jurors in this cause, and the sheriff having thereupon returned into court twenty four jurors as last commanded and the said twenty four jurors last returned into court by the sheriff being also exhausted, it was therefore further ordered by the court that the sheriff summons twenty four more jurors from among the bystanders to serve as jurors in this cause and the sheriff having returned into court twenty four jurors as last commanded, thereupon the following named persons were Elected, to wit: John Davis, Isaiah Williams, J.P. Lipham, Robert Anderson, H W Kent; Jacob Head; J Patton, Wm Hartzell, C Riggs, LD Jones, Isaac N Ware, E.B. Switt. Who being elected tried and sworn well and truly to try the issue joined after hearing the evidence and argument of counsel of both sides upon their oaths do say "We the jury agree to find the defendant guilty of manslaughter and as penalty eight years' service in the state penitentiary." It is therefore ordered by the court that the said defendant James H. Norris be sentenced to eight years hard labor in the penitentiary of the State of Illinois. It is further ordered by the court that J.P. West Sheriff of Mason County execute this judgment within ten days from the adjournment of this court. And afterwards to wit: on the same day the following proceedings were had and entered of record.

The People of the State of Illinois versus James H. Norris and William Armstrong: Indictment for Murder: Now on this day comes again the People by the state's attorney and the defendant William Armstrong by his attorneys and the court being fully advised as to defendant William Armstrong's motion hereinbefore entered for a change of venue, it is ordered by the court that the venue in this cause be changed to Cass County and that the clerk of this court certify and transmit the proceedings in this cause to the clerk of the circuit court of Cass County aforesaid. And thereupon the following named witnesses in this cause came and entered into a recognizance in the words and figures following to wit:

We Grigsby Z. Metzker, Charles Allen, William Killion, James P. Walker and B.F. Stevenson acknowledge ourselves to owe and be indebted to the People of the State of Illinois in the sum of two hundred dollars each, to be levied of our goods and chattels lands and tenements on the following condition, to wit: That if we Grigsby Z. Metzker, Charles Allen, William Killion, James P. Walker shall be and appear on the first day of the next term of the Circuit Court for the County of Cass and State of Illinois to give evidence in the case of the People of the state of Illinois versus James H. Norris and William Armstrong on a certain charge for murder then this recognizance to be null and void otherwise to remain in full force and virtue.

State of Illinois, Mason County: I Richard Ritter Clerk of the Circuit Court in and for the County aforesaid do certify that the foregoing is a true perfect and complete copy of all the proceedings of court in the case therein named as the same appears of Record in my office and that the papers transmitted herewith and marked A.B.C.D.E.F.G.H.I.J.K.L.M.

are all the original papers filed herein during the progress of this suit. Witness my hand and seal of office at Havana this 15th day of April AD 1858.

R. Ritter, Clerk.

Attachment for Contempt, May 6, 1858: State of Illinois: Cass County: The People of the State of Illinois.

To All the Sheriffs of said State of Illinois, Greeting.

We command you to take Charles Allen and B.F. Stevenson and them safely keep so that you have their bodies forthwith before the Circuit Court of said County, at the term now being held at Beardstown, to answer the People of the State of Illinois, for a contempt of court in not attending said court as a witness having been duly served with process. And have you then there this writ.

WITNESS, James Taylor clerk of our said court, at Beardstown, this 6th day of May A.D. 1858.

James Taylor, Clerk.

Endorsement: I return this writ having arrested the within named Charles Allen and now have him in Court this the 7th day of May AD 1858.

James A. Dick, Sheriff
By John Husted, Deputy
Serving .50
60 miles travel 3.00
Returning .10
$3.60

Judge's Docket, May 7, 1858: The People versus William Armstrong: Venue from Mason: 5th Day jury called and sworn. Verdicts not guilty. All the witnesses are necessary.

Jury Instruction, May 7, 1858: Instructions for People

1. The jury are instructed that if they believe from the evidence that the defendant William Armstrong struck the deceased James Preston Metzker the blow as charged in the indictment and if they further believe from the evidence that the deceased came to his death from the effects of said blow they will find the defendant guilty.

Endorsement: Given

2. The jury are further instructed that if they believe from the evidence that the defendant Armstrong killed the deceased James Preston Metzker without any considerable provocation the law will imply malice on the part of the defendant and they will find the defendant guilty.

Endorsement: Given

3. The jury are instructed that if they believe from the evidence that the defendant Armstrong struck the deceased Metzker in the right eye and thereby gave to the deceased a mortal bruise as charged in the indictment and that the deceased died in consequence of such bruise as charged in the indictment they will find the defendant guilty.

Endorsement: Given

Jury Instruction, May 7, 1858: [For the People] The jury are further instructed that they may acquit the defendant Armstrong of the charge of murder and find him guilty of manslaughter. And further if they should acquit the defendant of the charge of murder and find him guilty of manslaughter, they will fix the time of his confinement in the penitentiary any time not exceeding eight years.

Endorsement: Given

Jury Instruction, May 7, 1858: [for the Defense] The Court instructs the jury. That if they have any reasonable doubt as to whether Metzker came to his death by the blow on the eye, or by the blow on the back of the head, they are to find the defendant "not guilty" unless they also believe from the evidence, beyond reasonable doubt, that Armstrong and Norris acted in concert, against Metzker, and that Norris struck the blow on the back of the head.

Endorsement: Given

Jury Instruction, May 7, 1858: [for the Defense] That if they believe from the evidence that Norris killed Metzker, they are to acquit Armstrong, unless they also believe beyond a reasonable doubt that Armstrong acted in concert with Norris in the killing, or purpose to kill or hurt Metzker.

Endorsement: Given

Jury Verdict, May 7, 1858: We the jury acquit the defendant from all charges preferred against him in the Indictment.

Milton Logan Foreman

Court Minutes, May 7, 1858: May Term AD 1858: Friday May 7, 1858 (5th day): The Court met pursuant to adjournment: The People versus William Armstrong: Venue from Mason: And now on this seventh day of May, being the fifth day of this term of the court, come the People by their state's attorney Hugh Fullerton Esquire, prosecuting attorney for the Twenty First Judicial District and the prisoner William Armstrong who is brought here to the bar in proper person by the sheriff of Cass

County aforesaid, and also appearing by his counsel, the said attorney for the People furnished thereupon to the said prisoner a list of the regular panel of petit jurors at the present term of the court. And forthwith being demanded concerning the premises of the said indictment charged against him the said Armstrong says that he is "not guilty" thereof and puts himself upon the country and the People do likewise. And thereupon came a jury to wit: Horace Hill, Milton Logan, Nelson Graves, Charles D Marcy, John T Brady, Thornton M Cole, George F. Seilschott, SamI W. Neely, Matthew Armstrong, Benjamin Eyre, John M. Johnston and Augustus Hoyer, who having been elected tried and sworn, and having heard the evidence of the witnesses produced sworn and examined in this cause; the arguments of counsel, and the instructions of the court, retired to consider of their verdict, in charge of an officer duly sworn by the court. And afterwards, to wit: on the same day, the said jurors came into court in charge of the officer aforesaid, and the said prisoner Armstrong being brought into court in proper person, by the sheriff of the said County of Cass, the said jurors for verdict on their oaths do say, that the said defendant is not guilty, in the following words, to wit: "We the jury acquit the defendant from all charges preferred against him in the indictment." It is therefore ordered by the court that the said defendant be discharged, and that he go hence without day. And it is certified by the court that all the witnesses in this cause were necessary.

Appendix C

The Oral History of the Armstrongs

In the main body of our inquiry, most of our witnesses were people who gave their information with the expectation that it would be made public.[1] We have another body of information that purportedly comes from witnesses speaking in confidence—the oral history of the Armstrongs and their friends. All families of any size maintain an oral tradition that gets handed down to younger friends and relatives, and the Armstrong family was no exception. Such tradition may be very good, or it may be worthless. We should exercise extreme care in weighing such evidence, but if we are cautious we can sometimes unearth something of value. In this appendix we will review what we have discovered of this secondary tradition, attempt to evaluate it, and leave it to you, the reader, to determine what weight it deserves. The ultimate sources of this information will be friends and relatives of the Armstrong family who spoke with an expectation that their words would be more or less private, but their statements have been brought to our attention by listeners who, for various reasons, decided to publicize these confidential communications.

In 1914, when on his deathbed, A. P. Armstrong allegedly told the true story of the Almanac Trial to his nephew Randall James Plunkett. According to Plunkett, Jack Armstrong had become friends with Lincoln long before the famous wrestling match, which he and Lincoln contested to placate a group of roughnecks called the Clary's Grove Boys. Years later a Clary's Grove Boy named James Preston Metzker made an unprovoked attack on Duff Armstrong. It seems that Armstrong and his good friend James H. Norris were attending a camp meeting to listen to the preaching of Peter Cartwright, whom they both admired. While Armstrong and Norris were wetting their whistles at a bar, Armstrong and Metzker became embroiled in a disagreement about Cartwright's qualities as a preacher. Metzker attacked Armstrong, and Norris came to Armstrong's rescue by hitting Metzker with a neck yoke. A. P. Armstrong allegedly went on to give a fanciful description of the trial in which he made a number of preposterous claims, the most outlandish of which were: (1) Lincoln did not recognize the need for a change of venue and did not move for one until Duff prompted him to do so. (2) After Lincoln produced the almanac, he had Charles Allen arrested for perjury. (3) The jury deliberated for two days before returning a verdict of not guilty. Because Plunkett did not commit A. P. Armstrong's story to writing until 1962, we may be generous and attribute the outlandish details to faulty memory on Plunkett's part. It does seem more likely, however, that either Plunkett or A.P. Armstrong made the story up out of whole cloth.[2]

Plunkett may have been encouraged to put his account on paper because he had read a newspaper account of the trial given by Charles W. Smith, a nephew of Duff Armstrong. Smith claimed to have heard Uncle Duff speak often about the case. Smith said that the published accounts of the trial were "fairly accurate," but he did add some previously unreported details about the case. Armstrong purportedly told Smith that Metzker bullied him until "Uncle Duff socked him." Armstrong hit Metzker with his bare fist. Although the punch did not seriously injure Metzker, it knocked him down, and he received his fatal injury when his face struck a drainpipe on ground. Smith's account supports the contention that Lincoln did not procure the almanac until after Allen had testified. Although the circumstances related by Smith have more verisimilitude than Plunkett's, Smith places the fight outside a bar in Hall's Grove. Smith was 85 years old when he told this story, which he had heard over 60 years before.[3] While Smith's story may be interesting, it would be ill advised to give it much weight.

We have another story from a young woman who, although not a member of the Armstrong family, lived under the same roof with Duff Armstrong in the 1880s. John Armstrong opened his door to her because of friendship with her father; he opened his door to Duff Armstrong because they were both sons of Jack and Hannah Armstrong. The young lady looked upon Duff with awe. She would later write, "[H]e was like a character out of a book, more fascinating than any of the yellow-backed novels I kept hidden in the hay mow." She encouraged him to tell her stories of his youth, and he obliged her. One spring night they sat together on the front porch, she on the top step, he in his favorite chair. As the old man sat there with his feet propped up on the porch rail, he drew smoke into his lungs from his pipe and exhaled it into the night air. For a time she did not interrupt the silence because he seemed to her to be in a pensive mood. They sat there for a time lost in their own thoughts until, on impulse, she asked him a question. "Uncle Duff, tell me about Abraham Lincoln." He told her of the Almanac Trial, ending his story by saying, "Folks made talk afterward saying the almanac was for another year, but I don't know about that. All I know is that Abe came over to Ma and me and said 'Aunt Hannah, I'm giving your boy back to you.' " He lapsed into a long, thoughtful silence, which she finally broke with another question. Did he know how Pres Metzker was killed. Calling her by name, he said, "I always knew what happened. I wasn't too drunk to remember everything. I killed him with the neck yoke, just as they said. God knows I didn't mean to kill him. He was my friend." He closed his story of the Almanac Trial with the words, "I'd have told the truth except for the two people who died believing me innocent—Ma and Abe Lincoln."[4]

The story comes to us from a single source—a newspaper article written in 1988 by John Whiteside, a reporter for the *Joliet* (Illinois) *Herald*. The young woman who claimed to have sat at the feet of Duff Armstrong and heard his confession was Nora Senter Fry. She had gone to Oakford at the age of 18 to embark upon a life-long career as a schoolteacher. We do not know why she waited until she was in her sixties to write of this conversation she had with Duff Armstrong, nor do we know her intentions in putting the story on paper. As far as we know, she did nothing with her written account, and it was found among her papers after she died in the 1960s. A copy of the story eventually made its way into the hands of one of Fry's nieces—Alice Senter Kosick. Kosick learned of the story in 1988 and decided to share it with John Whiteside. Whiteside wrote an article about Fry's story, which appeared on page four of the *Lincoln* (Illinois) *Courier*. Paul J. Beaver noticed the article and commented on it in the *Lincoln Newsletter*, a publication of Lincoln College in Lincoln, Illinois.[5] Elizabeth W. Matthews included a reference to Beaver's comment in her work on Lincoln's legal career.[6] It appears that no one else took any further notice of this singular story.

What are we to make of Nora Fry's story? First let us tally the points against it:

(1) We know nothing about the circumstances surrounding the writing of the story. Context can radically alter the meaning and the credibility of statements. As we shall soon see when we investigate the veracity of another report, context can have great influence upon how a statement is received and whether it is believed.

(2) The very next year, Armstrong made a detailed public statement about the killing to J. McCan Davis, and that statement received

widespread publicity. In that statement Armstrong defended the authenticity of Lincoln's almanac and emphatically asserted that he hit Metzker with his fist and nothing more. Of course, what people tell their friends in confidence often differs from what they tell the world at large.

(3) Fry has Armstrong calling Lincoln "Abe." Other sources report that Armstrong called him "Uncle Abe."

(4) She reports Duff Armstrong as admitting, "I killed him with the neck yoke, just as they said." Up to this point, we have found no sources that say Armstrong used a neck yoke; on the contrary, all our evidence points to James Norris as the man who struck with the neck yoke. Nor do we have any record of Armstrong ever confessing to anyone else. It may be, however, that when Fry wrote her story decades later, her faulty memory simply transferred the neck yoke from Norris's hand to Armstrong's.

(5) Fry quotes Armstrong as saying, "Folks made talk afterward saying the almanac was for another year, but I don't know about that." In every other reported statement he made, Duff Armstrong argued for the authenticity of the almanac. He told the story of Lincoln sending his cousin for the almanac, and other witnesses corroborated his story.

(6) She wrote the story four decades after the fact. People's memories fade. Although the gist of a significant event can be well remembered, the devil is in the details. For many years I told the story of a masterful cross-examination I had witnessed. As I told and retold it, I recounted how the cross-examiner completely devastated the witness's credibility with four succinct questions. A quarter century after hearing the cross, I had occasion to go back to the court file and read the transcript of the brilliant cross-examination. The four questions I remembered were the four key points of the cross-examination, but the making of these four points consumed several pages of transcript and many more than four questions. The gist of my recollection was accurate, but the details of the cross were not as I remembered. The passage of time therefore can be used to argue either for or against crediting the statement of Nora Fry. She got the gist of Armstrong's confession right, but she misremembered the details.

We can find some corroboration for Fry's story in a statement purportedly made by John Armstrong in what he thought was a private conversation. At some time around the year 1916 Edgar Lee Masters and Theodore Dreiser made a trip to Oakford, Illinois, for the express purpose of meeting John Armstrong, the younger brother who had opened his doors to the aged Duff Armstrong. At this time John Armstrong was well advanced in years, having been born in 1846. Armstrong invited them into his modest home, fed them a meal, played his fiddle for them, and regaled them with memories of his youth. Dreiser was especially interested in whether Armstrong had ever met Lincoln. Armstrong said that when he was nine years old he traveled to Beardstown where his brother was jailed, and he saw Lincoln at that time. Inevitably, the talk turned to the Almanac Trial. Dreiser virtually cross-examined Armstrong about the almanac without learning anything new. Then Dreiser asked the question—did Duff hit Metzker? "You bet he did," came the reply. Armstrong explained that Duff had hit Metzker with a neck yoke, but somebody else had also hit him with a slungshot. "But what Duff did didn't kill him. It was the slungshot."[7]

We have two witnesses whom we must assess—John Armstrong, who told the story, and Edgar Lee Masters, who repeated it. Let us look at John Armstrong first. We have a record of Armstrong telling the story of the Almanac Trial on one other occasion. In 1912 the Lincoln Centennial Association invited him to speak at their annual gathering in Springfield, Illinois. He accepted, and the association included the text of his speech in a booklet commemorating the occasion. Armstrong told of Neil Watkins's testimony about the slungshot, and he spoke of the almanac, strongly defending its authenticity. He also told of Lincoln's releasing Duff from the army during the Civil War. There was one thing he never said—he never said his brother was innocent.[8] The Springfield speech does not contradict in any way Armstrong's later assertion that Duff struck Metzker with a neck yoke. In Springfield Armstrong spoke to a group of strangers. In Oakford he spoke to Edgar Lee Masters, the son of his (Armstrong's) best friend. As we shall see, Masters kept Armstrong's secret.

Masters wrote about the Almanac Trial on at least three occasions over a period of 20 years. His first and most complete retelling of the story came shortly after hearing it. In 1920 Masters published a work of fiction entitled *Mitch Miller*. In the novel young Mitch meets and befriends John Armstrong, and Armstrong gives a lengthy recitation of the facts of the Almanac Trial. In his account of the fight, Armstrong says, "[Metzker] pulled Duff off'n a barl where he was sleepin', and Duff got up and whooped him." Duff certainly gave Metzker a "whooping" if he hit him with a neck yoke, but Masters doesn't mention the neck yoke.[9] We mention this passage from a work of fiction because Masters, in his controversial 1931 biography *Lincoln the Man*, attests to its truth. His exact words are: "If anyone would know exactly how John Armstrong told about the part that Lincoln played in the case, and about John's visit to Duff in jail at Beardstown, let him read *Mitch Miller*."[10]

When Masters returned to the story of the Almanac Trial in *Lincoln the Man*, he did so with a vengeance. Almost nothing Lincoln did merited

Masters's approval. According to Masters, Lincoln did nothing extraordinary because "The case was one not hard to win." He notes that Lincoln did not participate in the hearing on the motion for change of venue and suggests that a more skillful lawyer handled the change of venue because Lincoln lacked the talent to handle such a complex proceeding. The court record belies Masters's claim that a change of venue was a complex proceeding. The inexperienced Dilworth won the change of venue with little fanfare. Masters finds it unusual that Lincoln would have helped Hannah Armstrong because Lincoln was "not a man of the liveliest gratitude." Masters notes that when Lincoln went to Beardstown to argue for Duff Armstrong's release on bail, he did not mention his involvement in the case until he stood up to argue the motion. Masters suggests that Lincoln might have done this to trick the prosecutor into leaving court early so that he could argue for bail unopposed. We have already seen that Lincoln's appearance at the bond hearing was most likely a spur-of-the-moment decision occasioned not by Fullerton's absence, but by Dilworth's. Masters's hostility toward Lincoln did not, however, cloud his judgment on the accusation of the faked almanac. Masters says that although Lincoln had a reputation as a "cunning lawyer" and was certainly "not above reproach as a practitioner," he was cunning enough to realize that he couldn't get away with faking the almanac. Masters finishes Lincoln off with two more jibes. He observes that other lawyers have won harder cases and that Lincoln's use of the almanac required no special abilities because "any practitioner of criminal law who knew his business" would conduct a sufficient investigation to uncover the issue. Masters, it seems, has 20/20 hindsight. In my estimation, based upon having tried a few murder cases, the Almanac Trial was a close run thing, and Armstrong could well have hanged for the killing. Masters's assessment of the Almanac Trial is so negative that one wonders why he didn't claim that Lincoln subverted justice by getting a guilty man acquitted. If his interview with John Armstrong actually happened, he would have had the ammunition. We must search for a reason why Masters did not include this detail in *Lincoln the Man*.

No story is ever the complete story of anything. All storytellers make choices about what to tell and when to keep silent. Sometimes they withhold details because they do not wish to weaken the point they are trying to make. Sometimes they withhold details they believe to be irrelevant or unimportant. Sometimes they do so because they do not want to embarrass or harm someone. When the danger of embarrassment or harm dissipates, they no longer see a need to keep silent. The Biblical scholar Gerd Theissen sees this tendency at work in the story of Jesus's arrest in the Garden of Gethsemane. Mark, who wrote the earliest Gospel, simply said that a disciple cut off the ear of one of the men in the arrest party. John, who wrote the latest, names Peter as the disciple. Theissen calls this an example of "protective anonymity." When Mark wrote Peter was still alive and subject to arrest for the crime. When John wrote he was dead. We can find a more modern example of protective anonymity in "Deep Throat," the shadowy figure who fed information to the authors of *All the President's Men*.

Masters may well have had a similar motive for suppressing the story of the neck yoke in his first two books, but the motive no longer existed when he wrote his third account of the Almanac Trial. Masters counted John Armstrong and his wife as friends, and he did not want to embarrass them. In *The Sangamon*, Masters tells of his last meeting with John Armstrong shortly before Armstrong's death in 1926. He then concludes his account of the Armstrong family by saying, "Aunt Caroline [John Armstrong's wife] lingered on until 1935, when she died, and thus ended the Armstrong family. ..." Masters did not tell the story of the neck yoke in either *Mitch Miller* (1920) or *Lincoln the Man* (1931) because he did not want to cause pain to his good friends, the Armstrongs. When he wrote *The Sangamon* in 1942, he could tell the story of the neck yoke without fear of embarrassing either John or Caroline, who were both dead. He also felt free in *The Sangamon* to give details of Duff Armstrong's later life that he had heretofore concealed. He described how after the Civil War, Duff wasted himself with alcohol. He quotes John Armstrong as saying, "Duff kept a-drinking. He got so that anybody could whup him. He went around showin' his discharge from the army and pickin' up money for drinks on it."[11]

We can see remarkable points of similarity between Nora Fry's story of the 1888 revelation of Duff Armstrong and Edgar Lee Masters's story of the 1919 revelation of John Armstrong. They both occurred in Oakford, they both occurred under the roof of John Armstrong's house, they both have Duff Armstrong hitting Pres Metzker with a neck yoke. They even corroborate each other on the detail of Duff's later life. Masters tells of Duff wasting his life as an alcoholic. Fry tells of an old man living with the family of his younger brother—a situation that often arises when a more successful sibling takes in a wayward brother who has become homeless due to alcoholism. They could hardly have collaborated on the story. The most likely source of the similarities between the two stories is Duff Armstrong himself, who told his brother John the truth about what happened at the whiskey camp. Why has the story of the neck yoke gone virtually unnoticed by Lincoln biographers? We can find it easy to understand why Nora Senter Fry's account went unnoticed, owing to its limited publication on the fourth page of a small-town newspaper, but Edgar Lee Masters was the renowned author of *Spoon River Anthology* and a Lincoln biographer himself. How could his version go unnoticed? Masters may have been a good poet, but he was not a good historian or biographer. He wrote his 498-page Lincoln biography in 47 days and then took 10 more to revise and edit it[12]—it is therefore not a scholarly work, and his animosity toward Lincoln became the dominant theme of the book. It was so vitriolic that a bill was introduced in Congress to declare the book "obscene, lewd, lascivious, filthy, and indecent. . ." and to ban it from the mail.[13] The furor over the book effectively ended Masters's literary career. When he published *The Sangamon*, it sold poorly, and Masters never again published a book with a major publisher.[14] Because Masters wrote *The Sangamon* after his career imploded, nobody took notice of his accusation against Armstrong.

The combined stories of Fry and Masters merit greater weight than the stories of Plunkett and Smith, but even if we accord them great weight, the stories do not change the conclusions we reached in Chapter 14. Regardless of whether he was guilty, Duff Armstrong should have been acquitted on the evidence adduced at trial, and the attorney who persuaded the jury to do their duty and acquit did nothing wrong.

Notes

CHAPTER 1

1. Donald W. Olson and Russell Doescher, "Lincoln and the Almanac Trial," *Sky and Telescope*, August 1999, 186–188, 187, inset, http://media.skyand telescope.com/documents/Almanac_Trial.pdf (accessed August 5, 2011).

2. Daniel W. Stowell, "Moonlight Offers Little Light," *Journal of the Abraham Lincoln Association* 24, no. 1 (Winter 2003): 66–74, 71, http://www .jstor.org/stable/20149041, (accessed July 9, 2010).

3. Daniel W. Stowell, "Murder at a Methodist Camp Meeting: The Origins of Abraham Lincoln's Most Famous Trial," *Journal of the Illinois State Historical Society* 101, no. 3–4 (2008): 219–234, 224, http://www.jstor.org/discover/10 .2307/40204737?uid=3739600&uid=2&uid=4&uid=3739256&sid=21101628 515497 (accessed January 6, 2013).

4. Ronald C. White, *A. Lincoln: A Biography* (New York: Random House, 2009), 244.

5. Richard B. Morris, *Fair Trial: Fourteen Who Stood Accused* (New York: Harper and Row, 1967).

6. Alexander Jacob, "Shot-Loaded Whips," 2008, http://cobrawhips.com/ g-shotloadedwhips.php (accessed March 8, 2013).

7. "Lincoln's Famous Case: Duff Armstrong's Story of His Own Murder Trial," *New York Sun*, June 7, 1896, *People v. Armstrong*, in *The Law Practice of Abraham Lincoln: Complete Documentary Edition*, 2nd ed. Martha L. Benner and Cullom Davis et al., eds. (Springfield: Illinois Historic Preservation Agency, 2009), http://www.lawpracticeofabrahamlincoln.org/Documents.aspx, hereafter cited as *LPAL* (accessed July 12, 2012).

8. William E. Barton, *The Life of Abraham Lincoln* (Boston: Books, Inc., 1943/1925), 513.

9. My first two murder trials followed this scenario—my client suffered a beating at a bar, went and found a weapon, and returned to exact fatal vengeance on his assailant. I have handled scores, if not hundreds, of such cases, most of them involving nonfatal assaults with deadly weapons.

10. Daniel W. Stowell et al., eds., *The Papers of Abraham Lincoln: Legal Documents and Cases*, Vol. 4 (Charlottesville: University of Virginia Press, 2008).

11. Carl Sandburg, *Abraham Lincoln: The Prairie Years*, Vol. 2 (New York: Harcourt, Brace, and World, 1926), 55.

12. William H. Townsend, "Lincoln's Defense of Duff Armstrong," *American Bar Association Journal* 11 (1925): 81–84, 81, http://heinonline.org (accessed July 10, 2012).

13. Barton, *Life of Abraham Lincoln*, 513.

14. This was the case in Illinois until 1966, when the Illinois Supreme Court confronted an extreme case where representing an indigent client would result in the attorney's financial ruin. The court decided that trial courts could require the state to pay the attorney despite the lack of statutory authorization. *People ex rel. Conn v. Randolph*, 35 Ill.2d 24, 219 N.E.2d 337 (1966).

15. Instruction 2.5, *Florida Grand Jury Instructions*, 2013, http://www.floridasupremecourt.org/jury_instructions/chapters/entireversion/onlinejurryinstructions.pdf (accessed January 20, 2013).

16. Larry Laudan, *Truth, Error, and Criminal Law: An Essay in Legal Epistemology* (New York: Cambridge University Press, 2006), 29–62.

17. "A reasonable doubt is not a mere possible doubt, a speculative, imaginary or forced doubt." Instruction 3.7, *Florida Standard Jury Instructions in Criminal Cases*, 2013, http://www.floridasupremecourt.org/jury_instructions/chapters/entireversion/onlinejurryinstructions.pdf (accessed January 20, 2013).

18. Instruction 2.03, *Florida Standard Jury Instructions: Involuntary Civil Commitment of Sexually Violent Predators*, 2013, http://www.floridasupreme court.org/jury_instructions/chapters/entireversion/onlinejurryinstructions.pdf (accessed January 20, 2013).

19. See Appendix A for the statements of the witnesses most heavily relied upon.

20. "The Promises and Pitfalls of Reminiscences as Historical Documents: A Case in Point," *Documentary Editing* 27 (2005): 153–171, 153.

21. The rules of evidence will be the same as used in my investigation of the prosecution of Jesus of Nazareth. *The Case against Christ: A Critique of the Prosecution of Jesus* (Newcastle upon Tyne, UK: Cambridge Scholars Publishing, 2011), 27–32.

CHAPTER 2

1. Francis L. Wellman, *The Art of Cross-Examination: With the Cross-Examinations of Important Witnesses in Celebrated Cases* (New York: Collier, 1970).

2. Justin Lovill, ed., *Notable Historical Trials, Volume 4: From Burke and Hare to Oscar Wilde* (London: Folio Society, 1999), 495–509.

3. See, for example, Roger C. Park, "Adversarial Influences on the Interrogation of Trial Witnesses," in *Adversarial versus Inquisitorial Justice: Psychological Perspectives on Criminal Justice Systems,* Peter J. van Koppen and Steven D. Penrod, eds. (New York: Kluwer Academic, 2003), 148.

4. Ronald H. Clark, George R. Dekle Sr., and William S. Bailey, *Cross-Examination Handbook: Persuasion, Strategies, and Techniques* (New York: Wolters-Kluwer, 2011), 111–113. It was while assisting in the writing of this book that I was inspired to conduct a thorough investigation of the Almanac Trial.

5. Steven Lubet, *Lawyer's Poker: 52 Lessons that Lawyers Can Learn from Card Players* (New York: Oxford University Press, 2006), 149–151.

6. Lovill, *Notable Historical Trials,* 495.

7. J. W. Donovan, *Tact in Court: Containing Sketches of Cases Won by Art, Skill, Courage and Eloquence,* 6th ed. (Rochester, NY: Williamson Law Book Co., Law Publishers, 1898), 173–175, http://archive.org/details/tactincourt00donogoog (accessed October 1, 2010).

8. Donovan, *Tact in Court.*

9. Donovan, *Tact in Court,* 175.

10. Walter B. Stevens, *A Reporter's Lincoln* (St. Louis: Missouri Historical Society, 1916), title page, http://www.archive.org/details/reporterslincoln00s (accessed September 30, 2010).

11. David W. Bartlett, *The Life and Public Services of Hon. Abraham Lincoln: To Which Is Added a Biographical Sketch of Hon. Hannibal Hamlin,* (New York: H. Dayton, Publisher, 1860), http://archive.org/details/lifeandpublics er00bartrich (accessed October 1, 2010).

12. Bartlett, *Life of Lincoln,* 110–115.

13. "A Sensation Story Spoilt," *Daily Illinois State Register,* June 26, 1860, *People v. Armstrong, LPAL,* http://www.lawpracticeofabrahamlincoln.org (accessed October 4, 2010).

CHAPTER 3

1. Earl Schenck Miers and William E. Baringer, *Lincoln Day by Day: A Chronology, 1809–1865,* Vol. 2 (Washington, DC: Lincoln Sesquicentennial Commission, 1960), 280, http://www.questia.com/PM.qst?a=o&d=1150449 (accessed June 1, 2012).

2. "Our Late President: A Chapter in the Private History of Abraham Lincoln," *New York Times,* January 22, 1866, http://query.nytimes.com/mem/archive-free/pdf?res=9B05E3D6123DE53BBC4A51DFB766838D679FDE (accessed January 17, 2013).

3. *Janesville* (Wisconsin) *Gazette,* http://newspaperarchive.com/janesville -daily-gazette/1860-05-25/page-4?tag=janesville+gazette+thrilling+episode +lincoln&rtserp=tags/janesville-gazette-thrilling-episode-lincoln?psb=dateasc (accessed June 1, 2012).

4. *Appleton* (Wisconsin) *Motor*, July 19, 1860, http://www.newspaperarchive .com/PdfViewerTags.aspx?img=6234118&firstvisit=true&src=search&currentResult =0&currentPage=0&fpo=False (accessed October 3, 2010); *Citizen* (Smethport, Pennsylvania), June 16, 1860, http://www.newspaperarchive.com/PdfViewer Tags.aspx?img=46544386&firstvisit=true&src=search&currentResult=0&current Page=0&fpo=False (accessed October 3, 2010); *Kenosha* (Wisconsin) *Telegraph*, June 7, 1860, http://www.newspaperarchive.com/PdfViewerTags.aspx?img =53892465&firstvisit=true&src=search&currentResult=0&currentPage=0&fpo =False (accessed October 3, 2010); *Racine* (Wisconsin) *Daily Journal*, June 11, 1860, http://www.newspaperarchive.com/PdfViewerTags.aspx?img=5327974 1&firstvisit=true&src=search&currentResult=1&currentPage=0&fpo=False (accessed 3 October 2010).

5. "Thrilling Episode from the Life of Abe Lincoln," *Appleton* (Wisconsin) *Motor*, July 19, 1860, http://www.newspaperarchive.com/PdfViewerTags.aspx? img=6234118&firstvisit=true&src=search&currentResult=0&currentPage=0&fpo =False (accessed October 3, 2010).

6. The two that included the "Western man's" story were Joseph H. Barrett, *Life of Abraham Lincoln with a Condensed View of His Most Important Speeches* (Cincinnati: Moore, Wilstach, Keys, and Company, 1860), http:// archive.org/details/cu31924032777413 (accessed February 24, 2013); and David W. Bartlett, *The Life and Public Services of Hon. Abraham Lincoln: To Which Is Added a Biographical Sketch of Hon. Hannibal Hamlin* (New York: H. Dayton, Publisher, 1860), http://archive.org/details/lifeandpublicser00 bartrich (accessed October 1, 2010).

7. Bartlett, *Life and Public Services of Hon. Abraham Lincoln*, 110.

8. "[A] ball of shot or metal covered with leather, and a band of elastic or leather attached to such ball, and made so that the same could be attached to the wrist or arm of a person." *Geary v. State*, 108 S.W. 379 (Ct.Crim.App., Texas, 1908).

9. Bartlett, *Life of Lincoln*, 110–115.

10. *The Law Practice of Abraham Lincoln*, http://www.lawpracticeofabraham lincoln.org (accessed July 12, 2012).

11. Newton Bateman, Paul Selby, and Charles A. Martin, eds., *Historical Encyclopedia of Illinois and History of Cass County*, Vol. 2 (Chicago: Munsell Publishing Company, 1915), 692, http://archive.org/details/historicencyclop 02bate (accessed October 1, 2010).

12. J. N. Gridley, *Lincoln's Defense of Duff Armstrong: The Story of the Trial and the Celebrated Almanac* (Virginia, IL: Illinois State Historical Society reprint, 1910), 2, http://www.archive.org/details/lincolnsdefenseo00grid (accessed July 27, 2011).

13. Mrs. T. J. Schweer, "Abraham Lincoln and the Armstrong Case," Lincoln Collection, William E. Barton Papers 1780–1976, Box 39, Folder 9, Special Collections Research Center, University of Chicago Library (February 12, 1909).

14. William E. Barton, Personal Note, Lincoln Collection, William E. Barton Papers 1780–1976, Box 39, Folder 9, Special Collections Research Center, University of Chicago Library (September 28, 1920).

15. Beardstown Courthouse, Abraham Lincoln Online (2010), http://showcase. netins.net/web/creative/lincoln/sites/beards.htm (accessed January 17, 2013).

16. *Lincoln Courthouse and Museum Photos* (Beardstown, IL: The Old Lincoln Courtroom and Museum Commission, 2012), http://www.lincolnin beardstown.org/photos.html (accessed August 22, 2012).

CHAPTER 4

1. "A Sensation Story Spoilt," *Daily Illinois State Register*, June 26, 1860, *People v. Armstrong, LPAL,* http://www.lawpracticeofabrahamlincoln.org (accessed July 12, 2012).

2. Actually, Lincoln was a teetotaler. Douglas L. Wilson and Rodney O. Davis, eds., *Herndon's Informants: Letters, Interviews, and Statements about Lincoln* (Chicago: University of Illinois Press, 1998), 15, 73, 90.

3. Abram Bergen, "Personal Recollections of Abraham Lincoln as a Lawyer," *American Lawyer* 5 (1897): 212–215, 214, http://heinonline.org/HOL/ LandingPage?collection=journals&handle=hein.journals/amlyr5&div=108&id =&page= (accessed July 6, 2012).

4. Donald W. Olson and Russell Doescher, "Lincoln and the Almanac Trial," *Sky and Telescope,* August 1999, 187, http://media.skyandtelescope.com/ documents/Almanac_Trial.pdf (accessed August 5, 2011).

5. William T. Alderson and Kenneth K. Bailey, "Correspondence between Albert J. Beveridge and Jacob M. Dickinson on the Writing of Beveridge's Life of Lincoln," *Journal of Southern History* 20, no. 2 (May 1954): 210–237, 220.

6. Ward H. Lamon, *The Life of Abraham Lincoln from His Birth to His Inauguration as President* (Boston: James R. Osgood and Company, 1872), 328, http://archive.org/details/lifeofabrahamlin00lamouoft (accessed April 20, 2009).

7. Goldwyn Smith, *Lectures and Essays* (Toronto: Hunter, Rose, and Company, 1881), 257, http://archive.org/details/lecturesessays00smit (accessed April 16, 2009).

8. Newton Bateman, Paul Selby, and Charles A. Martin, eds., *Historical Encyclopedia of Illinois and History of Cass County*, Vol. 2 (Chicago: Munsell Publishing Company, 1915), 691, http://archive.org/details/historicencyclop 02bate (accessed October 1, 2010).

9. James L. King, "Lincoln's Skill as a Lawyer," *North American Review* 166, n. 495 (February 1898): 186–195, 195, http://www.jstor.org/pss/25118955 (accessed July 9, 2010).

10. King, "Lincoln's Skill as a Lawyer," 193.

11. Bergen, "Personal Recollections of Lincoln as a Lawyer," 212–215, 214.

12. "Lincoln's Almanac," *Waterloo* (Iowa) *Courier*, November 10, 1886, http://www.newspaperarchive.com/PdfViewerTags.aspx?img=88428377&firstvisit =true&src=search&currentResult=0&currentPage=0&fpo=False (accessed May 13, 2009).

13. Albert J. Beveridge, *Abraham Lincoln 1809–1858*, Vol. 2 (Boston: Houghton Mifflin Company, 1928), 274n2.

14. "An Almanac with a History," *Alton* (Illinois) *Evening Telegraph*, May 19, 1896, http://www.newspaperarchive.com/PdfViewerTags.aspx? img=117617543&firstvisit=true&src=search&currentResult=0&currentPage =0&fpo=False (accessed January 9, 2008).

15. Walter B. Stevens, *A Reporter's Lincoln* (St. Louis: Missouri Historical Society, 1916), http://www.archive.org/details/reporterslincoln00s (accessed September 30, 2010).

16. Beveridge, *Abraham Lincoln*, 274n2.

17. Lehrman Institute and the Lincoln Institute, "Ward H. Lamon," *Mr. Lincoln and Friends*, http://www.mrlincolnandfriends.org/inside_search.asp?pageID=44 &subjectID=3&searchWord=Ward%20%H.%20%Lamon (accessed June 11, 2012).

18. Lamon, *Life of Abraham Lincoln*.

19. Lamon, *Life of Abraham Lincoln*, 329n1.

20. Lamon, *Life of Abraham Lincoln*, 329n1.

21. James Ram, *A Treatise on Facts as Subjects of Inquiry by a Jury*, first American edition by John Townshend (New York: Baker, Voorhis and Co., Publishers, 1870), 243, http://archive.org/details/treatiseonfactsa00ramj (accessed June 8, 2012).

22. James Ram, *A Treatise on Facts as Subjects of Inquiry by a Jury*, fourth American edition by John Townshend and Charles F. Beach (New York: Baker, Voorhis and Co., Publishers, 1890), 269n1, 505.

CHAPTER 5

1. For example, Charles Godfrey Leland, *Abraham Lincoln and the Abolition of Slavery in the United States* (New York: G. P. Putnam's Sons, 1879), 61, http:// archive.org/details/abrahamlinc1595lela (accessed June 4, 2012).

2. For example, J. G. Holland, *The Life of Abraham Lincoln* (Springfield: Gurdon Bill, 1866), 16, http://archive.org/details/lifeofabraham00inholl (accessed June 4, 2012).

3. Ida M. Tarbell, "Lincoln's Important Law Cases," *McClure's Magazine*, Vol. 7 (New York: S. S. McClure Co., 1896), 272–281, 277, 278, http://archive .org/details/mccluresmagazinev7mccl (accessed December 17, 2012).

4. See, for example, George P. Costigan, *Cases and Other Authorities on Legal Ethics* (St. Paul: West Publishing Company, 1917), 352, http://archive.org/ details/casesandotherau00costgoog (accessed October 1, 2010); Silas G. Pratt, ed., *Lincoln in Story: The Life of the Martyr-President Told in Authenticated Anecdotes* (New York: D. Appleton and Company, 1901), 79, http://www .archive.org/details/lincolninstor2086prat (accessed April 20, 2009).

5. Joseph H. Barrett, *Abraham Lincoln and his Presidency*, Vol. 1 (Cincinnati: Robert Clarke Company, 1904), 153, http://archive.org/details/abehispresidency 01barrrich (accessed September 30, 2010); James L. King, "Lincoln's Skill as a Lawyer," *North American Review* 166, no. 495 (February 1898): 186–195, 195, http://www.jstor.org/pss/25118955 (accessed July 9, 2010).

6. *Cobb v. State*, 27 Ga. 648, 651 (1859); *Geary v. State*, 108 S.W. 379 (Ct.Crim.App. Texas, 1908).

7. Diagram Group, *Weapons: An International Encyclopedia from 5000 B.C. to 2000 A.D.* (New York: St. Martin's Press: 1980), 17.

8. *People v. Gudino*, 2008 WL 4368877 (Cal.Super.Ct.No. 07CM7087, September 26, 2008).

9. Author's personal experience.

10. David W. Bartlett, *The Life and Public Services of Hon. Abraham Lincoln: To Which Is Added a Biographical Sketch of Hon. Hannibal Hamlin* (New York: H. Dayton, Publisher, 1860), 110, http://archive.org/details/lifeandpublicser 00bartrich (accessed October 1, 2010).

11. J. G. Holland, *The Life of Abraham Lincoln* (Springfield: Gurdon Bill, 1866), 45, http://archive.org/details/lifeabrahamlinc02hollgoog (accessed October 1, 2010).

12. Holland, *Life of Abraham Lincoln*, 129.

13. Isaac N. Arnold, *The History of Abraham Lincoln and the Overthrow of Slavery* (Chicago: Clarke & Co., Publishers, 1866), 87, http://archive.org/ details/historyabrahaml01arnogoog (accessed June 11, 2012).

14. Harriett Beecher Stowe, *Men of Our Times: Or Leading Patriots of the Day* (Hartford: Hartford Publishing Company, 1868), 24, 25, http://archive .org/details/menourtimesorle01stowgoog (accessed April 16, 2009).

15. Ward H. Lamon, *The Life of Abraham Lincoln from His Birth to His Inauguration as President* (Boston: James R. Osgood and Company, 1872), 327, 328, http://archive.org/details/lifeofabrahamlin00lamouoft (accessed April 20, 2009).

16. Lamon, *Life of Abraham Lincoln*, 329n1.

17. J. B. McClure, ed., *Anecdotes of Abraham Lincoln and Lincoln's Stories* (Chicago: Rhodes and McClure, Publisher, http://archive.org/details/ anecdotesabraha00mcclgoog (accessed April 16, 2009).

18. *Abraham Lincoln and the Abolition of Slavery in the United States* (New York: G. P. Putnam's Sons, 1879), 61, http://archive.org/details/abraham linc1595lela (accessed June 4, 2012).

19. Goldwyn Smith, *Lectures and Essays* (Toronto: Hunter, Rose, and Company, 1881), 257, http://archive.org/details/lecturesessays00smit (accessed 16 April 2009).

20. We shall undertake a detailed analysis of Thayer's transcript in Chapter 11.

21. W. M. Thayer, *The Pioneer Boy, and How He became President: The Story of the Life of Abraham Lincoln* (London: Hodder and Stoughton, 1882), 238–245, http://archive.org/details/pioneerboyhow2070thay (accessed June 9, 2012).

22. *The Life of Abraham Lincoln* (Chicago: Jansen, McClurg, and Company, 1885), 87, http://archive.org/details/historyabrahaml01arnogoog (accessed April 20, 2009).

23. *Life of Abraham Lincoln*, 88.

24. Lehrman Institute and the Lincoln Institute, "William O. Stoddard," *Mr. Lincoln and Friends,* http://www.mrlincolnandfriends.org/inside.asp?pageID=96&subjectID=9 (accessed June 11, 2012).

25. William O. Stoddard, *Abraham Lincoln: The True Story of a Great Life, Showing the Inner Growth, Special Training, and Peculiar Fitness of the Man for His Work* (New York: Fords, Howard, and Hulbert, 1885), 165, http://archive.org/details/abrahamlincoln00unkngoog (accessed April 16, 2009).

26. Noah Brooks, *Abraham Lincoln: The Nation's Leader in the Great Struggle through which was Maintained the Existence of the United States* (New York: G.P. Putnam and Sons, 1888), 27, http://archive.org/details/abrahamlincolnn00broo (accessed October 1, 2010).

27. John Robert Irelan, *The Republic: Or, a History of the United States of America in the Administrations, from the Monarchic Colonial Days to the Present Times,* Vol. 16 (Chicago: Fairbanks and Palmer Publishing Company, 1888), 142, http://www.archive.org/details/republicorahist00irelgoog (accessed April 20, 2009).

28. Lehrman Institute and the Lincoln Institute, "William H. Herndon," *Mr. Lincoln and Friends,* http://www.mrlincolnandfriends.org/inside.asp?pageID=43&subjectID=3 (accessed June 11, 2012).

29. William H. Herndon and Jesse William Weik, *Herndon's Lincoln: The True Story of a Great Life,* Vol. 2 (Chicago: Belford, Clarke and Company, 1889), 357–359, http://archive.org/details/herndonslincoln02hernrich (accessed October 1, 2010).

30. Earnest Foster, *Abraham Lincoln* (London: Cassell & Company Limited, 1893), 58, http://archive.org/details/abrahamlincoln00fostgoog (accessed October 7, 2010).

31. Charles Wallace French, *Abraham Lincoln the Liberator: A Biographical Sketch* (New York: Funk and Wagnalls, 1891), 76, http://archive.org/details/abrahamlincolnl00frengoog (accessed August 3, 2011).

32. Charles Carleton Coffin, *Abraham Lincoln* (New York: Harper and Brothers Publishers, 1893), 163, http://archive.org/details/cu31924030983963 (accessed October 1, 2010).

33. *Lawyer Lincoln* (New York: Carroll and Graf Publishers, 2001/1936), 122, 123.

34. *The Real Abraham Lincoln: A Complete One-Volume History of His Life and Times* (Englewood Cliffs, NJ: Prentice Hall), 167.

35. Stephen B. Oates, *With Malice toward None: A Life of Abraham Lincoln* (New York: Harper Collins, 1994/1977), 141, 142.

36. *Lincoln* (New York: Simon and Schuster Paperbacks), 151.

37. *Moonlight: Abraham Lincoln and the Almanac Trial* (New York: St. Martin's Press), 51–55.

38. *A. Lincoln Esquire: A Shrewd, Sophisticated Lawyer in His Time* (Macon, GA: Mercer University Press, 2002), 157, 158.

39. *Creating Winning Trial Strategies and Graphics* (Chicago: American Bar Association), 84, 85.

40. *Abraham Lincoln: A Life,* Vol. 1 (Baltimore: Johns Hopkins University Press), 344, 345.

41. *Lincoln the Lawyer* (Chicago: University of Illinois Press), 118.

42. *A. Lincoln: A Biography* (New York: Random House), 245

43. *Lincoln's Counsel: Lessons from America's Most Persuasive Speaker* (Chicago: ABA Publishing, 2010), 50, 51.

44. *The Graysons: A Story of Illinois* (New York: Century Company, 1887), 300–309, http://archive.org/details/graysonsastoryi00egglgoog (accessed August 3, 2011).

45. Herndon and Weik, *Herndon's Lincoln,* 357fn.

46. For example, *A First Book in American History* (New York: American Book Company, 1899), http://archive.org/details/afirstbookiname01unkngoog (accessed December 12, 2012);*The Household History of the United States and its People: For Young Americans* (New York: D. Appleton and Company, 1901), http://archive.org/details/householdhistor01egglgoog (accessed December 22, 2012); *The Transit of Civilization from England to America in the Seventeenth Century* (New York: D. Appleton and Company, 1901), http://archive.org/details/transitciviliza01egglgoog (accessed December 23, 2012); *The Beginners of a Nation: A History of the Source and Rise of the Earliest English Settlements in America with Special Reference to the Life and Character of the People* (New York: D. Appleton and Company, 1914), http://archive.org/details/beginnersanatio03egglgoog (accessed December 22, 2012).

47. The trial was fictionalized at least twice more. Mary Hazelton Wade told the story of the trial in *Abraham Lincoln: A Story and a Play* (Boston: Gorham Press, 1914), http://archive.org/details/abrahamlincolna00wadegoog (accessed September 30, 2010), as did the John Ford movie *Young Mr. Lincoln* (1939). In both stories Lincoln obtains an acquittal by the dramatic use of an almanac during the cross-examination of his client's principal accuser.

CHAPTER 6

1. Douglas L. Wilson and Rodney O. Davis, eds., *Herndon's Informants: Letters, Interviews, and Statements about Lincoln* (Chicago: University of Illinois Press, 1998), xx, xxi.

2. Lehrman Institute and the Lincoln Institute, "Ward Hill Lamon," http://www.mrlincolnandfriends.org/inside_search.asp?pageID=44&subjectID=3&searchWord=William%20%Herndon (accessed June 11, 2012).

3. Arthur L. Lowrie, *Ida M. Tarbell: Investigative Journalist Par Excellence* (Meadville, PA: Pelletier Library of Allegheny College, 1997), http://tarbell.allegheny.edu/biobib.html (accessed July 3, 2012).

4. See, for example, "Lincoln's Important Law Cases," *McClure's Magazine,* Vol. 7 (New York: S.S. McClure Co., 1896), 273–280, http://archive.org/details/mccluresmagazinev7mccl (accessed August 6, 2011).

5. *The Life of Abraham Lincoln: Drawn from Original Sources and Containing Many Speeches, Letters, and Telegrams Hitherto Unpublished and Illustrated with Many Reproductions from Original Paintings, Photographs, etc.* (New York: Lincoln History Society, 1907), Volume 1, http://archive.org/details/cu31924092901069; Volume 2, http://archive.org/details/cu31924092901077; Volume 3, http://archive.org/details/cu31924092901085; Volume 4, http://archive.org/details/cu31924092901093 (accessed December 17, 2012).

6. Lowrie, *Ida M. Tarbell."*

7. John Braeman, "Albert J. Beveridge and Demythologizing Lincoln," *Journal of the Abraham Lincoln Association* 25, no. 2 (Summer 2004): 1–24, 7, www.jstor.org/stable/20149061 (accessed September 7, 2010).

8. *The Life of Abraham Lincoln: Drawn from Original Sources and Containing Many Speeches, Letters, and Telegrams Hitherto Unpublished and Illustrated with Many Reproductions from Original Paintings, Photographs, etc.*, Vol. 2 (New York: Lincoln History Society, 1907), 66, 67, http://archive.org/details/cu31924092901077 (accessed August 6, 2011).

9. *The Life of Abraham Lincoln: Drawn from Original Sources and Containing Many Speeches, Letters, and Telegrams Hitherto Unpublished and Illustrated with Many Reproductions from Original Paintings, Photographs, etc.*, Vol. 2 (New York: Lincoln History Society, 1907), 66, 67, http://archive.org/details/cu31924092901077 (accessed August 6, 2011).

10. James L. King, "Lincoln's Skill as a Lawyer," *North American Review* 166, no. 495 (February 1898): 186–195, http://www.jstor.org/pss/25118955 (accessed July 9, 2010).

11. Abram Bergen, "Reminiscences of Abraham Lincoln as a Lawyer," *American Lawyer* 5 (1897): 212, 213, http://heinonline.org/HOL/LandingPage?collection=journals&handle=hein.journals/amlyr5&div=108&id=&page= (accessed July 6, 2012). See also Abram Bergen, "Abraham Lincoln as a Lawyer," *A.B.A. Journal* 12 (1926): 393, http://heinonline.org/HOL/LandingPage?collection=journals&handle=hein.journals/abaj12&div=110&id=&page= (accessed July 6, 2012).

12. T. G. Onstot, *Pioneers of Menard and Mason Counties* (Forest City, IL: T. G. Onstot, 1902), 13, http://archive.org/stream/pioneersofmenar00onst (accessed April 20, 2009).

13. John G. Nicolay and John Hay, *Complete Works of Abraham Lincoln*, Vol. 11 (New York: Francis D. Tandy Company, 1904), 297, http://archive.org/stream/completeworksofa11linc (accessed July 4, 2012).

14. (Dayton, OH: Press of United Brethren Publishing House, 1906), http://archive.org/stream/lincolnyearbookc00inlinc (accessed July 4, 2012).

15. (Dayton, OH: Otterbein Press, 1909), http://www.archive.org/details/footprintsofabra00inhobs (accessed October 10, 2010).

16. J. T. Hobson, *Footprints of Abraham Lincoln: Presenting Many Interesting Facts, Reminiscences and Illustrations Never Before Published* (Dayton, OH: Otterbein Press, 1909), 45, http://www.archive.org/details/footprintsofabra00inhobs (accessed October 10, 2010).

17. J. N. Gridley, *Lincoln's Defense of Duff Armstrong: The Story of the Trial and the Celebrated Almanac* (Virginia, IL: Illinois State Historical Society reprint, 1910), 6, 7, http://www.archive.org/details/lincolnsdefenseo00grid (accessed July 27, 2011).

18. Gridley, *Lincoln's Defense of Duff Armstrong*, 19.

19. Gridley, *Lincoln's Defense of Duff Armstrong*, 19.

20. Gridley, *Lincoln's Defense of Duff Armstrong*, 19, 23.

21. *Guide to the Lincoln Collection, William E. Barton Papers, 1780–1976*, Special Collections Research Center, University of Chicago Library, http://www.lib.uchicago.edu/e/scrc/findingaids/view.php?eadid=ICU.SPCL.BARTONWE (accessed May 5, 2013).

22. William E. Barton, *The Life of Abraham Lincoln* (Boston: Books, Inc., 1943/1925), 310–318.

23. S. Mendelsohn, *The Criminal Jurisprudence of the Ancient Hebrews: Compiled from the Talmud and Other Rabbinical Writings, and Compared with Roman and English Penal Jurisprudence* (Baltimore: M. Curlander, 1891), 135, 136, http://archive.org/stream/criminaljurispru00mend#page/n5/mode/2up (accessed January 13, 2013).

24. John Braeman, "Albert J. Beveridge and Demythologizing Lincoln," *Journal of the Abraham Lincoln Association,* Volume 25, No. 2 (Summer, 2004), 1–25, 23, www.jstor.org/stable/20149061 (accessed September 7, 2010).

25. Sandburg, Carl, *Abraham Lincoln: The Prairie Years*, Volume 2 (New York: Harcourt, Brace, and World, Inc., 1926), 56.

26. Ibid, 57.

27. Braeman, "Albert J. Beveridge and Demythologizing Lincoln," 1–25, 3.

28. Braeman, "Albert J. Beveridge and Demythologizing Lincoln," 10.

29. William T. Alderson and Kenneth K. Bailey, "Correspondence between Albert J. Beveridge and Jacob M. Dickinson on the Writing of Beveridge's Life of Lincoln," *Journal of Southern History* 20, no. 2 (May, 1954): 210–237, 220, www.jstor.org/stable/10.2307/2954915 (accessed September 7, 2010).

30. *Abraham Lincoln, 1809–1858*, Vol. 2 (Boston: Houghton Mifflin Company, 1928), 273, 274.

31. *Abraham Lincoln, 1809–1858*, 263n2. His sources included the Armstrong case file, J. Henry Shaw, William Walker, Judge James Harriot, Abram Bergen, John Armstrong, George T. Saunders, and J. N. Gridley's article on the case.

32. *Abraham Lincoln, 1809–1858*, 268.

33. *The Art of Cross Examination* (New York: The Macmillan Company, 1908), 56–58, http://www.archive.org/details/artcrossexamina00wellgoog (accessed July 27, 2011).

34. Francis L. Wellman, *The Art of Cross Examination*, 4th ed. (New York: Macmillan Company, 1944), 59. In attempting to set the record straight, however, Wellman has Lincoln confronting the witness with a calendar, which is hardly an improvement on Donovan's version.

35. Godfrey Rathbone Benson Charnwood, *Abraham Lincoln* (London: Constable and Company, 1921/1916), 106, http://archive.org/details/abraham 00char (accessed July 11, 2012).

36. Emil Ludwig, *Lincoln*, Eden Paul and Cedar Paul, translators (Boston: Little, Brown, and Company, 1930), 192.

37. *Lincoln the Lawyer* (New York: Century Company, 1913/1905), http://www.archive.org/details/lincolnlawyer00hillgoog (accessed August 3, 2011).

38. *Lincoln the Lawyer*, 233n1.

39. (New York: Carroll and Graf Publishers, 2001/1930), 122, 123.

40. (New York: Rinehart and Company, 1960).

41. (Chicago: University of Illinois Press, 2009), 118.

CHAPTER 7

1. Abraham Lincoln, *The Autobiography of Abraham Lincoln* (New York: Francis D. Tandy Company, 1905), 8.

2. Douglas L. Wilson and Rodney O. Davis, *Herndon's Informants: Letters, Interviews, and Statements about Abraham Lincoln* (Chicago: University of Illinois Press, 1998), 11.

3. Wilson and Davis, *Herndon's Informants*, 457.

4. Jason Emmerson, *Lincoln the Inventor* (Carbondale: Southern Illinois University Press, 2009), 5–8.

5. Ward H. Lamon, *The Life of Abraham Lincoln from His Birth to His Inauguration as President* (Boston: James R. Osgood and Company, 1872), 88, 89, http://archive.org/details/lifeofabrahamlin00lamouoft (accessed December 13, 2012).

6. Norman Hapgood, *Abraham Lincoln: The Man of the People* (New York: Macmillan Company, 1899), 186, http://archive.org/details/abrahamlincolnm 02hapggoog (accessed December 8, 2012).

7. *Kentucky Barrels, LLC*, http://www.kentuckybarrels.com/RainBarrels.html (accessed December 8, 2012).

8. John G. Sotos, *The Physical Lincoln: Finding the Genetic Cause of Abraham Lincoln's Height, Homeliness, Pseudo-Depression, and Imminent Cancer Death* (Mt. Vernon, VA: Mt. Vernon Book Systems, 2008), 282n.e79.

9. Lamon, *Life of Abraham Lincoln*, 154.

10. The chimes are the lips on the top and bottom of a barrel formed by the staves overlapping the lids.

11. Wayne Whipple, *The Story of Young Abraham Lincoln* (Philadelphia: Henry Altemus Company, 1915), 113–114, http://archive.org/details/storyof younga1978whip (accessed December 11, 2012).

12. William M. Thayer, *The Pioneer Boy and How He Became President* (Boston: H.B. Fuller and Company, 1868), 249–253, http://archive.org/details/ pioneerboyhow2070thay (accessed December 11, 2012).

13. Wilson and Davis, *Herndon's Informants*, 387.

14. Wilson and Davis, *Herndon's Informants*, 7, 13.

15. Randall J. Strossen, "Mike Jenkins Wins the Arnold Strongman," *Ironmind,* March 4, 2012, http://www.ironmind.com/ironmind/opencms/ Articles/2012/Mar/Mike_Jenkins_Wins_the_Arnold_Strongman.html (accessed December 12, 2012).

16. Lamon, *Life of Abraham Lincoln*, 154. We find Lincoln's feat much easier to believe in light of the fact that the modern world record for the harness lift is 3,515 pounds. Thom Van Vleck, "Harness Lift, Part 1," *USAWA: United States All-Around Weightlifting Association,* May 5, 2010, http://www.usawa.com/ harness-liftingpart-1/ (accessed December 12, 2012).

17. For example, Ida N. Tarbell, *The Life of Abraham Lincoln Drawn from Original Sources*, Vol. 1 (New York: Lincoln History Society, 1907), 62, 63, http://archive.org/details/lifeabrahamlinc01tarbgoog (accessed December 13, 2012).

18. T. G. Onstot, *Pioneers of Menard and Mason Counties* (Peoria, IL: J. W. Franks and Sons, 1902), 81, 82, http://archive.org/details/pioneersofmenar 00onst (accessed December 14, 2012).

19. Lamon, *Life of Abraham Lincoln*, 83, 84.

20. John G. Nicolay and John Hay, *Abraham Lincoln: A History*, Vol. 1 (New York: The Century Company, 1890), 79, http://archive.org/details/ abrahamlincolna07haygoog (accessed December 13, 2012).

21. William Litt, *Wrestliana: An Historical Account of Ancient and Modern Wrestling* (Whitehaven: Michael and William Alsop, 1860), 18, http://archive. org/details/wrestlianahistor00litt (accessed December 14, 2012).

22. Lamon, *Life of Abraham Lincoln*, 83, 84, 92, 93, 110; Nicolay and Hay, *Abraham Lincoln*, 132; Wilson and Davis, *Herndon's Informants*, 19, 439, 451; Douglas L. Wilson, *Honor's Voice: The Transformation of Abraham Lincoln* (New York: Vintage Books, 1998), 26–30.

23. *The American Almanac, Year-Book, Cyclopaedia, and Atlas*, Vol. 2 (New York, Chicago, and San Francisco: New York American Journal, Hearst's Chicago American, and San Francisco Examiner, 1904), 704; Litt, *Wrestliana,* 18; Jacob Robinson and Sidney Gilpin, *Wrestling and Wrestlers: Biographical Sketches of Celebrated Athletes of the Northern Ring* (London: Bemrose and Sons, 1893), xlvi, xlvii, http://archive.org/details/wrestlingwrestle00robiiala (accessed December 14, 2012).

24. Wilson, *Honor's Voice*, 30.

25. Edgar Lee Masters, *The Sangamon* (Chicago: University of Illinois Press, 1988/1942), 154.

26. Sotos, *Physical Lincoln*, 50.

27. Harriett Beecher Stowe, *Men of Our Times: Or, Leading Patriots of the Day* (Hartford: Hartford Publishing Co., 1868), 58, http://archive.org/details/ menourtimesorle01stowgoog (accessed December 14, 2012).

28. William H. Herndon and Jesse Weik, *Abraham Lincoln: The True Story of a Great Life*, Vol. 1 (New York: D. Appleton and Company, 1913), 74, http:// archive.org/details/abrahamlincolnt01weikgoog (accessed December 15, 2012).

29. Tarbell, *Life of Abraham Lincoln*, 62, 63.

30. Noah Brooks, *Abraham Lincoln: The Nation's Leader in the Great Struggle through Which Was Maintained the Existence of the United States* (New York: G. P. Putman's Sons, 1888), 50, 51, http://archive.org/details/abrahamlincolnn00broo (accessed December 15, 2012).

31. Lamon, *Life of Abraham Lincoln*, 92, 93.

32. Wilson and Davis, *Herndon's Informants*, 80, 369.

33. J. G. Holland, *The Life of Abraham Lincoln* (Springfield, MA: Gurdon Bill, 1866), 44, 45, http://archive.org/details/lifeabrahamlinc02hollgoog (accessed December 15, 2012).

34. Wilson, *Honor's Voice*, 29, 31.

35. W. D. Howells, *Life of Abraham Lincoln* (Springfield, IL: Abraham Lincoln Association, 1938/1860), xii, http://archive.org/details/lifeofabrahamlin00howe (accessed December 19, 2012).

36. Howells, *Life of Abraham Lincoln*, 33–35.

37. This reconstruction is heavily indebted to the extensive study of the bout done by Douglas L. Wilson in *Honor's Voice*, 19–51.

38. This reconstruction has the virtue of adhering as closely as possible to the old legal maxim that "You should, if you can, reconcile all the testimony of all the witnesses so as to make them all speak the truth." *Jacksonville Electric Co. v. Sloan*, 52 Fla. 257, 42 So. 516, 519 (1908); *Atlantic Coast Line R. Co. v. Beazley*, 54 Fla. 311, 45 So. 761, 794 (1907).

39. Wilson, *Honor's Voice*, 20.

40. Howells, *Life of Abraham Lincoln*, 35.

41. Carl Sandburg, *Lincoln: The Prairie Years*, Vol. 1 (New York: Harcourt, Brace, and World, Inc., 1926), 154.

42. Howells, *Life of Abraham Lincoln*, 39.

43. The legend that Lincoln was torn between blacksmithing and lawyering has been pronounced a "humbug" by at least one person who knew the young Lincoln. Wilson and Davis, *Herndon's Informants*, 373.

44. For example, William H. Townsend, *Lincoln the Litigant* (Boston: Houghton Mifflin and Company, 1925); Howells, *Life of Abraham Lincoln*, 20, 31.

45. Caroline Owsley Brown, "Springfield Society before the Civil War," *Journal of the Illinois State Historical Society* (1908–1984) 15, no. 1/2 (April–July 1922): 477–500, 490, http://www.jstor.org/stable/40186857 (accessed December 21, 2012).

46. Anonymous, Statement: It has been said that the wife of Armstrong . . . *The Documents of Ida M. Tarbell: The Ida M. Tarbell Collection of Lincolniana: Correspondence, Research Materials, Writings, etc. about Abraham Lincoln*, Allegheny College, July 23, 2012, https://dspace.allegheny.edu/handle/10456/30457 (accessed December 28, 2012).

47. T. H. Stone, Letter to Ida M. Tarbell, February 12, 1896, *The Documents of Ida M. Tarbell*, August 8, 2012.

CHAPTER 8

1. The census declined from 67,643 to 61,351. Mark Galli, "Revival at Cane Ridge," *Christian History and Biography* 45 (January 1, 1995), http://www.christianitytoday.com/ch/1995/issue45/4509.html (accessed December 28, 2012).

2. Nathan Bangs, *A History of the Methodist Episcopal Church*, Vol. 2 (New York: T. Mason and G. Lane, 1839), 101–104, http://archive.org/details/ahistorymethodi00banggoog (accessed December 28, 2012).

3. Bangs, *History of the Methodist Episcopal Church*, 104, 105.

4. Peter Cartwright, *Autobiography of Peter Cartwright: The Backwoods Preacher* (New York: Carlton and Porter, 1857), 30, 31, http://archive.org/details/autobiographype01cartgoog (accessed December 30, 2012).

5. David L. Goetz, "Christianity on the Early American Frontier: A Gallery of Trendsetters in the Religious Wilderness," *Christian History and Biography* 45 (January 1, 1995), http://www.christianitytoday.com/ch/1995/issue45/4526.html (accessed December 28, 2012).

6. Timothy K. Beougher, "Camp Meetings and Circuit Riders: Did You Know?" *Christian History and Biography* 45 (January 1, 1995), http://www.christianitytoday.com/ch/1995/issue45/4508.html (accessed December 28, 2012).

7. R. W. Gorham, *Camp Meeting Manual: A Practical Book for the Campground in Two Parts* (Boston: H. V. Degen, 1854), 121–135, http://archive.org/details/campmeetingmanu00gorhgoog (accessed January 6, 2013).

8. Daniel W. Stowell, "Murder at a Methodist Camp Meeting: The Origins of Abraham Lincoln's Most Famous Trial," *Journal of the Illinois State Historical Society* 101, no. 3–4 (2008): 221, http://www.jstor.org/discover/10.2307/40204737?uid=3739600&uid=2&uid=4&uid=3739256&sid=21101628515497 (accessed January 6, 2013).

9. Gorham, *Camp Meeting Manual*, 121–135.

10. Cartwright, *Autobiography of Peter Cartwright*, 34–38.

11. "Peter Cartwright, 1785–1872," *Mr. Lincoln and Friends*, http://www.mrlincolnandfriends.org/inside.asp?pageID=98&subjectID=10 (accessed January 6, 2013).

12. Doris Kearns, *Team of Rivals: The Political Genius of Abraham Lincoln* (New York: Simon and Schuster, 2005), 209.

13. Stowell, "Murder at a Methodist Camp Meeting," 219–234, 221.

14. "Peter Cartwright, 1785–1872."

15. Emil Ludwig, *Lincoln*, Eden Paul and Cedar Paul, translators (Boston: Little, Brown, and Company, 1930), 190.

16. Stowell, "Murder at a Methodist Camp Meeting," 219–234, 225.

17. *Daily Illinois State Journal*, September 9, 1857, *People v. Armstrong, LPAL,* http://www.lawpracticeofabrahamlincoln.org (accessed July 12, 2012).

18. Daniel W. Stowell, "Moonlight Offers Little Light," *Journal of the Abraham Lincoln Association* 24, no. 1 (Winter 2003): 66–74, 72, http://www.jstor.org/stable/20149041 (accessed July 7, 2010).

19. *Curtenius v. Wheeler*, 10 Ill. 462 (1849).

20. "Lincoln's Famous Case: Duff Armstrong's Story of His Own Murder Trial," *New York Sun*, June 7, 1896, *People v. Armstrong, LPAL,* http://www.lawpracticeofabrahamlincoln.org (accessed July 12, 2012).

21. Walter B. Stevens, *A Reporter's Lincoln* (St. Louis: Missouri Historical Society, 1916), 19, 20, http://www.archive.org/details/reporterslincoln00s (accessed September 30, 2010).

22. "Lincoln's Almanac: The True Inwardness of a Story That Has Been Told Time and Again," *Waterloo* (Iowa) *Courier*, November 10, 1886, http://newspaperarchive.com/waterloo-courier/1886-11-10/page-6?tag=duff+armstrong&rtserp=tags/duff-armstrong?py=1860&pey=1900 (accessed June 14, 2012); Ida M. Tarbell, *The Life of Abraham Lincoln: Drawn from Original Sources and Containing Many Speeches, Letters, and Telegrams Hitherto Unpublished and Illustrated with Many Reproductions from Original Paintings, Photographs, etc.*, Vol. 2 (New York: Lincoln History Society, 1907), 65, http://archive.org/details/cu31924092901077 (accessed December 17, 2012); J. T. Hobson, *Footprints of Abraham Lincoln: Presenting Many Interesting Facts, Reminiscences and Illustrations Never Before Published* (Dayton, OH: Otterbein Press, 1909), 48, 49, http://www.archive.org/details/footprintsofabra00inhobs (accessed October 10, 2010).

23. Douglas L. Wilson and Rodney O. Davis, eds., *Herndon's Informants: Letters, Interviews, and Statements about Lincoln* (Chicago: University of Illinois Press, 1998).

24. Finding Guide for the Papers of Ida N. Tarbell, Special Collections, Pelletier Library, Allegheny College (April 13, 2004), http://webpub.allegheny.edu/employee/j/jwestenf/MS_Tarbell/Index.htm (accessed January 18, 2013).

25. Guide to the Lincoln Collection, William E. Barton Papers 1780–1976, University of Chicago Library, Special Collections Research Center (2009), http://www.lib.uchicago.edu/e/scrc/findingaids/view.php?eadid=ICU.SPCL.BARTONWE (accessed January 18, 2013).

26. James Norris Pardon Papers, Illinois Digital Archives, http://www.idaillinois.org/cdm/compoundobject/collection/isa/id/2707 (accessed January 17, 2013).

27. John Armstrong, Speech, *Lincoln Centennial Association Addresses: Delivered at the Annual Banquet Held at Springfield, Illinois, February Twelfth Nineteen Hundred and Twelve, Commemorating the One Hundred and Third Anniversary of the Birth of Abraham Lincoln* (Springfield: Abraham Lincoln Association, 1912), 59, 60, http://archive.org/details/lincolncentennia00lodg (accessed June 12, 2012); Carl Sandburg, *Abraham Lincoln: The Prairie Years*, Vol. 2 (New York: Harcourt, Brace, and World, Inc., 1926), 55, 56.

28. Nelson Bateman, Paul Selby, and Charles E. Martin, eds., *Historical Encyclopedia of Illinois and History of Cass County*, Vol. 2 (Chicago: Munsell Publishing Company, 1915), http://archive.org/details/lincolncentennia00lodg (accessed January 6, 2013).

29. The "reach" is the pole that runs under the wagon and connects the front and rear axles.

30. J. N. Gridley, *Lincoln's Defense of Duff Armstrong: The Story of the Trial and the Celebrated Almanac* (Virginia, IL: Illinois State Historical Society reprint, 1910), 21, http://www.archive.org/details/lincolnsdefenseo00grid (accessed July 27, 2011).

31. Gridley, *Lincoln's Defense of Duff Armstrong.*

32. John J. Duff, *A. Lincoln: Prairie Lawyer* (New York: Rinehart and Company, Inc., 1960), 356; Reinhard H. Luthin, *The Real Abraham Lincoln: A Complete One Volume History of His Life and Times* (Englewood Cliffs, NJ: Prentice-Hall, Inc., 1960), 167.

33. Luthin, *Real Abraham Lincoln,* 700.

34. Allen D. Spiegel, *A. Lincoln Esquire: A Shrewd, Sophisticated Lawyer in His Time* (Macon, GA: Mercer University Press, 2002), 158.

35. Gridley, *Lincoln's Defense of Duff Armstrong,* 6, 7.

36. Wilson and Davis, *Herndon's,* 332–334.

37. "Buffalo Chips," *The Compact Edition of the Oxford English Dictionary,* Vol. 1 (New York: Oxford University Press, 1971), 1157.

38. John T. Brady, Letter to J. McCan Davis, May 23, 1896, *The Ida M. Tarbell Collection of Lincolniana* (March 22, 2013), https://dspace.allegheny.edu/handle/10456/33821 (accessed April 12, 2013).

39. "Lincoln's Almanac."

40. Bateman, Selby, and Martin, *Historical Encyclopedia of Illinois and History of Cass County,* 688.

41. George P. Costigan, *Cases and Other Authorities on Legal Ethics* (St. Paul: West Publishing Company, 1917), 352, http://archive.org/details/casesandotherau00costgoog (accessed October 1, 2010); Wayne Whipple, *The Story Life of Lincoln* (Philadelphia: John C. Winston Company, 1908), 264, http://archive.org/details/storylifelincol02whipgoog (accessed March 8, 2013).

42. Daniel W. Stowell et al., eds., *The Papers of Abraham Lincoln: Legal Documents and Cases,* Vol. 4 (Charlottesville: University of Virginia Press, 2008), 39, 40.

CHAPTER 9

1. "You, as foreman to this inquest, do solemnly swear that you will diligently inquire, and true presentment make, how, in what manner, and by whom or what, the body which here lies dead, came to its death; and that you will deliver to me, the coroner of this county, a true inquest thereof according to such evidence as shall be given you, and according to the best of your knowledge and belief: so help you God." N. H. Purple, *A Compilation of the Statutes of the State of Illinois of a General Nature* (Chicago: Keene and Lee, Booksellers, 1856), 1122, *LPAL,* http://www.lawpracticeofabrahamlincoln.org/Reference.aspx?ref=Reference%20html%20files/index%20for%20statutes.html (accessed February 21, 2013).

2. Daniel W. Stowell et al., eds., *The Papers of Abraham Lincoln: Legal Documents and Cases*, Vol. 4 (Charlottesville: University of Virginia, 2008), 40.

3. Stowell, *Papers of Abraham Lincoln*, 2.

4. Purple, *Compilation of the Statutes of the State of Illinois*, 654.

5. Richard Ritter, Transcript, *People v. Norris and Armstrong*, April 15, 1858, *LPAL*, http://www.lawpracticeofabrahamlincoln.org (accessed July 12, 2012).

6. "You, as foreman of this inquest, do solemnly swear (or affirm, as the case may be), that you will diligently inquire into, and true presentment make, of all such matters and things which should be given you in charge, or shall otherwise come to your knowledge touching the present service; you shall present no person through malice, hatred or ill will; nor shall you leave any unpresented through fear, favor or affection, or for any fee or reward, or for any hope or promise thereof; but in all your presentments, you shall present the truth, the whole truth, and nothing but the truth, according to the best of your skill and understanding: So help you God." Purple, *A Compilation of the Statutes of the State of Illinois*, 654.

7. Stowell, *Papers of Abraham Lincoln*, 3n10.

8. Joseph Cochrane, *Centennial History of Mason County* (Springfield, IL: Rokker's Steam Printing House, 1876), 204, http://archive.org/details/centennialhisto00cochgoog (accessed March 9, 2013).

9. John Armstrong, Speech, *Lincoln Centennial Association Addresses: Delivered at the Annual Banquet Held at Springfield, Illinois, February Twelfth Nineteen Hundred and Twelve, Commemorating the One Hundred and Third Anniversary of the Birth of Abraham Lincoln* (Springfield, IL: Abraham Lincoln Association, 1912), 59, http://archive.org/details/lincolncentennia00lodg (accessed June 12, 2012).

10. Stowell, *Papers of Abraham Lincoln*, 7n19.

11. Henry J. Aten, *History of the 85th Illinois Regiment Illinois Volunteer Infantry* (Hiawatha, KS: Regimental Association, 85th Illinois Volunteers, 1901), 333, 334, http://archive.org/details/historyofeightyf00aten (accessed March 9, 2013).

12. Stowell, *Papers of Abraham Lincoln*, 8n21.

13. William Armstrong, Affidavit, *People v. Norris and Armstrong*, November 5, 1857, *LPAL*, http://www.lawpracticeofabrahamlincoln.org (accessed July 12, 2012).

14. John J. Duff, *A. Lincoln: Prairie Lawyer* (New York: Rinehart and Company, Inc., 1960), 352.

15. James H. Norris, Letter to Governor Richard Yates, February 22, 1863, http://www.idaillinois.org/cdm/compoundobject/collection/isa/id/2707/rec/1 (accessed February 22, 2013).

16. William E. Barton, *The Life of Abraham Lincoln* (Boston: Books, Inc., 1943/1925), 311.

17. Barton, *Life of Abraham Lincoln*, 311.

18. William Walker, Letter to Governor Richard Yates, July 10, 1863, http://www.idaillinois.org/cdm/compoundobject/collection/isa/id/2707/rec/1 (accessed February 22, 2013).

19. Court Minutes, *People v. Norris and Armstrong*, October 31, 1857, *LPAL*, http://www.lawpracticeofabrahamlincoln.org (accessed July 12, 2012).

20. Dilworth and Campbell, Motion to Quash Indictment, *People v. Norris and Armstrong*, October 30, 1957, *LPAL*, http://www.lawpracticeofabraham lincoln.org (accessed July 12, 2012).

21. David Ott, Affidavit, *People v. Norris and Armstrong*, November 5, 1857, *LPAL*, http://www.lawpracticeofabrahamlincoln.org (accessed July 12, 2012).

22. Purple, *Compilation of the Statutes of the State of Illinois*, 654.

23. James McCowan, Affidavit, *People v. Norris and Armstrong*, November 5, 1857, *LPAL*, http://www.lawpracticeofabrahamlincoln.org (accessed July 12, 2012).

24. James Harriott, Judge's Docket, *People v. Norris and Armstrong*, November 5, 1857, *LPAL*, http://www.lawpracticeofabrahamlincoln.org (accessed July 12, 2012).

25. John H. Havinghorst and Hugh Fullerton, Indictment, *People v. Norris and Armstrong*, November 5, 1857, *LPAL*, http://www.lawpracticeofabraham lincoln.org (accessed July 12, 2012).

26. Purple, *Compilation of the Statutes of the State of Illinois*, 654.

27. Havinghorst and Fullerton, Indictment.

28. William Blackstone, *Commentaries on the Laws of England, Book the Fourth, of Public Wrongs* (Oxford: Clarendon Press, 1779), Appendix ii, iii, http://archive.org/details/lawsofenglandc04blacuoft (accessed February 22, 2013).

29. The witnesses were Grigsby Z. Metzker, Charles Allen, James P. Walker, William M. Hall, Joseph A. Douglas, William Douglas, B. F. Stephenson, Hamilton Rogers, William Killion, Joseph Speltz, and William Haines. Havinghorst and Fullerton, Indictment.

30. Ambrose Bierce, *The Devil's Dictionary* (New York: Dover Publishing Company, 1958/1911), 132.

31. Purple, *Compilation of the Statutes of the State of Illinois*, 362. The wording of Georgia's current murder statute is almost identical to the old Illinois law. O.C.G.A. § 16-5-1 (2012), http://www.lexisnexis.com/hottopics/gacode/Default .asp (accessed February 23, 2013).

32. Richard Ritter, Court Minutes, *People v. Norris and Armstrong*, November 5, 1858, *LPAL*, http://www.lawpracticeofabrahamlincoln.org (accessed July 12, 2012).

33. Purple, *Compilation of the Statutes of the State of Illinois*, 655.

34. Norris, Letter to Governor Richard Yates.

35. John Davis et al., Verdict, *People v. Norris and Armstrong*, November 7, 1858, *LPAL*, http://www.lawpracticeofabrahamlincoln.org (accessed July 12, 2012).

36. Richard Ritter, Transcript, *People v. Norris and Armstrong*, April 15, 1858, *LPAL*, http://www.lawpracticeofabrahamlincoln.org (accessed July 12, 2012).

37. Nelson Bateman, Paul Selby, and Charles E. Martin, eds., *Historical Encyclopedia of Illinois and History of Cass County*, Vol. 2 (Chicago: Munsell

Publishing Company, 1915), 688, http://archive.org/details/lincolncentennia 00lodg (accessed January 6, 2013).

38. J. N. Gridley, *Lincoln's Defense of Duff Armstrong: The Story of the Trial and the Celebrated Almanac* (Virginia, IL: Illinois State Historical Society reprint, 1910), 14, http://www.archive.org/details/lincolnsdefenseo00grid (accessed July 27, 2011).

39. Noah Brooks, *Abraham Lincoln: The Nation's Leader in the Great Struggle through Which Was Maintained the Existence of the United States* (New York: G. P. Putman's Sons, 1888), 128, http://archive.org/details/abrahamlincolnn00broo (accessed December 15, 2012); J. T. Hobson, *Footprints of Abraham Lincoln: Presenting Many Interesting Facts, Reminiscences and Illustrations Never Before Published* (Dayton, OH: Otterbein Press, 1909), 42, http://www.archive.org/details/footprintsofabra00inhobs (accessed October 10, 2010).

40. W. M. Thayer, *The Pioneer Boy, and How He Became President: The Story of the Life of Abraham Lincoln* (London: Hodder and Stoughton, 1882), 240, http://archive.org/details/pioneerboyhow2070thay (accessed June 9, 2012).

41. *The Lincoln Log: A Daily Chronology of the Life of Abraham Lincoln* (Illinois Historic Preservation Agency and the Abraham Lincoln Presidential Library and Museum, 2013), http://www.thelincolnlog.org/Home.aspx (accessed February 24, 2013).

42. *Lincoln Log.*

43. "Thrilling Episode from the Life of Abe Lincoln," *Appleton* (Wisconsin) *Motor*, July 19, 1860, http://www.newspaperarchive.com/PdfViewerTags.aspx ?img=6234118&firstvisit=true&src=search&currentResult=0&currentPage=0 &fpo=False (accessed October 3, 2010).

44. David W. Bartlett, *The Life and Public Services of Hon. Abraham Lincoln: To Which Is Added a Biographical Sketch of Hon. Hannibal Hamlin* (New York: H. Dayton, Publisher, 1860), 111, http://archive.org/details/lifeandpublicser 00bartrich (accessed October 1, 2010); Joseph H. Barrett, *Life of Abraham Lincoln with a Condensed View of His Most Important Speeches* (Cincinnati: Moore, Wilstach, Keys, and Company, 1860), http://archive.org/details/ cu31924032777413 (accessed February 24, 2013).

45. J. G. Holland, *The Life of Abraham Lincoln* (Springfield, IL: Gurdon Bill, 1866), 129, http://archive.org/details/lifeofabraham00inholl (accessed June 4, 2012); Harriett Beecher Stowe, *Men of Our Times: Or Leading Patriots of the Day* (Hartford: Hartford Publishing Company, 1868), 24, http://archive.org/ details/menourtimesorle01stowgoog (accessed April 16, 2009); Earnest Foster, *Abraham Lincoln* (London: Cassell & Company Limited, 1893), 57, http:// archive.org/details/abrahamlincoln00fostgoog (accessed October 7, 2010); Helen Nicolay, *The Boy's Life of Abraham Lincoln* (New York: Appleton-Century-Crofts, Inc., 1933/1905), 94; John T. Richards, *Abraham Lincoln: The Lawyer-Statesman* (Boston: Houghton Mifflin Company, 1916), 45, http:// archive.org/details/abrahamlincolnl01richgoog (accessed February 24, 2013); Mrs. T. J. Schweer, *History of Beardstown and Cass County* (Beardstown, IL:

Beardstown Public Schools, 1925), 15, http://archive.org/details/historyof beardst00schw (accessed February 24, 2013).

46. Hobson, *Footprints of Abraham Lincoln*, 41, 42.

47. J. Otis Humphreys, Introduction of John Armstrong, *Lincoln Centennial Association Addresses: Delivered at the Annual Banquet Held at Springfield, Illinois, February Twelfth Nineteen Hundred and Twelve, Commemorating the One Hundred and Third Anniversary of the Birth of Abraham Lincoln* (Springfield, IL: Abraham Lincoln Association, 1912), 57, http://archive.org/details/lincolncentennia00lodg (accessed June 12, 2012).

48. John Armstrong, Speech, *Lincoln Centennial Association Addresses: Delivered at the Annual Banquet Held at Springfield, Illinois, February Twelfth Nineteen Hundred and Twelve, Commemorating the One Hundred and Third Anniversary of the Birth of Abraham Lincoln* (Springfield, IL: Abraham Lincoln Association, 1912), 58–61, http://archive.org/details/lincolncentennia00lodg (accessed June 12, 2012).

49. Alonzo Rothschild, *Honest Abe: A Study in Integrity Based on the Early Life of Abraham Lincoln* (Boston: Houghton Mifflin Company, 1917), 344n31, http://archive.org/details/honestabestudy1258roth (accessed February 24, 2013).

50. Abraham Lincoln, *Collected Works of Abraham Lincoln*, Vol. 8, Roy P. Basler, ed. and Marion Dolores Pratt and Lloyd A. Dunlap, asst. eds. (New Brunswick, NJ: Rutgers University Press, 1953), 452, http://quod.lib.umich.edu/l/lincoln/lincoln8/1:875?rgn=div1;singlegenre=All;sort=occur;subview=detail;type=simple;view=fulltext;q1=hannah+armstrong (accessed January 17, 2013).

51. Reinhard H. Luthin, *The Real Abraham Lincoln: A Complete One Volume History of His Life and Times* (Englewood Cliffs, NJ: Prentice-Hall, Inc., 1960), 166.

52. Rothschild, *Honest Abe*, 344n31.

53. Brian Dirck, *Lincoln the Lawyer* (Chicago: University of Illinois Press, 2009), 117.

54. Michael Burlingame, *Abraham Lincoln: A Life*, Vol. 1 (Baltimore: Johns Hopkins University Press, 2008), 343.

55. Ida M. Tarbell, *The Life of Abraham Lincoln: Drawn from Original Sources and Containing Many Speeches, Letters, and Telegrams Hitherto Unpublished and Illustrated with Many Reproductions from Original Paintings, Photographs, etc.*, Vol. 2 (New York: Lincoln History Society, 1907), 65, http://archive.org/details/cu31924092901077 (accessed December 17, 2012).

56. Edgar Lee Masters, *Lincoln the Man* (Columbia, SC: Foundation for American Education, 1997/1931), 131.

57. Douglas L. Wilson and Rodney O. Davis, eds., *Herndon's Informants: Letters, Interviews, and Statements about Lincoln* (Chicago: University of Illinois Press, 1998), 482. I have inferred the identity of John Armstrong as Lincoln's putative son because he was the youngest son of Jack and Hannah Armstrong.

58. Wilson and Davis, *Herndon's Informants*, 527.

59. Dirck, *Lincoln the Lawyer*, 116.

60. John Mortimer, *The First Rumpole Omnibus* (New York: Penguin Books, 1983), 176.

61. Undated, Unsigned Order, *People of the State of Illinois v. William Frain,* *LPAL,* http://www.lawpracticeofabrahamlincoln.org (accessed July 12, 2012).

62. Abraham Lincoln, "The Trailor Murder Case" (1846), *The Collected Works of Abraham Lincoln,* Vol. 1, Roy P. Baisler, ed. (New Brunswick, NJ: Rutgers University Press, 1953), 371–376, http://archive.org/details/collected worksof015581mbp (accessed March 10, 2013).

CHAPTER 10

1. N. H. Purple, *A Compilation of the Statutes of the State of Illinois of a General Nature* (Chicago: Keene and Lee, Booksellers, 1856), 495, *LPAL,* http://www.lawpracticeofabrahamlincoln.org/Reference.aspx?ref=Reference%20html%20files/index%20for%20statutes.html (accessed February 21, 2013).

2. Ruth A. Gill, Bill of Divorce, *Ruth A. Gill v. Jonathan Gill,* Cass County Circuit Court, September 7, 1856, *LPAL,* http://www.lawpracticeofabraham lincoln.org (accessed July 12, 2012).

3. Jonathan Gill, Answer, *Ruth A. Gill v. Jonathan Gill,* Cass County Circuit Court, November 7, 1856, *LPAL,* http://www.lawpracticeofabrahamlincoln .org (accessed July 12, 2012).

4. Albert J. Beveridge, *Abraham Lincoln, 1809–1858,* Vol. 2 (Boston: Houghton Mifflin Company, 1928), 265; William H. Townsend, "Lincoln's Defense of Duff Armstrong," *American Bar Association Journal* 11 (1925): 81–84, 82, http://heinonline.org (accessed July 10, 2012).

5. John T. Brady, Letter to J. McCan Davis, May 23, 1896, *The Ida M. Tarbell Collection of Lincolniana* (March 22, 2013), https://dspace.allegheny.edu/handle/10456/33821 (accessed April 12, 2013).

6. William Henry Perrin, ed., *History of Cass County, Illinois* (Chicago: O. L. Baskin and Company, 1882), http://archive.org/details/historyofcasscou00perr (accessed March 9, 2013).

7. Edgar Lee Masters, *Lincoln the Man* (Columbia, SC: Foundation for American Education, 1997/1931), 131, 132.

8. Daniel W. Stowell et al., eds., *The Papers of Abraham Lincoln: Legal Documents and Cases,* Vol. 4 (Charlottesville: University of Virginia Press, 2008), 24.

9. *Jacksonville Electric Co. v. Sloan,* 52 Fla. 257, 42 So. 516, 519 (Fla. 1906).

10. James Taylor, Court Minutes, *People v. Armstrong,* Cass County Circuit Court, November 16, 1857, *LPAL,* http://www.lawpracticeofabrahamlincoln. org (accessed July 12, 2012).

11. James Taylor, Writ of Certiorari, *People v. Armstrong,* Cass County Circuit Court, November 17, 1857, *LPAL,* http://www.lawpracticeofabraham lincoln.org (accessed July 12, 2012).

12. R. Ritter, Transcript, *People v. Armstrong,* Mason County Circuit Court, April 15, 1858, *LPAL,* http://www.lawpracticeofabrahamlincoln.org (accessed July 12, 2012).

13. James Taylor, Court Minutes, *People v. Armstrong*, Cass County Circuit Court, November 19, 1857, *LPAL,* http://www.lawpracticeofabrahamlincoln .org (accessed July 12, 2012).

14. Taylor, Court Minutes, November 19, 1857.

15. Stowell et al., *Papers of Abraham Lincoln*, 40.

16. Earl Schenck Miers and William E. Baringer, *Lincoln Day by Day: A Chronology, 1809–1865*, Vol. 2 (Washington, DC: Lincoln Sesquicentennial Commission, 1960), 215, http://archive.org/stream/lincolndaybydayc02unit #page/n5/mode/2up (accessed March 11, 2013).

17. J. T. Hobson, *Footprints of Abraham Lincoln: Presenting Many Interesting Facts, Reminiscences and Illustrations Never Before Published* (Dayton, OH: Otterbein Press, 1909), 46, http://www.archive.org/details/footprintsof abra00inhobs (accessed October 10, 2010).

18. Albert J. Beveridge, *Abraham Lincoln, 1809–1858*, Vol. 2 (Boston: Houghton Mifflin Company, 1928), 265; John J. Duff, *A. Lincoln: Prairie Lawyer* (New York: Rinehart and Company, Inc., 1960), 354.

19. Stowell et al., *Papers of Abraham Lincoln*, 40.

20. David C. Rubin, Robert W. Schrauf, and Daniel L. Greenberg, "Belief and Recollection of Autobiographical Memories," *Memory & Cognition* 31, no. 6 (2003): 887–901, 894, http://link.springer.com/article/10.3758%2FBF03196 443?LI=true#page-1 (accessed March 11, 2013).

21. The witnesses who were summoned to appear were James P. Watkins, Joseph A. Douglas, William Douglas, William Haines, Joseph Spitts, Hamilton Rogers, William Killion, A.J. Killion, Andrew Killion, William P. Havens, Grigsby Z. Metzker, Charles Allen, Benjamin F. Stevenson, Hamilton Rogers, and Joseph Spelts. James Taylor, Subpoenas, *People v. Armstrong*, Cass County Circuit Court, April 23, 1857, *LPAL,* http://www.lawpracticeofabraham lincoln.org (accessed July 12, 2012).

22. We know this from a study of the witness payment affidavits executed by the witnesses on May 8, claiming six days per diem for their appearance. See, for example, A. J. Killion, Witness Payment Affidavit, *People v. Armstrong*, Cass County Circuit Court, May 8, 1858, *LPAL,* http://www.lawpracticeofabraham lincoln.org (accessed July 12, 2012).

23. J. N. Gridley, *Lincoln's Defense of Duff Armstrong: The Story of the Trial and the Celebrated Almanac* (Illinois State Historical Society reprint, 1910), 22, http://www.archive.org/details/lincolnsdefenseo00grid (accessed July 27, 2011).

24. I say this on the basis of my experience in having prepared thousands of witnesses to testify.

25. James Taylor, Subpoena, *People v. Armstrong*, Cass County Circuit Court, May 5, 1857, *LPAL,* http://www.lawpracticeofabrahamlincoln.org (accessed July 12, 2012).

26. James Taylor, Writ of Attachment, *People v. Armstrong*, Cass County Circuit Court, May 6, 1857, *LPAL,* http://www.lawpracticeofabrahamlincoln .org (accessed July 12, 2012).

27. Gridley, *Lincoln's Defense of Duff Armstrong*, 4; Nelson Bateman, Paul Selby, and Charles E. Martin, eds., *Historical Encyclopedia of Illinois and History of Cass County*, Volume 2 (Chicago: Munsell Publishing Company, 1915), 690, http://archive.org/details/lincolncentennia00lodg (accessed January 6, 2013).

28. John Husted, Endorsement on Writ of Attachment, *People v. Armstrong*, Cass County Circuit Court, May 6, 1857, *LPAL,* http://www.lawpracticeof abrahamlincoln.org (accessed July 12, 2012).

29. Nelson Bateman, Paul Selby, and Charles E. Martin, eds., *Historical Encyclopedia of Illinois and History of Cass County*, Vol. 2 (Chicago: Munsell Publishing Company, 1915), 690, http://archive.org/details/lincolncentennia 00lodg (accessed January 6, 2013).

30. John Husted, Statement to J. McCan Davis, June 5, 1896, *The Ida M. Tarbell Collection of Lincolniana* (March 22, 2013), https://dspace.allegheny. edu/handle/10456/33843 (accessed March 31, 29013).

31. Stowell et al., *Papers of Abraham Lincoln*, 41.

32. Jean Myers, "Justice Served: Abraham Lincoln and the Melissa Goings Case," (June 15, 2007), http://www.villageofmetamora.com/?hiscourt (accessed March 13, 2013).

33. Bateman, Selby, and Martin, *Historical Encyclopedia of Illinois and History of Cass County*, 691.

34. Abram Bergen, "Reminiscences of Abraham Lincoln as a Lawyer," *American Lawyer* 5 (1897): 212–215, 212, http://heinonline.org/HOL/Landing Page?collection=journals&handle=hein.journals/amlyr5&div=108&id=&page= (accessed July 6, 2012).

35. Duff, *A. Lincoln: Prairie Lawyer*, 354.

36. Ronald C. White, *A. Lincoln: A Biography* (New York: Random House: 2009), 244; Brian Dirck, *Lincoln the Lawyer* (Chicago: University of Illinois Press, 2009), 117; Albert Woldman, *Lawyer Lincoln* (New York: Carroll and Graf Publishers, 2001/1936), 122; Duff, *A. Lincoln: Prairie Lawyer*, 354; R. M. Wanamaker, *The Voice of Lincoln* (New York: Charles Scribner's Sons, 1920/ 1918), 104, http://archive.org/details/voiceoflinc2074wana (accessed March 17, 2013); Frederick Trevor Hill, *Lincoln the Lawyer* (New York: Century Company, 1913/1905), 232.

37. Ida M. Tarbell, *The Life of Abraham Lincoln: Drawn from Original Sources and Containing Many Speeches, Letters, and Telegrams Hitherto Unpublished and Illustrated with Many Reproductions from Original Paintings, Photographs, etc.*, Vol. 2 (New York: Lincoln History Society, 1907), 65, http:// archive.org/details/cu31924092901077 (accessed December 17, 2012).

38. J. McCan Davis, Notes of interview with William Douglas, *The Ida M. Tarbell Collection of Lincolniana* (March 22, 2013), https://dspace.allegheny .edu/handle/10456/33824 (accessed March 31, 2013).

39. "How Abraham Lincoln Selected the Jury in the Famous Almanac Trial," *Daily Pantagraph* (Bloomington, IL, February 12, 1927), Almanac Trial Papers,

wallet 3 of 5, The Papers of Abraham Lincoln, Abraham Lincoln Presidential Library, Springfield, IL.

40. Caleb Dilworth, Letter to J. McCan Davis, May 18, 1896, *The Ida M. Tarbell Collection of Lincolniana* (March 22, 2013), https://dspace.allegheny .edu/handle/10456/33789 (accessed March 27, 2013).

41. William Walker, Letter to J. McCan Davis, May 15, 1896, *The Ida M. Tarbell Collection of Lincolniana* (March 22, 2013), https://dspace.allegheny .edu/handle/10456/33752 (accessed March 27, 2013).

42. James C. Riley, "Estimates of Regional and Global Life Expectancy, 1800–2001," *Population and Development Review* 31, no. 3 (September, 2005): 537–543, 538, http://www.jstor.org/stable/3401478 (accessed March 18, 2013).

43. Tarbell, *Life of Abraham Lincoln*, 65.

44. Stowell et al., *Papers of Abraham Lincoln*, 39.

45. "Complete Sun and Moon Data for One Day," U.S. Naval Observatory (March 30, 2012), http://aa.usno.navy.mil/data/docs/RS_OneDay.php (accessed March 17, 2013).

46. Charles Allen et al., Witness Payment Affidavits, *People v. Armstrong*, Cass County Circuit Court, May 8, 1858, *LPAL,* http://www.lawpracticeof abrahamlincoln.org (accessed July 12, 2012).

47. John McCan Davis, "Manuscript: The Armstrong Trial," *The Ida M. Tarbell Collection of Lincolniana* (March 22, 2013), https://dspace.allegheny .edu/handle/10456/33829 (accessed March 24, 2013).

48. James L. King, "Lincoln's Skill as a Lawyer," *North American Review* 166, no. 495 (February 1898): 186–195, 195, http://www.jstor.org/pss/25118955 (accessed July 9, 2010).

49. Phil Berger, "Tyson Hurts Right Hand in Scuffle with a Boxer," *New York Times,* August 24, 1988, http://www.nytimes.com/1988/08/24/sports/tyson -hurts-right-hand-in-scuffle-with-a-boxer.html?n=Top%2fReference%2fTimes %20Topics%2fPeople%2fT%2fTyson%2c%20Mike (accessed March 25, 2013).

50. McCan Davis, "Manuscript: The Armstrong Trial."

CHAPTER 11

1. (1893), 6 R. 67 (H.L.).

2. *R. v. Lyttle*, [2004] 1 R.C.S. 193, 212, http://www.canlii.org/en/ca/scc/doc/ 2004/2004scc5/2004scc5.html (accessed February 20, 2013).

3. *Supreme and District Court Bench Book* (Queensland, Australia: Queens- land Courts, 2011), 32.1, http://www.canlii.org/en/ca/scc/doc/2004/2004scc5/ 2004scc5.html (accessed February 20, 2013).

4. John Evangelist Walsh, *Moonlight: Abraham Lincoln and the Almanac Trial* (New York: St. Martin's Press), 50–55.

5. *Peloponnesian War,* 1:22. Benjamin Jowett, trans., *Thucydides*, Vol. 1 (Oxford: Clarendon Press, 1900), 16, http://www.archive.org/details/thucydides 01thucuoft (accessed January 14, 2011).

6. Richard H. Underwood, "John Walsh, Moonlight: Abraham Lincoln and the Almanac Trial," *Northern Kentucky Law Review* 29, no. 2 (n.d.): 237–249, 241, 242, http://chaselaw.nku.edu/documents/law_review/v29/nklr_v29n2.pdf (accessed March 23, 2013).

7. *The Pioneer Boy, and How He Became President: The Story of the Life of Abraham Lincoln* (London: Hodder and Stoughton, 1882), 238–245, http://archive.org/details/pioneerboyhow2070thay (accessed June 9, 2012).

8. *Abraham Lincoln* (New York: Harper and Brothers Publishers, 1893), 163, http://archive.org/details/cu31924030983963 (accessed October 1, 2010).

9. *The Story Life of Abraham Lincoln: A Biography Composed of Five Hundred True Stories Told by Abraham Lincoln and His Friends* (Philadelphia: J. C. Winston Company, 1908), 261–265, http://archive.org/details/storylifeoflin 1967whip (accessed March 23, 2013).

10. *Abraham Lincoln* (New York: Harper and Brothers Publishers, 1893), 163, http://archive.org/details/cu31924030983963 (accessed October 1, 2010).

11. *Pioneer Boy,* 238–240.

12. *Story Life of Abraham Lincoln,* 263–265.

13. *Story Life of Abraham Lincoln,* 262, 263.

14. *Gospel Parallels: A Comparison of the Synoptic Gospels,* 5th ed. (Nashville: Thomas Nelson Publishers, 1995).

15. *Synopsis of the Four Gospels* (New York: United Bible Society, 1985).

16. G. Christopher Ritter, *Creating Winning Trial Strategies and Graphics* (Chicago: ABA Publishing, 2004), 84, 85.

17. Albert Woldman, *Lawyer Lincoln* (New York: Carroll and Graf Publishers, 2001/1936), 122, 123.

18. *Cedar Rapids* (Iowa) *Evening Gazette,* June 6, 1906, http://newspaperarchive.com/cedar-rapids-evening-gazette/1909-06-08/page-6?tag=milton+logan+lincoln+armstrong+almanac&rtserp=tags/milton-logan-lincoln-armstrong-almanac?pci=7 (accessed June 14, 2012).

19. Michael Burlingame, *Abraham Lincoln: A Life,* Vol. 1 (Baltimore: Johns Hopkins University Press, 2008), 345.

20. Ward H. Lamon, *The Life of Abraham Lincoln from His Birth to His Inauguration as President* (Boston: James R. Osgood and Company, 1872), 330, http://archive.org/details/lifeofabrahamlin00lamo (accessed December 13, 2012).

21. J. N. Gridley, *Lincoln's Defense of Duff Armstrong: The Story of the Trial and the Celebrated Almanac* (Illinois State Historical Society reprint, 1910), 18–22, http://www.archive.org/details/lincolnsdefenseo00grid (accessed July 27, 2011).

22. Gridley, *Lincoln's Defense of Duff Armstrong,* 18–22.

23. J. McCan Davis, Interview with William A. Douglas, *The Ida M. Tarbell Collection of Lincolniana* (March 22, 2013), https://dspace.allegheny.edu/handle/10456/33824?show=full (accessed March 27, 2013).

24. Joseph Benjamin Oakleaf, *Abraham Lincoln as a Criminal Lawyer* (Rock Island, IL: Augustana Book Concern, 1923), 6.

25. Joseph H. Barrett, *Abraham Lincoln and His Presidency*, Vol. 1 (Cincinnati: Robert Clark Company, 1904), 122, http://archive.org/details/abehispresidency01barrrich (accessed March 27, 2013).

26. Caleb Dilworth, Letter to J. McCan Davis, May 18, 1896, *The Ida M. Tarbell Collection of Lincolniana* (March 22, 2013), https://dspace.allegheny.edu/handle/10456/33789 (accessed March 27, 2013).

27. John Armstrong, Speech, *Lincoln Centennial Association Addresses: Delivered at the Annual Banquet Held at Springfield, Illinois, February Twelfth Nineteen Hundred and Twelve, Commemorating the One Hundred and Third Anniversary of the Birth of Abraham Lincoln* (Springfield, IL: Abraham Lincoln Association, 1912), 60, http://archive.org/details/lincolncentennia00lodg (accessed June 12, 2012).

28. "Lincoln's Famous Case: Duff Armstrong's Story of His own Murder Trial," *New York Sun*, June 7, 1896, *People v. Armstrong, LPAL*, http://www.lawpracticeofabrahamlincoln.org (accessed July 12, 2012).

29. Rule 3.220, Florida Rules of Criminal Procedure (2012).

CHAPTER 12

1. J. T. Hobson, *Footprints of Abraham Lincoln: Presenting Many Interesting Facts, Reminiscences and Illustrations Never Before Published* (Dayton, OH: Otterbein Press, 1909), 48, http://www.archive.org/details/footprintsofabra00inhobs (accessed October 10, 2010) (Letter: Lyman Lacey to Hobson, September 1, 1908).

2. David W. Bartlett, *The Life and Public Services of Hon. Abraham Lincoln: To Which Is Added a Biographical Sketch of Hon. Hannibal Hamlin* (New York: H. Dayton, Publisher, 1860), 113, http://archive.org/details/lifeandpublicser00bartrich (accessed October 1, 2010).

3. Ward H. Lamon, *The Life of Abraham Lincoln from His Birth to His Inauguration as President* (Boston: James R. Osgood and Company, 1872), 329, http://archive.org/details/lifeofabrahamlin00lamo (accessed December 13, 2012).

4. Lamon, *Life of Abraham Lincoln*, 329n.1.

5. William E. Barton, *The Life of Abraham Lincoln* (Boston: Books, Inc., 1943/1925), 312; J. N. Gridley, *Lincoln's Defense of Duff Armstrong: The Story of the Trial and the Celebrated Almanac* (Virginia, IL: Illinois State Historical Society reprint, 1910), 5, http://www.archive.org/details/lincolnsdefenseo00grid (accessed July 27, 2011).

6. "Complete Sun and Moon Data for One Day," U.S. Naval Observatory (March 30, 2012), http://aa.usno.navy.mil/data/docs/RS_OneDay.php (accessed March 28, 2013).

7. *Boatwright v. State*, 452 So.2d 666, 668 (4th DCA Fla. 1984).

8. *Jacksonville Electric Co. v. Sloan*, 52 Fla. 257, 42 So. 516, 519 (Fla. 1906).

9. Abram Bergen, "Reminiscences of Abraham Lincoln as a Lawyer," *American Lawyer* 5 (1897): 212–215, 214, http://heinonline.org/HOL/

LandingPage?collection=journals&handle=hein.journals/amlyr5&div=108&id
=&page= (accessed July 6, 2012).

10. Gridley, *Lincoln's Defense of Duff Armstrong*, 19.

11. *Iliad* 1:245–283.

12. Caleb Dilworth, Letter to J. McCan Davis, May 18, 1896, *The Ida M. Tarbell Collection of Lincolniana* (March 22, 2013), https://dspace.allegheny .edu/handle/10456/33789 (accessed March 27, 2013).

13. Wayne Whipple, *The Story Life of Lincoln* (Philadelphia: John C. Winston Company, 1908), 262, http://archive.org/details/storylifelincol02whipgoog (accessed March 8, 2013) (9:00–10:00); Earnest Foster, *Abraham Lincoln* (London: Cassell & Company Limited, 1893), 58, http://archive.org/details/ abrahamlincoln00fostgoog (accessed October 7, 2010) (9:30); Duncan Ferguson, "True Story of the Almanac Used by Abraham Lincoln in the Famous Trial of Duff Armstrong," *Journal of the Illinois State Historical Society* 15, no. 3/4 (October 1922), 688–691, 688, http://www.jstor.org/stable/40186950 (accessed January 6, 2012) (10:00); Ida M. Tarbell, *The Life of Abraham Lincoln: Drawn from Original Sources and Containing Many Speeches, Letters, and Telegrams Hitherto Unpublished and Illustrated with Many Reproductions from Original Paintings, Photographs, etc.*, Vol. 2 (New York: Lincoln History Society, 1907), 66, http://archive.org/details/cu31924092901077 (accessed December 17, 2012) (10:00–11:00); Albert J. Beveridge, *Abraham Lincoln, 1809–1858*, Vol. 2 (Boston: Houghton Mifflin Company, 1928), 268 (11:00).

14. Donald W. Olson and Russell Doescher, "Lincoln and the Almanac Trial," *Sky and Telescope*, August 1999, 186–188, 187, http://media.skyandtelescope .com/documents/Almanac_Trial.pdf (accessed August 5, 2011).

15. "Lincoln's Famous Case: Duff Armstrong's Story of His Own Murder Trial," *New York Sun*, June 7, 1896.

16. J. McCan Davis, Notes of interview with William Douglas, *The Ida M. Tarbell Collection of Lincolniana* (March 22, 2013), https://dspace.allegheny .edu/handle/10456/33824 (accessed March 31, 2013).

17. James P. O'Shea, Martin S. Banks, and Maneesh Agrawala. "The Assumed Light Direction for Perceiving Shape from Shading." *Proceedings of the 5th Symposium on Applied Perception in Graphics and Visualization*, 135–142, 136 (Association for Computing Machinery, 2008).

18. Rhiannon Thomas, Marko Nardini, and Denis Mareschal, "Interactions between 'Light-from-Above' and Convexity Priors in Visual Development," *Journal of Vision* 10, no. 8 (2010): 6, 1–7, 2, http://www.journalofvision.org/ content/10/8/6 (accessed September 13, 2012).

19. Charles Wallace French, *Abraham Lincoln the Liberator: A Biographical Sketch* (New York: Funk and Wagnalls, 1891), 76, http://archive.org/details/ abrahamlincolnl00frengoog (accessed August 3, 2011).

20. Michael Burlingame, *Abraham Lincoln: A Life*, Vol. 1 (Baltimore: Johns Hopkins University Press, 2008), 345.

21. Caleb J. Dilworth, Letter to J. McCan Davis, June 5, 1896, *The Ida M. Tarbell Collection of Lincolniana* (March 22, 2013), https://dspace.allegheny .edu/handle/10456/33942 (accessed March 31, 2013).

22. Standard 4-7.6(b), *American Bar Association Standards for Criminal Justice: The Defense Function* (Washington, DC: American Bar Association Criminal Justice Standards Committee, Criminal Justice Section, 1993), 223, http://www.americanbar.org/content/dam/aba/publications/criminal_justice _standards/prosecution_defense_function.authcheckdam.pdf (accessed March 31, 2013).

23. "Thrilling Episode from the Life of Abe Lincoln," *Janesville* (Wisconsin) *Gazette*, http://newspaperarchive.com/janesville-daily-gazette/1860-05-25/page -4?tag=janesville+gazette+thrilling+episode+lincoln&rtserp=tags/janesville -gazette-thrilling-episode-lincoln?psb=dateasc (accessed June 1, 2012).

24. Alan Dershowitz, *Letters to a Young Lawyer* (New York: Basic Books, 2001), 157.

25. J. McCan Davis, Manuscript: How the Almanac "Forgery" Was Discovered, n.d., *The Ida M. Tarbell Collection of Lincolniana* (March 22, 2013), https://dspace.allegheny.edu/handle/10456/33692 (accessed March 31, 2013); J. McCan Davis, Notes: Corrections for Almanac, n.d., *The Ida M. Tarbell Collection of Lincolniana* (March 22, 2013), https://dspace.allegheny.edu/ handle/10456/33722 (accessed March 31, 2013).

26. Caleb J. Dilworth, Letter to J. McCan Davis, June 5, 1896, *The Ida M. Tarbell Collection of Lincolniana* (March 22, 2013), https://dspace.allegheny .edu/handle/10456/33942 (accessed April 12, 2013).

27. John Husted, Statement to J. McCan Davis, June 5, 1896, *The Ida M. Tarbell Collection of Lincolniana* (March 22, 2013), https://dspace.allegheny .edu/handle/10456/33843 (accessed March 31, 2013).

28. Davis, Manuscript.

29. T. L. Mathews, Letter to Lincoln National Life Foundation dated May 23, 1939, Almanac Trial Papers, wallet 3 of 5, The Papers of Abraham Lincoln, Abraham Lincoln Presidential Library, Springfield, IL.

30. An accurate 1853 almanac would show that in Mason County the moon set around 3:55 p.m. on August 29, 1857, and didn't come back up until 1:09 a.m. on August 30. "Complete Sun and Moon Data for One Day," U.S. Naval Observatory (March 30, 2012), http://aa.usno.navy.mil/data/docs/RS_OneDay .php (accessed March 28, 2013).

31. William T. Alderson and Kenneth K. Bailey, "Correspondence between Albert J. Beveridge and Jacob M. Dickinson on the Writing of Beveridge's Life of Lincoln," *The Journal of Southern History*, Volume 20:2 (May, 1954), 210–237, 220, http://www.jstor.org/stable/2954915 (accessed July 9, 2010).

32. *Abraham Lincoln* 1809–1858, Volume 2 (Boston: Houghton Mifflin Company, 1928), 274.

CHAPTER 13

1. J. N. Gridley, *Lincoln's Defense of Duff Armstrong: The Story of the Trial and the Celebrated Almanac* (Virginia, IL: Illinois State Historical Society reprint, 1910), 22, http://www.archive.org/details/lincolnsdefenseo00grid (accessed July 27, 2011).

2. "Lincoln's Famous Case: Duff Armstrong's Story of His own Murder Trial," *New York Sun*, June 7, 1896, *People v. Armstrong, LPAL,* http://www.lawpracticeofabrahamlincoln.org (accessed July 12, 2012).

3. James H. Norris, Letter to Governor Richard Yates (February 22, 1863), http://www.idaillinois.org/cdm/compoundobject/collection/isa/id/2707/rec/1 (accessed February 22, 2013).

4. As Brady recollected, Allen proved a credible witness before his impeachment with the almanac. Gridley, *Lincoln's Defense of Duff Armstrong*, 22.

5. David W. Bartlett, *The Life and Public Services of Hon. Abraham Lincoln: To Which Is Added a Biographical Sketch of Hon. Hannibal Hamlin* (New York: H. Dayton, Publisher, 1860), 113, 114, http://archive.org/details/lifeand publicser00bartrich (accessed October 1, 2010).

6. "Lincoln's Famous Case," *New York Sun.*

7. Douglas L. Wilson and Rodney O. Davis, eds., *Herndon's Informants: Letters, Interviews, and Statements about Lincoln* (Chicago: University of Illinois Press, 1998), 326.

8. Gridley, *Lincoln's Defense of Duff Armstrong*, 22.

9. James Norris Pardon Papers, 25, 26, Illinois Digital Archives, http://www.idaillinois.org/cdm/compoundobject/collection/isa/id/2707 (accessed January 17, 2013).

10. James Taylor, Instanter Subpoena, *People v. Armstrong*, Cass County Circuit Court (May 6, 1858), *LPAL,* http://www.lawpracticeofabrahamlincoln.org (accessed July 12, 2012).

11. Albert J. Beveridge, *Abraham Lincoln, 1809–1858,* Vol. 2 (Boston: Houghton Mifflin Company, 1928), 269.

12. Daniel W. Stowell et al., eds., *The Papers of Abraham Lincoln: Legal Documents and Cases*, Vol. 4 (Charlottesville: University of Virginia Press, 2008), 40.

13. Wilson and Davis, *Herndon's Informants*, 341.

14. Abraham Lincoln, Proposed Jury Instructions, *People v. Armstrong*, Cass County Circuit Court (May 7, 1858), *LPAL,* http://www.lawpracticeof abrahamlincoln.org (accessed July 12, 2012).

15. Stowell et al., *Papers of Abraham Lincoln*, 40, 41.

16. Wilson and Davis, *Herndon's Informants*, 22.

17. Wilson and Davis, *Herndon's Informants*, 704.

18. Gridley, *Lincoln's Defense of Duff Armstrong*, 22.

19. Reinhard H. Luthin, *The Real Abraham Lincoln: A Complete One Volume History of His Life and Times* (Englewood Cliffs, NJ: Prentice-Hall, Inc., 1960), 167.

20. Stowell et al., *Papers of Abraham Lincoln*, 41.

21. "The Famous Armstrong Case: Milton Logan, Only Survivor, Tells How Lincoln Cleared Defendant and Won Case," *Cedar Rapids* (Iowa) *Evening Gazette,* June 6, 1906, http://newspaperarchive.com/cedar-rapids-evening -gazette/1909–06–08/page-6?tag=milton+logan+lincoln+armstrong+almanac&rtserp =tags/milton-logan-lincoln-armstrong-almanac?pci=7 (accessed June 14, 2012).

22. Wilson and Davis, *Herndon's Informants,* 23.

23. Wilson and Davis, *Herndon's Informants,* 332–334.

24. Aristotle, *On Rhetoric,* 3:19 (March 15, 2004), http://rhetoric.eserver.org/ aristotle/rhet3–19.html (accessed April 7, 2013).

25. John T. Brady, Letter to J. McCan Davis, May 23, 1896, *The Ida M. Tarbell Collection of Lincolniana* (March 22, 2013), https://dspace.allegheny .edu/handle/10456/33821 (accessed April 12, 2013).

26. "The Famous Armstrong Case," *Cedar Rapids Evening Gazette.*

27. Gridley, *Lincoln's Defense of Duff Armstrong,* 21, 22.

28. 373 U.S. 83 (1963).

29. Andrew L. Reisman, "An Essay on the Dilemma of 'Honest Abe': The Modern Day Professional Responsibility Implications of Abraham Lincoln's Representations of Clients He Believed to Be Culpable," *Nebraska Law Review* 72 (1993): 1205–1235, 1211, http://heinonline.org (accessed April 10, 2013).

30. John T. Brady, Letter to J. McCan Davis, May 23, 1896, *The Ida M. Tarbell Collection of Lincolniana* (March 22, 2013), https://dspace.allegheny .edu/handle/10456/33821 (accessed April 12, 2013).

31. Rule 611(b), Federal Rules of Evidence.

32. *Skomoroske v. Marcotte,* 255 Ill. App. 1 (2nd Dist. 1929).

33. *Philadelphia & Trenton R. Co. v. Stimpson,* 39 US 448, 461 (1840).

34. Stephan Lorant, "A Day in Lincoln's Life: How Honest Abe Saved a Man's Life and Repaid a Debt of Gratitude," *Life* 24, no. 6 (February 9, 1948): 111–112, 115–116, 118.

35. Walter B. Stevens, *A Reporter's Lincoln* (St. Louis: Missouri Historical Society, 1916), title page, http://www.archive.org/details/reporterslincoln00s (accessed September 30, 2010).

CHAPTER 14

1. "Lincoln's Famous Case: Duff Armstrong's Story of His own Murder Trial," *New York Sun,* June 7, 1896, *People v. Armstrong, LPAL,* http://www .lawpracticeofabrahamlincoln.org (accessed July 12, 2012).

2. John T. Brady, Letter to J. McCan Davis, May 23, 1896, *The Ida M. Tarbell Collection of Lincolniana* (March 22, 2013), https://dspace.allegheny.edu/ handle/10456/33821 (accessed April 12, 2013).

3. John McCan Davis, "Manuscript: The Armstrong Trial," *The Ida M. Tarbell Collection of Lincolniana* (March 22, 2013), https://dspace.allegheny .edu/handle/10456/33829 (accessed March 24, 2013).

4. "Lincoln's Famous Case," *New York Sun.*

5. J. N. Gridley, *Lincoln's Defense of Duff Armstrong: The Story of the Trial and the Celebrated Almanac* (Virginia, IL: Illinois State Historical Society reprint, 1910), 18–22, http://www.archive.org/details/lincolnsdefenseo00grid (accessed July 27, 2011).

6. Davis, "Manuscript."

7. John T. Brady, Letter to J. McCan Davis.

8. Gridley, *Lincoln's Defense of Duff Armstrong*, 18–22.

9. Davis, "Manuscript."

10. Caleb J. Dilworth, Letter to J. McCan Davis, May 18, 1896, *The Ida M. Tarbell Collection of Lincolniana* (March 22, 2013), https://dspace.allegheny.edu/handle/10456/33789 (accessed March 27, 2013).

11. *Hopkinson v. People*, 18 Ill. 264 (1857).

12. We do not discuss excusable homicide because under Illinois law at the time, a killing was excusable only if it was an "unfortunate or accidental killing" committed "without intention, [while] doing a lawful act with ordinary circumspection. ..." *Hopkinson v. People*, 18 Ill. 264, 1857 WL 5554 (1857).

13. *Schnier v. People*, 23 Ill. 17, 1859 WL 6956 (1859).

14. See, for example, *Heiney v. State*, 447 So.2d 210, 212 (Fla. 1984).

15. N. H. Purple, *A Compilation of the Statutes of the State of Illinois of a General Nature* (Chicago: Keene and Lee, Booksellers, 1856), 362, *LPAL*, http://www.lawpracticeofabrahamlincoln.org/Reference.aspx?ref=Reference%20html%20files/index%20for%20statutes.html (accessed February 21, 2013).

16. *Nix v. Whiteside*, 475 U.S. 157, 166, 106 S.Ct. 988, 994, 89 L.Ed.2d 123 (1986).

APPENDIX A

1. "Lincoln's Almanac: The True Inwardness of a Story That Has Been Told Time and Again," *Waterloo* (Iowa) *Courier,* November 10, 1886, http://newspaperarchive.com/waterloo-courier/1886-11-10/page-6?tag=duff+armstrong&rtserp=tags/duff-armstrong?py=1860&pey=1900 (accessed June 14, 2012).

2. "Lincoln's Famous Case: Duff Armstrong's Story of His Own Murder Trial," *New York Sun,* June 7, 1896, *People v. Armstrong, LPAL,* http://www.lawpracticeofabrahamlincoln.org (accessed July 12, 2012).

3. Walter B. Stevens, *A Reporter's Lincoln* (St. Louis: Missouri Historical Society, 1916), 19, 20, http://www.archive.org/details/reporterslincoln00s (accessed September 30, 2010).

4. "Reminiscences of Abraham Lincoln as a Lawyer," *American Lawyer* 5 (1897): 212–215, http://heinonline.org/HOL/LandingPage?collection=journals&handle=hein.journals/amlyr5&div=108&id=&page= (accessed July 6, 2012).

5. *The Ida M. Tarbell Collection of Lincolniana* (March 22, 2013), https://dspace.allegheny.edu/handle/10456/33821 (accessed April 12, 2013).

6. *Ida M. Tarbell Collection of Lincolniana.*

7. J. N. Gridley, *Lincoln's Defense of Duff Armstrong: The Story of the Trial and the Celebrated Almanac* (Virginia, IL: Illinois State Historical Society reprint,

1910), 18–22, http://www.archive.org/details/lincolnsdefenseo00grid (accessed July 27, 2011).

8. *The Ida M. Tarbell Collection of Lincolniana* (March 22, 2013), https://dspace.allegheny.edu/handle/10456/33789 (accessed March 27, 2013).

9. *Ida M. Tarbell Collection of Lincolniana.*

10. *Ida M. Tarbell Collection of Lincolniana.*

11. Douglas L. Wilson and Rodney O. Davis, eds., *Herndon's Informants: Letters, Interviews, and Statements about Lincoln* (Chicago: University of Illinois Press, 1998), 703, 704.

12. *Ida M. Tarbell Collection of Lincolniana.*

13. "The Famous Armstrong Case: Milton Logan, Only Survivor, Tells How Lincoln Cleared Defendant and Won Case," *Cedar Rapids* (Iowa) *Evening Gazette,* June 6, 1906, http://newspaperarchive.com/cedar-rapids-evening-gazette/1909-06-08/page-6?tag=milton+logan+lincoln+armstrong+almanac&rtserp=tags/milton-logan-lincoln-armstrong-almanac?pci=7 (accessed June 14, 2012).

14. James Norris Pardon Papers, 3, 19–22, Illinois Digital Archives, http://www.idaillinois.org/cdm/compoundobject/collection/isa/id/2707 (accessed January 17, 2013).

15. Wilson and Davis, *Herndon's Informants,* 316, 317.

16. Wilson and Davis, *Herndon's Informants,* 332–334.

17. James Norris Pardon Papers, 25, 26.

18. Wilson and Davis, *Herndon's Informants,* 22, 23.

19. Wilson and Davis, *Herndon's Informants,* 325, 326.

20. Wilson and Davis, *Herndon's Informants,* 341.

APPENDIX B

1. *People v. Armstrong, LPAL,* http://www.lawpracticeofabrahamlincoln.org (accessed July 12, 2012) (this document and all subsequent documents in Appendix B).

APPENDIX C

1. Nelson Watkins occupies a unique position among our witnesses because he made his revelations to John T. Brady with no expectation that he was speaking to a wider audience.

2. Randall James Plunkett, "Were You There, Charlie?" n.d., Unpublished manuscript, *People v. Armstrong* Case Files, Wallet 3 of 5, The Papers of Abraham Lincoln, Abraham Lincoln Presidential Library, Springfield, Illinois.

3. Les Ernst, "Peorian's Uncle Defendant in Abe's 'Almanac Trial,'" *Peoria Journal Star,* February 10, 1961, *People v. Armstrong* Case Files, Wallet 3 of 5, The Papers of Abraham Lincoln, Abraham Lincoln Presidential Library, Springfield, Illinois.

4. John Whiteside, "The Rest of the Duff Armstrong Story?" *Lincoln* (Illinois) *Courier,* August 29, 1988, 4.

5. Paul J. Beaver, "Another Look at the Duff Armstrong–Alamanac Trial," *Lincoln Newsletter* 7, no. 4 (1988), 1–3.

6. *Lincoln as a Lawyer: An Annotated Bibliography* (Carbondale: Southern Illinois University Press, 1991), 130.

7. Edgar Lee Masters, *The Sangamon* (Chicago: University of Illinois Press, 1988/1942), 96–106.

8. John Armstrong, Speech, *Lincoln Centennial Association Addresses: Delivered at the Annual Banquet Held at Springfield, Illinois, February Twelfth Nineteen Hundred and Twelve, Commemorating the One Hundred and Third Anniversary of the Birth of Abraham Lincoln* (Springfield, IL: Abraham Lincoln Association, 1912), 58–61.

9. Edgar Lee Masters, *Mitch Miller* (New York: Macmillan Company, 1920), 159, 160, http://archive.org/details/mitchmillerillu00mastgoog (accessed February 16, 2013).

10. Edgar Lee Masters, *Lincoln the Man* (Columbia, SC: Foundation for American Education, 1997/1931), 130.

11. Edgar Lee Masters, *The Sangamon* (Chicago: University of Illinois Press, 1988/1942), 105.

12. Herbert K. Russell, *Edgar Lee Masters: A Biography* (Chicago: University of Illinois Press, 2001), 274.

13. Russell, *Edgar Lee Masters*, 277.

14. Russell, *Edgar Lee Masters*, 344.

Selected Bibliography

What follows is a list of books consulted during the writing of this work. News articles, web pages, and journal articles cited in the endnotes are omitted from this bibliography.

Aland, Kurt. *Synopsis of the Four Gospels*. New York: United Bible Society, 1985.

The American Almanac, Year-Book, Cyclopaedia, and Atlas, Volume 2. New York, Chicago, and San Francisco: New York American Journal, Hearst's Chicago American, and San Francisco Examiner, 1904.

American Bar Association Standards for Criminal Justice: The Defense Function. Washington, DC: American Bar Association Criminal Justice Standards Committee, Criminal Justice Section, 1993. http://www.americanbar.org/content/dam/aba/publications/criminal_justice_standards/prosecution_defense _function.authcheckdam.pdf (accessed March 31, 2013).

Aristotle. *On Rhetoric*. http://rhetoric.eserver.org/aristotle/rhet3–19.html (accessed April 7, 2013).

Arnold, Isaac N. *The History of Abraham Lincoln and the Overthrow of Slavery*. Chicago: Clarke & Co., Publishers, 1866. http://archive.org/details/historyabrahaml01arnogoog (accessed June 11, 2012).

Arnold, Isaac N. *The Life of Abraham Lincoln*. Chicago: Jansen, McClurg, and Company, 1885. http://archive.org/details/historyabrahaml01arnogoog (accessed April 20, 2009).

Aten, Henry J. *History of the 85th Illinois Regiment Illinois Volunteer Infantry*. Hiawatha, KS: Regimental Association, 85th Illinois Volunteers, 1901. http://archive.org/details/historyofeightyf00aten (accessed March 9, 2013).

Bangs, Nathan. *A History of the Methodist Episcopal Church*, Volume 2. New York: T. Mason and G. Lane, 1839. http://archive.org/details/ahistory methodi00banggoog (accessed December 28, 2012).

Barrett, Joseph H. *Abraham Lincoln and his Presidency*, Volume 1. Cincinnati: Robert Clarke Company, 1904. http://archive.org/details/abehispresidency 01barrrich (accessed September 30, 2010).

Barrett, Joseph H. *Life of Abraham Lincoln with a Condensed View of His Most Important Speeches*. Cincinnati: Moore, Wilstach, Keys, and Company, 1860. http://archive.org/details/cu31924032777413 (accessed February 24, 2013).

Bartlett, David W. *The Life and Public Services of Hon. Abraham Lincoln: To Which Is Added a Biographical Sketch of Hon. Hannibal Hamlin*. New York: H. Dayton, Publisher, 1860. http://archive.org/details/lifeand publicser00bartrich (accessed October 1, 2010).

Barton, William E. *The Life of Abraham Lincoln*. Boston: Books, Inc., 1943/ 1925.

Bateman, Newton, Paul Selby, and Charles A. Martin, eds. *Historical Encyclopedia of Illinois and History of Cass County*, Volume 2. Chicago: Munsell Publishing Company, 1915. http://archive.org/details/historicencyclop02 bate (accessed October 1, 2010).

Benner, Martha L., Cullom Davis, et al., eds. *The Law Practice of Abraham Lincoln: Complete Documentary Edition*, 2nd ed. Springfield: Illinois Historic Preservation Agency, 2009. http://www.lawpracticeofabrahamlincoln.org (accessed July 12, 2012).

Beveridge, Albert J. *Abraham Lincoln, 1809–1858*, Volume 2. Boston: Houghton Mifflin Company, 1928.

Blackstone, William. *Commentaries on the Laws of England, Book the Fourth, Of Public Wrongs*. Oxford: Clarendon Press, 1779. http://archive.org/ details/lawsofenglandc04blacuoft (accessed February 22, 2013).

Brooks, Noah, *Abraham Lincoln: The Nation's Leader in the Great Struggle through Which Was Maintained the Existence of the United States*. New York: G.P. Putnam and Sons, 1888. http://archive.org/details/abraham lincolnn00broo (accessed October 1, 2010).

Burlingame, Michael, *Abraham Lincoln: A Life*, Volume 1. Baltimore: Johns Hopkins University Press, 2008.

Cartwright, Peter. *Autobiography of Peter Cartwright: The Backwoods Preacher*. New York: Carlton and Porter, 1857. http://archive.org/details/ autobiographype01cartgoog (accessed December 30, 2012).

Charnwood, Godfrey Rathbone Benson. *Abraham Lincoln*. London: Constable and Company, 1921/1916. http://archive.org/details/abraham00char (accessed July 11, 2012).

Clark, Ronald H., George R. Dekle Sr., and William S. Bailey. *Cross-Examination Handbook: Persuasion, Strategies, and Techniques*. New York: Wolters-Kluwer, 2011.

Cochrane, Joseph. *Centennial History of Mason County*. Springfield, IL: Rokker's Steam Printing House, 1876. http://archive.org/details/centennial histo00cochgoog (accessed March 9, 2013).

Coffin, Charles Carleton. *Abraham Lincoln*. New York: Harper and Brothers Publishers, 1893. http://archive.org/details/cu31924030983963 (accessed October 1, 2010).

Costigan, George P. *Cases and Other Authorities on Legal Ethics*. St. Paul, MN: West Publishing Company, 1917. http://archive.org/details/casesandotherau 00costgoog (accessed October 1, 2010).

Dekle, George R. *The Case against Christ: A Critique of the Prosecution of Jesus*. Newcastle upon Tyne, UK: Cambridge Scholars Publishing, 2011.

Dershowitz, Alan. *Letters to a Young Lawyer*. New York: Basic Books, 2001.

Diagram Group. *Weapons: An International Encyclopedia from 5000 B.C. to 2000 A.D.* New York: St. Martin's Press, 1980.

Dirck, Brian. *Lincoln the Lawyer*. Chicago: University of Illinois Press, 2009.

Donald, David Herbert. *Lincoln*. New York: Simon and Schuster Paperbacks, 1995.

Donovan, J. W. *Tact in Court: Containing Sketches of Cases Won by Art, Skill, Courage and Eloquence*, 6th ed. Rochester, NY: Williamson Law Book Co., Law Publishers, 1898. http://archive.org/details/tactincourt00 donogoog (accessed October 1, 2010).

Duff, John J. *A. Lincoln: Prairie Lawyer*. New York: Rinehart and Company, 1960.

Eggleston, Edward. *The Graysons: A Story of Illinois*. New York: Century Company, 1887. http://archive.org/details/graysonsastoryi00egglgoog (accessed August 3, 2011).

Emmerson, Jason. *Lincoln the Inventor*. Carbondale: Southern Illinois University Press, 2009.

Florida Grand Jury Instructions. 2013. http://www.floridasupremecourt.org/ jury_instructions/chapters/entireversion/onlinejurryinstructions.pdf (accessed January 20, 2013).

Florida Standard Jury Instructions in Criminal Cases. 2013. http://www .floridasupremecourt.org/jury_instructions/chapters/entireversion/onlinejurry instructions.pdf (accessed January 20, 2013).

Florida Standard Jury Instructions: Involuntary Civil Commitment of Sexually Violent Predators. 2013. http://www.floridasupremecourt.org/jury _instructions/chapters/entireversion/onlinejurryinstructions.pdf (accessed January 20, 2013).

Foster, Earnest. *Abraham Lincoln*. London: Cassell & Company Limited, 1893. http://archive.org/details/abrahamlincoln00fostgoog (accessed October 7, 2010).

French, Charles Wallace. *Abraham Lincoln the Liberator: A Biographical Sketch*. New York: Funk and Wagnalls, 1891. http://archive.org/details/ abrahamlincolnl00frengoog (accessed August 3, 2011).

Gorham, R. W. *Camp Meeting Manual: A Practical Book for the Campground in Two Parts*. Boston: H. V. Degen, 1854. http://archive.org/details/campmeetingmanu00gorhgoog (accessed January 6, 2013).

Gridley, J. N. *Lincoln's Defense of Duff Armstrong: The Story of the Trial and the Celebrated Almanac*. Virginia, IL: Illinois State Historical Society reprint, 1910. http://www.archive.org/details/lincolnsdefenseo00grid (accessed July 27, 2011).

Hapgood, Norman. *Abraham Lincoln: The Man of the People*. New York: Macmillan Company, 1899. http://archive.org/details/abrahamlincolnm02hapggoog (accessed December 8, 2012).

Herndon, William H., and Jesse William Weik. *Herndon's Lincoln: The True Story of a Great Life*, Volume 2. Chicago: Belford, Clarke and Company, 1889. http://archive.org/details/herndonslincoln02hernrich (accessed October 1, 2010).

Herndon, William H., and Jesse William Weik. *Abraham Lincoln: The True Story of a Great Life*, Volume 1. New York: D. Appleton and Company, 1913. http://archive.org/details/abrahamlincolnt01weikgoog (accessed December 15, 2012).

Hill, Frederick Trevor. *Lincoln the Lawyer*. New York: Century Company, 1913/1905. http://www.archive.org/details/lincolnlawyer00hillgoog (accessed August 3, 2011).

Hobson, J. T. *Footprints of Abraham Lincoln: Presenting Many Interesting Facts, Reminiscences and Illustrations Never Before Published*. Dayton, OH: Otterbein Press, 1909. http://www.archive.org/details/footprintsofabra00inhobs (accessed October 10, 2010).

Hobson, J. T. *The Lincoln Year Book: Containing Immortal Words of Abraham Lincoln Spoken and Written on Various Occasions, Preceded by Appropriate Scripture Texts and Followed by Choice Poetic Selections for Each Day in the Year, with Special Reference to Anniversary Dates*. Dayton, OH: Press of United Brethren Publishing House, 1906. http://archive.org/stream/lincolnyearbookc00inlinc (accessed July 4, 2012).

Holland, J. G. *The Life of Abraham Lincoln*. Springfield, MA: Gurdon Bill, 1866. http://archive.org/details/lifeabrahamlinc02hollgoog (accessed December 15, 2012).

Howells, W. D. *Life of Abraham Lincoln*. Springfield, IL: Abraham Lincoln Association, 1938/1860. http://archive.org/details/lifeofabrahamlin00howe (accessed December 19, 2012).

Irelan, John Robert. *The Republic: Or, a History of the United States of America in the Administrations, from the Monarchic Colonial Days to the Present Times*, Volume 16. Chicago: Fairbanks and Palmer Publishing Company, 1888. http://www.archive.org/details/republicorahist00irelgoog (accessed April 20, 2009).

Jowett, Benjamin, trans. *Thucydides*, Volume 1. Oxford: Clarendon Press, 1900. http://www.archive.org/details/thucydides01thucuoft (accessed January 14, 2011).

Kearns, Doris. *Team of Rivals: The Political Genius of Abraham Lincoln*. New York: Simon and Schuster, 2005.

Lamon, Ward H. *The Life of Abraham Lincoln from His Birth to His Inauguration as President*. Boston: James R. Osgood and Company, 1872. http://archive.org/details/lifeofabrahamlin00lamouoft (accessed April 20, 2009).

Laudan, Larry. *Truth, Error, and Criminal Law: An Essay in Legal Epistimology*. New York: Cambridge University Press, 2006.

Leland, Charles Godfrey. *Abraham Lincoln and the Abolition of Slavery in the United States*. New York: G. P. Putnam's Sons, 1879. http://archive.org/details/abrahamlinc1595lela (accessed June 4, 2012).

Lincoln Centennial Association Addresses: Delivered at the Annual Banquet Held at Springfield, Illinois, February Twelfth Nineteen Hundred and Twelve, Commemorating the One Hundred and Third Anniversary of the Birth of Abraham Lincoln. Springfield, IL: Abraham Lincoln Association, 1912. http://archive.org/details/lincolncentennia00lodg (accessed June 12, 2012).

Lincoln, Abraham. *Collected Works of Abraham Lincoln*, Volume 8, Roy P. Basler, ed. New Brunswick, NJ: Rutgers University Press, 1953. http://quod.lib.umich.edu/l/lincoln/lincoln8/1:875?rgn=div1;singlegenre=All;sort=occur;subview=detail;type=simple;view=fulltext;q1=hannah+armstrong (accessed January 17, 2013).

Lincoln, Abraham. *The Autobiography of Abraham Lincoln*. New York: Francis D. Tandy Company, 1905.

Lincoln, Abraham. *The Collected Works of Abraham Lincoln*, Volume 1, Roy P. Baisler, ed. New Brunswick, NJ: Rutgers University Press, 1953. http://archive.org/details/collectedworksof015581mbp (accessed March 10, 2013).

Litt, William. *Wrestliana: An Historical Account of Ancient and Modern Wrestling*. Whitehaven, UK: Michael and William Alsop, 1860. http://archive.org/details/wrestlianahistor00litt (accessed December 14, 2012).

Lovill, Justin, ed. *Notable Historical Trials, Volume 4: From Burke and Hare to Oscar Wilde*. London: Folio Society, 1999.

Lubet, Steven. *Lawyer's Poker: 52 Lessons That Lawyers Can Learn from Card Players*. New York: Oxford University Press, 2006.

Ludwig, Emil. *Lincoln*. Eden Paul and Cedar Paul, trans. Boston: Little, Brown, and Company, 1930.

Luthen, Reinhard H. *The Real Abraham Lincoln: A Complete One-Volume History of His Life and Times*. Englewood Cliffs, NJ: Prentice Hall, 1960.

Masters, Edgar Lee. *Lincoln the Man*. Columbia, SC: Foundation for American Education, 1997/1931.

Masters, Edgar Lee. *Mitch Miller*. New York: Macmillan Company, 1920. http://archive.org/details/mitchmillerillu00mastgoog (accessed February 16, 2013)

Masters, Edgar Lee. *The Sangamon*. Chicago: University of Illinois Press, 1988/1942.

Matthews, Elizabeth W. *Lincoln as a Lawyer: An Annotated Bibliography*. Carbondale: Southern Illinois University Press, 1991.

McClure, J. B., ed. *Anecdotes of Abraham Lincoln and Lincoln's Stories*. Chicago: Rhodes and McClure, Publisher, 1880. http://archive.org/details/anecdotesabraha00mcclgoog (accessed April 16, 2009).

Mendelsohn, S. *The Criminal Jurisprudence of the Ancient Hebrews: Compiled from the Talmud and Other Rabbinical Writings, and Compared with Roman and English Penal Jurisprudence*. Baltimore: M. Curlander, 1891. http://archive.org/stream/criminaljurispru00mend#page/n5/mode/2up (accessed January 13, 2013).

Miers, Earl Schenck, and William E. Baringer. *Lincoln Day by Day: A Chronology, 1809–1865*, Volume 2. Washington, DC: Lincoln Sesquicentennial Commission, 1960. http://archive.org/stream/lincolndaybydayc02unit#page/n5/mode/2up (accessed March 11, 2013).

Morris, Richard B. *Fair Trial: Fourteen Who Stood Accused*. New York: Harper and Row, 1967.

Mortimer, John. *The First Rumpole Omnibus*. New York: Penguin Books, 1983.

Nicolay, Helen. *The Boy's Life of Abraham Lincoln*. New York: Appleton-Century-Crofts, Inc., 1933/1905.

Nicolay, John G., and John Hay, *Complete Works of Abraham Lincoln*, Volume 11. New York: Francis D. Tandy Company, 1904. http://archive.org/stream/completeworksofa11linc (accessed July 4, 2012).

Nicolay, John G., and John Hay. *Abraham Lincoln: A History*, Volume 1. New York: The Century Company, 1890. http://archive.org/details/abrahamlincolna07haygoog (accessed December 13, 2012).

Oakleaf, Joseph Benjamin. *Abraham Lincoln as a Criminal Lawyer*. Rock Island, IL: Augustana Book Concern, 1923.

Oates, Stephen B. *With Malice toward None: A Life of Abraham Lincoln*. New York: Harper Collins, 1994/1977.

Onstot, T. G. *Pioneers of Menard and Mason Counties*. Forest City, IL: T. G. Onstot, 1902. http://archive.org/stream/pioneersofmenar00onst (accessed April 20, 2009).

Perrin, William Henry, ed. *History of Cass County, Illinois*. Chicago: O. L. Baskin and Company, 1882. http://archive.org/details/historyofcasscou00perr (accessed March 9, 2013).

Pratt, Silas G., ed. *Lincoln in Story: The Life of the Martyr-President Told in Authenticated Anecdotes*. New York: D. Appleton and Company, 1901. http://www.archive.org/details/lincolninstor2086prat (accessed April 20, 2009).

Purple, N. H. *A Compilation of the Statutes of the State of Illinois of a General Nature*. Chicago: Keene and Lee, Booksellers, 1856. http://www.lawpracticeofabrahamlincoln.org/Reference.aspx?ref=Reference%20html%20files/index%20for%20statutes.html (accessed February 21, 2013).

Ram, James. *A Treatise on Facts as Subjects of Inquiry by a Jury*, first American edition by John Townshend. New York: Baker, Voorhis and Co., Publishers, 1870. http://archive.org/details/treatiseonfactsa00ramj (accessed June 8, 2012).

Ram, James. *A Treatise on Facts as Subjects of Inquiry by a Jury*, fourth American edition by John Townshend and Charles F. Beach. New York: Baker, Voorhis and Co., Publishers, 1890.

Richards, John T. *Abraham Lincoln: The Lawyer-Statesman*. Boston: Houghton Mifflin Company, 1916. http://archive.org/details/abrahamlincolnl01 richgoog (accessed February 24, 2013).

Ritter, Christopher G. *Creating Winning Trial Strategies and Graphics*. Chicago: American Bar Association, 2004.

Rizer, Arthur L. *Lincoln's Counsel: Lessons from America's Most Persuasive Speaker*. Chicago: ABA Publishing, 2010.

Robinson, Jacob, and Sidney Gilpin. *Wrestling and Wrestlers: Biographical Sketches of Celebrated Athletes of the Northern Ring*. London: Bemrose and Sons, 1893. http://archive.org/details/wrestlingwrestle00robiiala (accessed December 14, 2012).

Rothschild, Alonzo. *Honest Abe: A Study in Integrity Based on the Early Life of Abraham Lincoln*. Boston: Houghton Mifflin Company, 1917. http:// archive.org/details/honestabestudy1258roth (accessed February 24, 2013).

Russell, Herbert K. *Edgar Lee Masters: A Biography*. Chicago: University of Illinois Press, 2001.

Sandburg, Carl. *Abraham Lincoln: The Prairie Years*, Volumes. 1 and 2. New York: Harcourt, Brace, and World, Inc., 1926.

Schweer, Mrs. T. J. *History of Beardstown and Cass County*. Beardstown, IL: Beardstown Public Schools, 1925. http://archive.org/details/historyofbeardst 00schw (accessed February 24, 2013).

Selby, Paul. *Anecdotal Lincoln: Speeches, Stories, and Yarns from the "Immortal Abe."* Chicago: Thompson and Thomas, 1900.

Smith, Goldwyn. *Lectures and Essays*. Toronto: Hunter, Rose, and Company, 1881. http://archive.org/details/lecturesessays00smit (accessed April 16, 2009).

Sotos, John G. *The Physical Lincoln: Finding the Genetic Cause of Abraham Lincoln's Height, Homeliness, Pseudo-Depression, and Imminent Cancer Death*. Mt. Vernon, VA: Mt. Vernon Book Systems, 2008.

Spiegel, Allen D. *A. Lincoln Esquire: A Shrewd, Sophisticated Lawyer in His Time*. Macon, GA: Mercer University Press, 2002.

Stevens, Walter B. *A Reporter's Lincoln*. St. Louis: Missouri Historical Society, 1916. http://www.archive.org/details/reporterslincoln00s (accessed September 30, 2010).

Stoddard, William O. *Abraham Lincoln: The True Story of a Great Life, Showing the Inner Growth, Special Training, and Peculiar Fitness of the Man for His Work*. New York: Fords, Howard, and Hulbert, 1885. http://archive .org/details/abrahamlincoln00unkngoog (accessed April 16, 2009).

Stowe, Harriett Beecher. *Men of Our Times, or Leading Patriots of the Day*. Hartford, CT: Hartford Publishing Company, 1868. http://archive.org/ details/menourtimesorle01stowgoog (accessed April 16, 2009).

Stowell, Daniel W. et al., eds. *The Papers of Abraham Lincoln: Legal Documents and Cases*, Volume. 4. Charlottesville: University of Virginia Press, 2008.

Supreme and District Court Bench Book. Queensland Courts, Queensland, Australia, 2011. http://www.canlii.org/en/ca/scc/doc/2004/2004scc5/2004scc5.html (accessed February 20, 2013).

Tarbell, Ida M. *The Life of Abraham Lincoln: Drawn from Original Sources and Containing Many Speeches, Letters, and Telegrams Hitherto Unpublished and Illustrated with Many Reproductions from Original Paintings, Photographs, Etc.*, Volume. 1. New York: Lincoln History Society, 1907. http://archive.org/details/cu31924092901069, Volume 2. http://archive.org/details/cu31924092901077, Volume 3. http://archive.org/details/cu31924092901085, Volume 4. http://archive.org/details/cu31924092901093 (accessed December 17, 2012).

Thayer, W. M. *The Pioneer Boy, and How He became President: The Story of the Life of Abraham Lincoln*. London: Hodder and Stoughton, 1882. http://archive.org/details/pioneerboyhow2070thay (accessed June 9, 2012).

Throckmorton, Burton. *Gospel Parallels: A Comparison of the Synoptic Gospels*, 5th ed. Nashville: Thomas Nelson Publishers, 1995.

Townsend, William H. *Lincoln the Litigant*. Boston: Houghton Mifflin and Company, 1925.

Van Koppen, Peter J., and Steven D. Penrod, eds. *Adversarial versus Inquisitorial Justice: Psychological Perspectives on Criminal Justice Systems*. New York: Kluwer Academic, 2003.

Wade, Mary Hazelton. *Abraham Lincoln: A Story and a Play*. Boston: Gorham Press, 1914. http://archive.org/details/abrahamlincolna00wadegoog (accessed September 30, 2010).

Walsh, John Evangelist. *Moonlight: Abraham Lincoln and the Almanac Trial*. New York: St. Martin's Press, 2000.

Wanamaker, R. M. *The Voice of Lincoln*. New York: Charles Scribner's Sons, 1920/1918. http://archive.org/details/voiceoflinc2074wana (accessed March 17, 2013).

Wellman, Francis L. *The Art of Cross Examination*. New York: Macmillan Company, 1908. http://www.archive.org/details/artcrossexamina00wellgoog (accessed July 27, 2011).

Wellman, Francis L. *The Art of Cross-Examination: With the Cross-Examinations of Important Witnesses in Celebrated Cases*. New York: Collier Books, 1970.

Whipple, Wayne. *The Story Life of Abraham Lincoln: A Biography Composed of Five Hundred True Stories Told by Abraham Lincoln and His Friends*. Philadelphia: J. C. Winston Company, 1908. http://archive.org/details/storylifeoflin1967whip (accessed March 23, 2013).

Whipple, Wayne. *The Story of Young Abraham Lincoln*. Philadelphia: Henry Altemus Company, 1915. http://archive.org/details/storyofyounga1978whip (accessed December 11, 2012).

White, Ronald C. *A. Lincoln: A Biography*. New York: Random House, 2009.

Wilson, Douglas L. *Honor's Voice: The Transformation of Abraham Lincoln*. New York: Vintage Books, 1998.

Wilson, Douglas L., and Rodney O. Davis, eds. *Herndon's Informants: Letters, Interviews, and Statements about Lincoln*. Chicago: University of Illinois Press, 1998.

Woldman, Albert, *Lawyer Lincoln*. New York: Carroll and Graf Publishers, 2001/1936.

Index

About the Author

GEORGE R. DEKLE, Sr. is a career prosecutor who has investigated and prosecuted hundreds of murder cases, including numerous death penalty cases. Since his retirement as a prosecutor, he has worked as a legal skills professor at the University of Florida, Levin College of Law; authored one book on prosecution; and co-authored a book on cross-examination. Dekle is the recipient of the Gene Berry Memorial Award as the outstanding prosecutor in Florida (1982), the Florida Prosecuting Attorneys Association Distinguished Faculty Award (1996, 2003), and the FPAA's Lifetime Achievement Award for efforts in continuing legal education for prosecutors (2005).

Dekle's books include *The Last Murder: The Investigation, Prosecution, and Execution of Ted Bundy* (Praeger, 2011) and *Prosecution Principles: A Clinical Handbook* (Thomson West, 2007), a handbook designed to describe the office and duties of the American prosecutor and to educate law students and rookie prosecutors in the skills necessary to fulfill the duties of the prosecutor. He is co-author of *Cross-Examination Handbook: Persuasion, Strategies, and Techniques* (Aspen, 2010), a handbook designed to educate trial advocacy students, clinical students, and continuing education students in the skills necessary to conduct successful cross-examinations.

CPSIA information can be obtained
at www.ICGtesting.com
Printed in the USA
LVHW051508280223
740497LV00004B/222

9 781440 830495